A HATHOR HOUSE BOOK

-:-:-:-:-:-:-

ON THE U.S.S. COLORADO

The U.S.S. COLORADO

ON THE

U.S.S. COLORADO

by

Ruby Parker Goodwin

Ruby Parker Goodwin

With Special Drawings

by

Bonnie Parker Engle

Hathor House Books
315 W. Grant - #2C
Douglas, Wyoming 82633
Copyright © 1988 Ruby Parker Goodwin
ISBN 0-934482-03-9
Library of Congress
Catalog Card Number: 87-091070

Beneath the meadow deep and cold
    Springtimes's bloom is dead;
O'er the lonely meadow memory still
    Seeks the dream that sped
In Springtime's frill across the hill
    On up the rugged heights ahead.

          ----Wilbur Allen Parker

All rights reserved. No part of the material protected by this copyright notice may be reproduced or utilized in any form or by any means, electronic or mechanical, including photocopying, recording, or by any informational storage and retrieval system without written permission from the copy-right owner. Printed in the United States of America.

I release this book to the public with pride as I place my brother in the annals of history.

.....The Author

TABLE OF CONTENTS

PAGE

FOREWORD and ACKNOWLEDGEMENTS xi

PART I:
Study Up! Wash! Ship Out!   1
Camp Ward, Farragut, Idaho 18

PART II:
Aboard the U.S.S. COLORADO . . . . ,174
Mindoro 178
The U.S.S. COLORADO DAILY, 1943 180
Orders for the Day, Wed., 8 December 1943 . 189
The U.S.S. COLORADO DAILY, 1944 191
June 1944 - Honolulu to Kawjalein 212
Saipan 215
Guam 220
Tinia, "We Caught It" 222
September 12, 1944, A Rated Leave 228
November 20, 1944 at Leyte 237
December 4, 1944, Anchor at Palau Island . .241
New Year's Eve, 1944-1945 248
Eulithi 266
April 1945, Okinawa 276
Tokyo Bay 324
The Home-Going 330

EPILOGUE 343
A Bit of Autobiography From the Author 345

LIST OF ILLUSTRATIONS

U.S. COLORADO Thanksgiving Menu 1943 84
Navy Department Certificate 182
V-MAIL .202
Zamboanga, World's Most Beautiful Paradise . . 203
Wilbur Parker in the Hawaiian Islands 209
"The Navy has marked it intolerable..." . . . 252
~~AMERICAN~~ Plane 254
"...the ships all lined out...." 257
Route of the U.S.S. COLORADO 273
"The plane came down in flames...." 280
President Franklin Roosevelt's Death 283
Hitler's Death 290
And Now You've Made History 317
The Japs Surrendered 323
"I'm not the same man I was...." 338

PHOTOGRAPHS

The U.S.S. COLORADO . . . . *frontispiece*
Samuel M. Parker & the Barncastle 78A
Wilbur Allen Parker EM 3/C 175
At the Zamboanga Cafe 204
War-Worn Wilbur in the Hawaiian Islands . . . 210

FOREWORD and ACKNOWLEDGEMENTS

ON the U.S.S. COLORADO is a family book.

It is *not* a smoothly-flowing novel. Its primary intention is a detailed account of the maneuvers of the battleship, the U.S.S. COLORADO of the United States Navy. Hence, the book is a compilation of historical data and facts, which I hope are in sequence and in a readable script.

Also, ON the U.S.S. COLORADO is a historical biography of a Wyoming (U.S.A.) man. This book is as true an account as possible of one man's experience during World War II.

All names of persons, places, ships, incidents, and wars are nonfictional. All writing is as near factual as the author can make it.

PART II features the diaries of Wilbur A. Parker, which he started October 1943 as the U.S.S. COLORADO made her way into the battle of Tarawa in the Central Pacific. Wilbur gives on-the-war-front accounts of battle scenes at Tarawa, Eniwetok, and the Philippines, particularly the battle of Okinawa before entering Tokyo Bay, September 1945.

I'm indebted to and wish to thank the following people who have helped me struggle through the past $2\frac{1}{2}$ years as I worked ON the U.S.S. COLORADO:

Al Leiser, Assistant Manager, of Farragut State Park, Idaho, for permission to use information concerning Camp Farragut in this book.

Pat Cole for her assistance in the gathering of material pertaining to Farragut Naval Training Base.

The Wyoming Council on the Arts for the helpful, critical comments.

Bonnie Parker Engle, my niece, for her enthusiasm and belief in my project. Her encouragement helped me carry through each time I faltered.

Mike Perrotti for the hours of laborious editing and proof-reading. I don't know what I'd done without him.

Ruby Parker Goodwin
March 17, 1988

PART I

STUDY UP!

WASH!

SHIP OUT!

by
Ruby Parker Goodwin

PART I

"REMEMBER PEARL HARBOR!" "REMEMBER PEARL HARBOR!" In the United States it was the hue and battle cry of 1942. Soon to follow was the plea, "REMEMBER BATAAN!" "REMEMBER THE DEATH MARCH!" How long do we remember? How long are we expected to remember? It's so easy for the participants of a war to remember the horrendous warfare that ruptured a lifetime; but what of the next generation? Must our progeny have their own war experience before they can come to know war as the most hidious of crimes?

It seems we learn only through our own experience...only after having the disease do we recognize the dire results of the malady. We fill our libraries with books on the atrocities of war. Are we hoping our youth will read and thereby come to know and hopefully avoid the horror their forefathers experienced? Or are words of warning mere incentive to try the tantalizing forbidden consequences? Are our children listening to what they believe it would be like to participate in some horror movie? Does anything exist until we experience the facts for ourselves?

Whatever the answers may be, it seems nearly every generation is sucked into the vortex of war and violence.

Since Hitler's war in Europe began in 1938, barely 20 years from the First World War, Wilbur Parker sensed an increasing restlessness in the United States. His friends and neighbors from all sides were saying, "We're bound to be drawn into it." While his co-workers asked, "Do you think we will be called into the Service?"

Despite the fierce and on-going war in Europe, year 1940, the United States was still trying to hold its peace. Nevertheless, only the other day on a radio broadcast, Wilbur heard President Roosevelt say, "We must be the arsenal of the democracies."

"How can any Country harbor an arsenal", Wilbur remarked to his brother, Les, "Without taking sides and ultimately being drawn into the conflict?"

Wilbur was born October 9, 1915, in a log cabin on the North Laramie River near Laramie Peak in the state of Wyoming. "Some of our greatest men were born in log cabins," his mother told him as he was growing up. "There's Abraham Lincoln for an example."

"I don't want to be President, Mother," he told her, "I just want to be a mountain man who roams free. I'll herd sheep, I'll carve wood, or I'll write my sister some poetry. She has such a hard time knowing what she wants to do. She says she wants to be a writer, but I don't think she knows how."

His father, Samuel M. Parker, built Wilbur's birthplace, a two-room, log-house on a homestead he acquired in 1906. It nestled in a deep canyon where two rivers divided...the North Laramie and a lesser tributary known as Bear Creek...all in Albany County, Wyoming, and in 1915 known as Wyman, Wyoming. Wyman was but a small Post Office of which Wilbur's mother, Ursa Menefee Parker, was the Post Mistress. She'd been commissioned to the job March 17, 1915 (seven months before Wilbur's birth) by Postmaster General of the United States of America, Albert S. Burleson.

Father, Samuel M. Parker, carried mail into Wyman by the way of horseback the thirty miles from Wheatland, Wyoming.

Wilbur Parker, at age 24, stood straight and lean...all 5 ft. 11 inches of him. Perhaps, his solidness was developed by climbing Wyoming peaks, or by the miles of walking in the mountains while hunting...or by fishing the rushing steams that gushed to the valley's floor. His soft, brown,

3a

hair rose in waves from a square forehead which showed a slight scar above the left temple. If anyone were to mention this flaw, he'd likely say with a laugh, "Oh, that? I ran my head into some ice to see if the ice was solid enough to skate on." His head may not have been strong as he wished, but the carriage of his whole body emanated strength as though he were in command of his destiny. His square shoulders he held proudly, while his liquid, brown eyes, looked into yours with a direct, honest look, as if to say, "I have nothing to hide, have you?"

Wilbur may have exuberated a confidence he didn't feel. However, he definitely knew what he wanted out of life, and he thought he need only steer his course and work hard to get what he wanted in this great land of opportunity,the United States of America. Besides, he didn't think his wants were outlandish or out-of-reach. The first thing on his want-list was to have a decent-paying job. After that with time and a little money, he could start on his second most-wanted dream...an education.

Nevertheless, Wilbur wasn't at all satisfied with the way his life was going here in December, 1940. "It could be worse," he thought,"What if I'm called to serve in a futile war?" Even the thought of it seemed to disrupt his actions and his plans.

What could be said about his life today? First, he did have a job. There were a number of free trade schools near his rooming house here in Los Angeles. He was paying only $28.00 a month for his room and board. He liked his tiny, gray-haired, landlady, and her son who was about his age...24. Besides he was close to his brother, Les,and wife, Dorothy. He'd stayed with them for three or four months after they all moved to California from Trojan, South Dakota, where he and Les had worked in the gold mines. When Dorothy talked of going to work, he thought it was time to move out. She didn't need an extra mouth to

3

cook for. Most of all, he didn't think it a good idea to live with relatives. It often strained an otherwise good relationship.

The thing to do if he were dis-satisfied with his life was to step out and take action to improve it. First, he took advantage of the trade schools and started a class in math. His working hours gave him a chance to study *if* he didn't fall asleep in the class room; for the late hours got to him. He went to work at 12:30 to reach home at 7:30 in the morning. He was getting 60¢ an hour, and he had a five-day week, although more and more he was working Saturdays, too; for, as the war grew hotter in Europe, more and more, it seemed, the United States was stepping up war production.

Inspite of his full schedule, however, Wilbur was managing to have some fun times, too. He and Harley and Louise DeWitt from Rapid City, South Dakota, liked to go places together. Just last Sunday they went to see a family by the name of Jones. After a very fine dinner prepared by Mrs. Jones, she jumped up from the table and said,"Now let's all go to church."

Ordinarily one does not find church attendance anything to write home about..."Dear Mom: Having a wonderful time. Went to church last Sunday." What more was there to say?

However, by attending services at *this* church there could be a lot more said. Wilbur chuckled remembering his surprise when the five of them stepped from the car before the temple of Aimee McPherson. Aimee's Angelus Temple, which seated over 5,000 people, was truly magnificent. So was Aimee who dramatized all her scriptures. She couldn't sing, but she was a good actress. "And she's so beautiful," thought Wilbur,"especially for one her age. I understand she's past 50, but she scarcely looks thirty. Most men find themselves wishing they were younger for a pretty, young, girl. Here I am wishing I were older!"

He watched her as she moved on stage, her dark,

burnished hair falling in shining waves to her shoulders. Her high heels moved in and out of the rustling satin of her gown.

Yes, she was gorgeous, and Wilbur caught himself wondering how many men found themselves enamored by her. It wasn't her physical beauty that really grabbed you so much as it was the dazzling, inner spark that emanated from her. This glow seemed contagious, and it sparked the congregation.

She was very responsive to all the joking going on around her. She could top everyone else when it came to repartees, even though no one ever got out-of-hand. "Is there such a thing as *reverent* joking?" Wilbur asked himself. Aimee made it seem like there was. She and her son went so far as to have a hog-calling contest, and surprisingly, it didn't seem sacrilegious. Instead, it was hilarious...giving an element of the pre-posterous in an otherwise serious situation. "Laughter is sacramental," proclaimed Aimee, "It restores the soul. If God had not intended us to laugh we'd be a gloom-ridden race. It's an *ill* man who cannot laugh, and who dreams up war. And when I say *laugh*, I don't mean make fun of your fellow man. When we lose our sense of humor, we're losers in all things. O.K. You over there," she called, at the same time pointing to a sleek gentleman in the crowd, "It's time to call in your hogs...a little louder, make them believe it!"

There was never anything vulgar about her speech nor her demeanor. It really should have been ridiculous, but she managed to look so regal poised on the stage in her high-necked, ecru-satin robe with the huge, flowing sleeves, and the skirt rustling about her high-heeled slippers. Her full lips puckered in leading the hog calling. Her good humour was contagious. The crowd bellowed with various loud imitations of what they thought hog-calling may sound like. Not one in the room remained sober. "And," thought Wilbur,"I bet not one person will go home gloomy." Some preachers made you fear the fire amd brimstone. This one gave you the laughter that washed over your life and your soul in a rare healing ointment.

He , for one, would remember Aimee and her words, "God didn't put us here on His good,green earth to weep and to war all the time,"she cried, "God gave us laughter. If you'll notice when we're laughing we're never hurting anyone.God would have us love our neighbor, so let's go out and laugh with Him and leave our axes and guns behind!"

At the remembrance of this *church* event,Wilbur laughed aloud into his silent little room. He looked up at the opposite wall where a 12"x 14" picture of Aimee and her son graced the otherwise blank and rather faded wallpaper. "We're giving pictures away to out-of-state folks," Aimee told him as she shook his hand. Where, but in Aimee's glowing presence could one ever find religion like this? Wilbur laughed again. Yes, laughter may be the best religion. At least, it made him feel better about people and the whole world. It even made him feel better about himself.

As Hitler's war in Europe progessed, the stress was felt world wide, and the people of the United States were realizing day by day more clearly the demands this struggle was making upon them. Everyone forgot to laugh.

The British evacuated Benghazi, in North Africa April 3, 1941;the Axis offensive was meeting with considerable success under the boldness of General Rommel. While back in the States, Wilbur, after settling to a life of work and study, received a notice from the Draft Board to report for a physical examination. He was working for Douglas Aircraft, Santa Monica, California. "I think I'll just let my boss see this,"he told Buck Parr, Les' brother-in-law, "Maybe it'll settle a few things." So long as he was in an important war-time industry, the air plant brought about a deferment for the time being.

Always in Wilbur's mind was the question,"How long will it be before I'm called?" He eased back into factory work, always wary and with the feeling when Uncle Sam really wanted him there'd be another notice. He knew he was merely putting off the inevitable.

Everything seemed to be pointing up to the United States' involvement in the great conflict that was bludgeoning other nations. By October the first, 1941, German armies began Operation Typhoon, an all-out drive against Moscow. Then right on the heels of this event, came the news the U.S.Navy destroyer, Reuben James, was torpedoed off the coast of Iceland by a German vessel. Was the United States going to stand for this sort of treatment?

As though no conflict were emminent other men went ahead with all the ordinary events one thinks of life as holding. Buck Parr married Ellen. It was a nice, quiet, little wedding with Les Parker as best man.

"All very happy, and peaceful now," thought Wilbur as he watched, "But what God has brought together may be ripped asunder by war. Will Buck be leaving a war bride behind?" He foolishly mentioned as much to Buck. Buck was fast with his reply,"Well, if you don't marry your girl before you leave for war, you may end up with one of those Dear John epistles. Man, alive,wake up! We'd better live while we can; we may not have a tomorrow! Don't you know that?"

"That's just why I don't want to leave a wife behind," retorted Wilbur,"You could be leaving her pregnant, you know. That will put a girl in a horrible spot."

"By, God, I want to know what it's like to be married and have kids," Buck's tone was a little heated, "I want to experience all the good things life has to offer, and I'm not going to be shortchanged if I can help it!"

Wilbur shut up. Buck believed what he said. Wilbur, also, believed in his words, "I don't want to do anything that's going to make a hardship on those I love."

All that had been dreaded swiftly came to a head with the date of December 7, 1941. Pearl Harbor blew the debacle cork. On December 8, 1941, the United States declared war against Japan. President Franklin D. Roosevelt, in asking Congress for a declaration of war, condemned the Japanese attack on Pearl Harbor. What the Japanese did there he said, "will live in infamy."

Rapidly, the United States pushed into high gear. Before the week of December the 7th was over, Hitler and Mussolini declared themselves to be at war with the United States.

Overnight, the United States preparations for defense were changed into preparedness for war. Factories which had made automobiles or other instruments for peace were turned over to the making of tanks or some other needed form of munitions. Thousands of troops with tanks, airplanes, and other needed equipment were sent nearer the fighting fronts. Mothers quaked and asked, "Will my sons have to go?"

On the job with Douglas Aircraft, Dept. 84, Wilbur found himself working 12 hours a day, which didn't leave him much time to study, especially when he had to get his own meals, and do his own washing. However, the 40-hour work week which went into effect under the Fair Labor Standards Act in October of 1940, meant that at least he received overtime pay.

After the war began all windows of the factory were blacked out, so his place of work afforded about as much light and sunshine as had the mine-tunnels in Trojan, South Dakota. He and the crew were working on DC3's, a large transport ship. Beside them another crew was working on a big B10 Super-Bomber. This bomber was an impressive sight. It dwarfed a motor car into insignificance. Its tires alone were gigantic. In fact, and this was no mere boast, the B 10's tires measured 96 inches in diameter with the largest casing of its sort ever made for an airplane. It had about a 500 ft. wingspread, and an average plane could set on each wing. The air in the tube weighed 28 lbs. while tire, tube, wheel, and brake top scale, sat at 2700 pounds! (The huge tire was a product of Firestone, not of Douglas Aircraft.) Bigger and better airplanes, better guns, and war implements were fast being materialized. Over in the Santa Monica plant nearing completion was the B-19 known as the "Guardian of a Hemisphere."

All this production meant thousands of people were needed on the assembly line, and Wilbur likened himself to an ant in an anthill. He had to keep busy on the production front or be quickly swamped by a busy crowd, thousandfold.

January 18, 1942, a newspaper in Williamsport, Pennsylvania, cried out in huge headlines: EVERY PLANE IN NATION NEEDED FOR VICTORY

"Plane, Gun, Tank, and Ship Builders must expand to meet record goals."

It went on to say, "Sweat and toil of 25,000,000 men...five times the number now employed...will be required to translate into planes and tanks and ships and guns the victory program of the United States. The cost in dollars and cents will amount to $427.48 for every man, woman, and child in the nation and will nearly double the current national debt of more than $58,000,000,000.

"In 12 months this country will spend: $56,000,000,000 on the victory program, to create arms not only for Uncle Sam but also for all the allies in the war against the Axis.

"It's an all-out mobilization for all-out victory for the United States."

As he worked in the manufacture of war planes, Wilbur was reminded daily, hourly, that his country *was* at war. Sometimes on his day off, he drove out to the beach, and up along the mountains taking pictures and enjoying the sunshine after the dark bustle of the factory, He recalled the mountains back home at Fletcher Park, Wyoming, where he had spent so many carefree hours growing up. He remem-

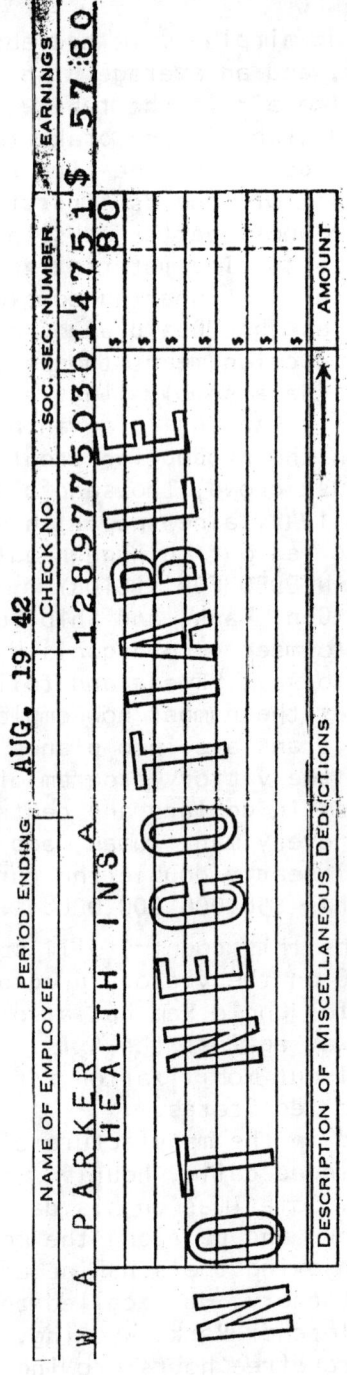

bered those halcyon days now as the black war cloud floated over his waking hours. He recalled how straight and tall the ponderosa pines stretched, heard in his mind their constant sighing unto the heavens...heavens so sunny and blue...while the trees spread their shade in protection of the boy trodding on the pine-needle carpet beneath. Ah, how he loved to hunt and fish along those mountain streams that headed in Laramie Peak country! As he grew older he found he was an avid hunter only when meat was needed for the family table. He far preferred hunting of the no-bloody type...let the pretty, agile deer roam free, he'd rather go searching for arrowheads in Cottonwood Park.

He finally succeeded in obtaining quite a collection of arrowheads. Ruby was always chiding him, "You can find Indian things when no one else can." He thought of his sister and how far their lives were drifting apart. "Hell," he mused, "One can't always remain a kid!" Nevertheless, he missed the dreams that were going so far astray.

His sister, Doris, was growing up on the old home place. She was so much younger than the rest of the family. "It's too bad," thought Wilbur, "She's really being cheated by not having brothers and sister her own age to share with." Well, all the pleasant home scenes were threatened now. "Yes," breathed Wilbur to himself as he kicked at the sand on Santa Monica Beach, "Yes, I'll *fight* if necessary to protect them!" He wasn't aware of voicing the sentiment of every patriotic, young man in the U.S.A.

Just one month from Pearl Harbor, January 7, 1942, the siege of Bataan was started. Lt. Johnathan M. Wainright was in charge of the defenders of Bataan. The shortage of food and medical supplies forced Bataan's surrender, April 9, 1942. The Japanese forced about 60,000 prisoners 70 miles to prisoner-of-war camps. About 10,000 American and Philipinos died from starvation and maltreatment during the march. Thus, the name,

Bataan Death March, was to go down in history as savage example as to what war is all about.
As the battle of Guadacanal raged in the Solomon Islands of the Southwest Pacific in August 1942, the draft board returned Wilbur to Class 1A. Without further procrastination, he went to take his physical examination.
It took longer to stand in line than the five minutes it took for the exam. "I feel like an old man compared to these boys," he thought as he looked down the line to estimate most of the "men" were between 18 and 20. Wilbur was 26, almost too old, all right, for the draft. He didn't know that the draft age in a few more months would be pushed up to age 42. He came away after the blood test and the simple questions, pondering, "Well, it looks as though it may not be long now before I'm in the fray. I'm not planning on it, but maybe I'll be killed before I have a chance to live. One thing is sure, there's one heck a lot of us running the same gauntlet." Then trying to find something good about his dilema, he thought, "I've felt so rotten lately, and I'm so run down maybe a shot of army life will do me good. They say the army builds one up."
Anyway, whether one liked it or not, there truly was no choice for any eligible, young man. Uncle Sam did the choosing. He recalled the recent letter he had from a cousin, Frank Hill, who wrote he was in Camp at Ft. McClellan, Alabama, "and it's not too bad," he said, "even if I don't know whether I really like it or not."
1942 was the true beginning of long years of brutal human extermination, not to mention the fiendish razing of tropical islands, and thriving countries. Nearing the end of August, 1942, all of Wilbur's indecisions came to an end. Notifying the Draft Board where he'd be, he quit his job at Douglas Aircraft. Then he persuaded his brother, Les and wife, Dorothy, to return to Wyoming with him...Les and Dorothy for a vacation, and Wilbur made up his mind he'd stay with his

folks in the mountains of Fletcher Park, Wyoming until he was called. He chose the Navy as the branch of the Service he wanted to be in. Now all he had to do was settle back and enjoy a good visit with his parents.

    Keeping track of the war was a little more difficult at Fletcher Park. Mail came to the little Post Office three times a week.There was no other means of communication with the outside world. His folks didn't even own a radio. Nevertheless, Wilbur's restlessness ebbed a bit. He put on some weight as he wandered about the old homeplace. Always before he'd felt that he had some control of his life...at least to a certain extent, like he could choose where he lived, what job he'd work at, and what he'd do for entertainment; for in America one had the right to choose one's course of direction. Now his life was out of his hands...his life was not his own...guess that was what fighting was all about...to protect your nation's freedoms, you lost your own. And because, he'd soon be the Devil's Advocate of War, he steeled himself to the implications that would mean. God, he hated to kill a deer, how could he kill a man?

    For a while he could roam the old mountain trails, traverse the paths along Cottonwood Creek, and inhale the good fresh mountain air. He helped his father, Samuel M. Parker, about the place, and he visited long hours with his mother, Ursa T. Parker. Doris, his sister, had much of his attention. Dark of hair, big brown eyes she was growing into a beautiful woman. They enjoyed some laughter and kidding, and at times, some serious talks. He could sense her great loneliness. She was growing up alone in the mountains with no one her age to talk to, or to do the things girls did...whatever that was. And Doris, as she listened to her brother and shared his laughter, alert to his moods and his thinking, always noting how great his love was for the mountains and the isolation they afforded, could never bring herself to confide what cried out in her heart, "Wilbur, these mountains you love are my prison!" Yes, she hated them! They were robbing her of all the things she wanted...most of all she wanted to be a girl. She wanted to do things, go places, learn the things that girls must learn to prepare for life. Here, life was passing her by. No one seemed to understand this, not even her parents. She could not talk to her parents about her great need. Much as she loved them, she could not hurt them for they truly believed they were rearing her in the best possible environment. They knew they were shielding her from all the cruel temptations of the outside world. Wilbur might understand, but he had enough on his mind faced, as he was, with entering the war. Wilbur may die in the war..."but will it," she wondered fiercely, "be any worse than shriveling up in isolation!"

That September, 1942, as Wilbur enjoyed the home scene, the bitter fighting in Guadacanal continued. By September 11, 6,000 Japanese had reached the island since August 29, via fast transports escorted by warships and landing by night. The Americans called these the "Tokyo Night Express." September 14, the Japanese broke off their assaults on Bloody Ridge leaving 600 dead men on the field. And on September 18, the Americans received reinforcements of vehicles, arms, ammunition, supplies, and petrol, besides the 4000 marines of the 7th Marine Regiment. By September 29, the American forces on Guadacanal numbered more than 19,000. The Seabee construction battalions were turning Henderson field into a fully operational airport, though the runway was often broken up by Japanese bombs. War was raging and bloody on all fronts. On the Eastern front the Russian counter-attack to the northwest of Stalingrad continued to make progress, with a report of bitter and gory hand-to-hand fighting.

At New Guinea, the Australians opened their counter-offensive in the mountains along the

Port Moresby-Kodak track, and in Madagascar the British could now boast they were in control of the Central part of that island. As September 1942 ended, the Japanese carried out the first nuisance raid on Adak Island.

On October 8, torrential rains forced the marines on Guadacanal to break off their attacks on the enemy beyond the river Matanikaw, and on Wilbur's 27th birthday, October 9, 1942, as he ate the birthday dinner his mother prepared for him, the Marines returned from the action on Matanikaw. The Japanese lost 700 men while the Americans counted 190 of their men dead or wounded.

Thus the battle of Guadacanal heightened as October advanced.

It was the latter part of October when Wilbur received his summons to appear in Cheyenne, Wyoming, to be inducted there. The date gave him time to go see his sister, Ruby, and her husband, Bill Goodwin, at Wendover, Wyoming, and to spend a day and night there. The time wasn't long enough for Ruby. She wanted to be with her brother long as possible. "I want to see you off," she told him, "but what will I do with Stanley? With gas rationing the way it is we can't take the car that far."

Quickly they solved the problem. They'd take the car as far as Wheatland, leave it there and take the bus on into Cheyenne. "We'll take little Stanley with us. He's too heavy for you to carry so I'll carry him." At three years old Stanley Goodwin was like carrying a 50-pound sack of flour for his mother. The thought of getting a baby sitter was preposterous. Even if there had not been a war going on to take all available man and woman power there were no baby-sitters unless one were to go thirty-eight miles or so into Guernsey. "I don't think there is such a thing as a baby sitter in the whole state of Wyoing," Ruby told her brother.

"We'll just take him with us,"Wilbur repeated.

The bus going into Cheyenne was packed. Ruby sat holding Stanley on her lap while Wilbur stood in the aisle beside them. Ruby recalled what had almost become a slogan..."Save the transportation for our servicemen." She felt very guilty taking up a seat.

Across the aisle from her a young sailor with the color high in his face kept repeating in a very loud voice, "Remember Bataan! Remember Bataan!" He made incomprehensible sounds, too, as he waved his arms and moved in his seat. "Hey," he called out to no one in particular,"REMEMBER BATAAN!" He seemed possessed by some inner image which threw him into a fever, "Remember Bataan!"

He's still in shock," someone spoke from the seat back of Ruby. "A lot of Navy men who fought on Bataan are being sent home"

"Yes," said another, "It seems the ones who didn't lose their lives there lost their minds."

Ruby felt a chill rising along her spine. What lay ahead for her brother? What good was war, even though it may bring freedom, if it left a demented nation?

Wilbur, Ruby, and Stanley arrived in Cheyenne to find that city packed with recruits from every branch of the service. It seemed everywhere they went service men moved in a sea flowing either to or from war.

She was thankful that Wilbur seemed to know where he was going. Carrying three-year old Stanley in strong, sheltering arms, and telling Ruby to stick closely to him, he forged ahead breaking through the crowds. To Ruby's amazement, Wilbur found out what he needed to know that October day of 1942. "My troop bus doesn't leave until tomorrow, so we may as well get something to eat before you board the return bus to Wheatland."

This turned into a major feat. All the cafes were packed with service men. All places were in an uproar. The fever of war was on rampage in every building and up and down the streets. Ruby, struggling to keep behind Wilbur with the mob jostling and pushing her, carried a sick feeling in the pit of her stomach. How could she stuff food on top of this God-awful war-sickness?

"Do we have to eat?" she yelled, hoping Wilbur could hear her above the noise. "Let's try this place," he yelled back,"It doesn't look quite so crowded."

When they worked their way inside the door, they actually spotted what appeared to be an empty booth in the back of the cafe. By the time they could reach it, it contained four sailors.

"Hey," called a soldier, "That's a good-looking wife and kid you got there, Buddy. It's too bad you can't take them with you."

"She's my sister," Wilbur kept saying to the many who asked, then he gave up on all answering of needless questioning to concentrate on finding a place to sit down.

Ruby was surprised that Stanley didn't cry as the crowd clamored and shoved. However, he hadn't even whimpered, and ordinarily he was a very timid child. He merely clung to his adored uncle, and when the jostling worsened, he clenched his tiny arms about Wilbur's neck and hung on.

As they were about to give up in the search for a table, a booth of sailors who had finished eating and were merely adding their shouting to the bedlam, relinquished their seats to Wilbur and his sister. Then, they were forever getting waited on.

"Maybe I'll miss the bus," remarked Ruby, as she watched the harried waitreses.They looked much as if they'd been out on a race track all day beneath a hot sun. Their hair and faces were damp, and their uniforms dirty and rumpled. When the ordered hamburgers finally arrived, they were cold and dried up. Stanley was so paralyzed by the confusion he couldn't eat no matter how his uncle coaxed. "Well, maybe we have time to plow out and get to your bus,"Wilbur shouted at his sister with a big grin.

Thus it happened, Ruby didn't get to see Wilbur depart for war. It was a hasty good-bye at the bus depot. It was late, not even a moment for tears, as Ruby, carrying Stanley and purse, crowded up the bus steps. The darkness and the crowd swallowed her brother while the war-pain jabbed her throat. She carried it with her as she forged down the bus aisle looking for a seat. There were none. She stood holding Stanley in the crowded aisle, numb with what was happening to so many by this war. She hugged her son to her, a little ashamed she was so glad he was too tiny for the service...not *now*, not *ever*, she hoped.

A voice called beside her, and a hand tugged at her sleeve, "Hey, little girl, you may have this seat." A sailor, handsome of features, a white cap on his black hair, was looking up at her.

"Oh, no," she objected recalling the patriotic slogan..."*Save our transportation*...."

"Yes," he said firmly, "It's the likes of you we're fighting for. I'll crowd in amongst my buddies back there," he said pointing towards the rear of the bus. With these words he arose and fairly planted her in the seat, Stanley on her lap.

"I love sailors," she thought, "I love all sailors who're risking their lives...all sailors who're going insane after fighting...all sailors who are protecting my son, all service men who are going to war." The enormity of what war was doing to the young men of the United States hit her like a thunderbolt, "Oh, my God, and my brother is one of them!" Tears stung her eyes and crawled down her aching throat.

Truly, there was no consolation for the agony Ruby, or other loved ones felt, as they watched their kin being shipped off to battle.

A few days after Wilbur's departure, she received a short letter fom him. As she read, her thought was, "He's safe as long as his training lasts." The address told her in what direction he was taken . She read eagerly, still feeling the frightful war-pain in her inwards.

W.A. Parker, A.S.
Co. 53, Barracks 18
2nd Regiment, U.N.T.S.
Camp Ward, Farragut, Idaho

October 25, 1942

Dear Ruby,
    We had a nice trip though it was a little cold through Douglas and Casper.(Wyo.) There was about 3 or 4 inches of snow there. It is nice here though.
    We got into camp about 7 o'clock Friday night. They looked our luggage over and we were given bunks and eats. Next day, Saturday, we were given our clothes, we took a medical exam and were assigned to our company and barracks. The medical exam was simple enough but my left arm is sore and stiff from the shots they gave me. We did some drilling yesterday, but, don't guess we will get much today it being Sunday. They say we have to go to church.
    I'm wondering how far it is to Grandpa and Grandma Parker's? They're in Couer de'Alene somewhere...can't be very far, or so I think.
    Camp Ward is a big place. I'm told it's supposed to accomodate 30,000 recruits when finished. There's a recreation center and a canteen where we can buy candy, stationery, etc. Then there's a movie picture theater and a swimming pool. In fact, I just heard some of the boys say we're allowed to go in the pool now, so think I'll put on my trunks and go over. Sure hope you and little Stanley made it home O.K.
    Write soon, Wilbur

    When Wilbur boarded the recruit bus in Cheyenne, Wyoming, he had no idea where he'd end up. As he noted the Highway signs, he learned he wasn't going East, for which he was grateful. He was at home in the West.
    About four miles east of Athol, Idaho, lay Farragut, Idaho, his destination. As Wilbur came down the steps of the bus that cold, October day and viewed the huge U.S. Naval Training Center of

which he was to become a part, he thought, "This is a bigger ant hill than the Douglas Aircraft factory. I'll truly feel like an ant here." As he barged into the buzzing, teeming, ant hill, it wasn't the last time he'd feel he'd lost his identity...all servicemen, he found, soon felt this way...one man was nothing...it was the regimented whole that belonged. Should one man fall it little mattered, he was so quickly replaced by another...the same as any army ant.

"This must be my first lesson," he mused, "in Naval indoctrination." Nevertheless, he experienced a feeling of thankfulness when he raised his eyes to look beyond the Center to see Farragut rimmed by trees, like a familiar scene from his Wyoming home. He'd also noted during the four-mile stretch from Athol to Farragut that the road was lined with jack pines. Farragut itself was constructed in a most scenic setting of ponderosa pine, white pine, and douglas fir, not to mention the western red cedar and the western tamarac. It was very much like the home country of Wyoming with the familiar trees and the mountains in the background. This huge Naval base was nestled at the foot of the Coer d'Alene and the Bitterroot Mountain Ranges. The forest land protected many species of wild life such as the whitetail deer, black bear, bobcat, coyote, mountain goat, and the badger...even an occasional elk roamed the secluded country side...making it hard to realize a war was impending and threatening, it was such a quiet, calm, sanctuary.

Wilbur came at the wrong season to see them, but Idaho natives told him, besides a wide variety of water fowl, there were many kinds of birds... the robin, owl, humming bird, bald eagle, and the kingfisher. Then there was Idaho's state bird, the Mountain Bluebird.

Later, as Wilbur became established in Camp-life, he discovered were he to walk straight South for six or seven-hundred yards from Camp Ward he'd run into Lake Pend Oreille, a deep, cold,

50-mile-long lake. Actually, the massive naval training base of Farragut was built on the southwestern tip of this lake. "Pend Oreill", an Idaho native told him, "is pronounced *Ponderay*. It's French for ear lobe."

Indeed, the lake *was* a vast ear lobe that curved among the beautiful, wooded terrain where the Kaniksu National Forest merged with the Couer d'Alene National Forest to insure a perpetual native atmosphere for many miles.

On the northeastern shore of the lake between Hope and Clark Fork the lake was rimmed by the Cabinet Mountains. A railroad went along this mountainous shore line amid thick trees and underbrush.

Precipitous slopes provided only a slim shoreline along the southeastern side where the lake was framed between native fir and yellow pine. At times, Wilbur was informed, Idaho's state flower, the Syringa, decked the verdant shore.

Wilbur with 100 or so other recruits had come all the way from Cheyenne by bus. However, most of the recruits arrived at Athol by train from their induction centers and were hauled the four miles to Farragut by large buses. "I felt as though they were taking me to the end of the world," a would-be sailor told Wilbur, "Especially as we cane from Athol down through those miles of trees before we got here!"

But Wilbur was accustomed to trees, and mountains. He'd grown up in isolation of this kind. What bothered him were the thousands of recruits, 300 of which were right in his own barracks, where there was no way of separation himself from them. To live totally without privacy was one of the toughest lessons he was to learn while in the Navy.

*"The barracks buildings were designed to house two companies of recruits, each consisting of about 150 men, with one company on the lower "deck" and the other "topside". There were 22 of these barracks buildings on the perimeter of each "camp" or regiment, with the center of activity being the huge drill hall and adjoining drill field, affectionately known as the "grinder". The barracks frequently looked desserted while recruits were out drilling or receiving other training.

*World War II was already in progress when construction of Farragut Naval Training Base first started. The Walter Butler Construction Co. undertook the gigantic task of building it in six months, starting April 10, 1942. 22,000 men were hired working 10 hours a day, and 13 out of every 14 days.

*"The orginal plans for Farragut called for a 20,000-man training facility costing $27 million. At the ground breaking the plan was revised to 30,000-man facility, costing $37 million.

"The naval station was commissioned in September 1942. After 5 months construction Camp Bennion was opened for recruits September 15, 1942, the first of the six training camps to be completed."*

Six training camps opened within six months of which Camp Ward was second, opening October 1, 1942, Wilbur arriving October 23, 1942.

**"Each of the self-contained camps was designed to house, feed, and train some 5,000 men at a time. Each camp was laid out in the form of an oval with the huge drill field or 'grinder' in the center. Along one side was the gigantic drill hall, large enough to accommodate six basketball courts, with a swimming pool, 75 foot square, attached to one end. Each camp had its own mess hall, 22 doubledeck barracks, two medical dispensaries, a recreation and ship's store building, indoor rifle range, regimental headquarters, Chief Petty Officers quarter, and service buildings."

*Information courtesy, Al Leiser, Assistant Manager, Farragut State Park, Idaho, Dept of Parks & Recreation, Athol, Idaho

** a quote from "Farragut State Park" Bulletin

   As Wilbur stepped inside his new home at Camp Ward, Barracks 18, he looked down the long interior at the long lines of bunks, 3 deep on either side of the isle that lined both walls, he thought, "I guess this may be something to write home about but I won't write it. My mother would be horrified. It reminds me of a rather big clean barn complete with stanchions."
   * "There was no semblance of carpeting, of course, but there were signs to tell you that the 'ceiling'was the overhead and 'front' was the 'bow'. And many other signs introduced the recruit to the Navy terminology of ship life. Each 'deck' of the barracks contained about 75 bunks to accomodate about 150 men. Each recruit was issued his own mattress, and they received heavy, canvas hammocks too, which they'd need on board ship.
   "Large communal shower and shave rooms adjoined the 'heads' at the end of the 'deck'...."
   Wilbur, following the other recruits, hung his canvas sailor's bag from the end of his bunk, thinking as he did so, "Hi, Mom, I'm home in my stanchion hanging up my harness."
   * Everyone in camp soon knew that Farragut, was named after Admiral David Glasgow Farragut, USN, famous for his achievements during the Civil war and the first Admiral of the United States Navy. The name "Farragut" was chosen by Commander-inChief of all the U.S. armed Forces, President Franklin D. Roosevelt. Admiral David Glasgow Farragut was born at Campbell's Station, near Knoxville, Tennesee on July 5, 1801, and died at Portsmouth, New Hampshire, on August 14, 1870, after 59 years of service in the Navy."

   * Information courtesy, Al Leiser, Assistant Manager, Farragut State Park, Idaho, Dept. of Parks & Recreation, Athol, Idaho

Wilbur also learned that Camp Ward was named after a James Richard Ward, S 1/C, U.S.N. However, the name was all he came to know about Camp Ward.

Immediately, almost before he hung his sea bag at its post, Wilbur was launched into the training life of Camp Ward. By November 5, 1942, he'd been on guard duty for nearly two weeks.*"Barracks Guard Duty was an essential phase of recruit training. All hands took turns standing these 3-hour watches around the clock and also tending the barracks furnace."

While Wilbur was on guard duty, November 5,1942, the American infrantry regiment was pushing south of Koli Point in an effort to surround the Japanese forces concentrated in the area. Wilbur would keep closer track of what was going on in the islands now that he was a Navy man. His mind was full of askance..."In what part of the ocean will I eventually be stationed...what gulf...what island, what water, what ship?"

"I think I've hit it pretty soft for these first few weeks, at least," he told himself. "I stand guard at regimental headquarters for six hours, then I'm off 18." And to top this he was permitted to stand in the boiler room most of the time where it was warm. His most difficult problem, it seemed, was remembering to salute all the officers that hung around. It seemed, everywhere he moved he bumped into one. Then after a while he became used to saluting and it seemed a natural thing to do.

Following the shots he wrote to his sister about, the recruits got a shot for typhoid. It proved to be a rugged injection, eight of the men passed out, some of them passing out several times, while two were taken to the dispensary. Wilbur had some fever the first night, but his

* Information courtesy, Al Leiser, Assistant Manager, Farragut State Park, Idaho Dept. of Parks & Recreation, Athol, Idaho

23

arm wasn't nearly as sore as it had been from those first shots. He noticed his sore arms mostly when he delved into that darned canvas sea bag. It was about 3 feet high and about 16 inches in diameter, so it was a heck of a thing to get into. They were given orders to keep *everything* but their blankes, mattresses, overshoes, and the blue caps in it. In order to get *anything* into it, all clothes must be properly folded and rolled.

In November, Wilbur recieved the good news that Brother Les was now working in Northrupt. Maybe he'd be deferred as he was working in an essential war industry...this and the fact he was married. Marital status made a difference with the Draft Board, especially those married *before* the war started so it didn't look as though marriage was a draft dodge.

November 19, 1942, was to be a big day in Camp Ward for Company 53. The recruits were to take an I.Q. test, which was to determine (as to grade) whether or not Mr. Recruit would get to go to school. * "After Boot Training many sailors who exhibited special aptitudes were assigned to Service Schools for 16 weeks of training in various specialties. Farragut had quite a number of such schools, preparing men for petty officer ratings as Electricians Mate, Gunner's Mate, Fire Controlmen, and Torpedoman in the Electrical and Ordance Depts., and Radioman, and Signalman, Quartermaster, Yeomen and Storekeeper in the Communications and Clerical Departments."

November 18 was DISASTER DAY for Wilbur who arose feeling so rotten he knew he was losing his mind. "Guess I'll catch one of those workers that are working on the station tonight and go AWOL," he moaned,"Very likely I'll be dead by the time they catch me! Ye Gods, I didn't think

    * Information courtesy, Al Leiser, Assistant Manager, Farragut State Park, Idaho Dept. of Parks & recreation, Athol, Idaho

24

I could pass the upcoming test even *if* I felt *good*. Now what? I'd think my head was wood if it didn't hurt so damned bad!" At 8:30 A.M. he found himself in the dispensary. After the doctor gave him a brief check-up, he growled at Wilbur, "Now get out of here and go to bed." Instead, Wilbur went to chow certain he'd feel better if he ate. "It's nothing serious or the doctor would have said." After eating a little, he actually did feel somewhat better, at least, good enough to worry some more. "My gosh, there must be 18 or 20 thousand recruits here, and I understand only about 125 so far are getting to go to school. My,gosh,if this doesn't go away, how am I going to stand a chance?"

Maybe if he kept moving around this awful feeling would gradually leave. If only he felt like washing. Washing was a special headache all its own, and there was always laundry to do. Really,he didn't mind scrubbing his own clothes, it was hasseling the other 120 men trying to do the same thing...all in one small washroom, no tubs, no wash boards...this, and the fact all washing was to be done between the hours of 4:30 and 9:00. The Navy really believed in you getting your clothes clean, too, and *keeping* them that way! There were two wash days a week in which time the men were to keep their clothes spotless.

The crucial day of November 19 arrived inspite of all fears and worries, finding Wilbur in the dispensary...the prognosis *measles*. Before he landed there, however, he screwed on his aching, block, head, and muddled through the awesome test. Fever was eating him up. He had difficulty reading the questions, and when he did, he couldn't concentrate on the meaning. "The questions are easy," he moaned to himself, "For they might as well not be where they are. I can't read them, much less understand them, so they make sense all right! Just write down something, just whatever's in this head, and hang onto it for God's sake. For God's sake, hang onto this damn, painful head!

It's the only one I'll ever have!"

He was never to know how he made it to the dispensary. After a week's passage he still lay feverish and cramped in the small confinement of a hospital on base. Why did they choose to put him in this one? Maybe only the deranged came here! Seems like even crazy people would need hot water to shave or take a bath. But then, heck, he wasn't able to shave or take a bath.

Wilbur's incapacitaion did not deter the war. The very night of the day he was stuck in the dispensary, the Japanese on Guadacanal launched an attack from Kukombona against the American positions in the sector west of the river, Matanikau. On the 21st the Americans succeeded in driving the Japanese out of Cruz Point, but made no further progress.

When at last Wilbur was released from the hospital, dirty and unshaven, he felt as though he were being freed from a run-down jail. None-theless, he'd been pretty glad to go in, and he came out to the discovery he was a lucky man to still be in Company 53; for some of the men who hadn't even been as ill or as long as he, had been sent back to a younger company.

He'd spent Thanksgiving in the hospital, which hadn't mattered. Although the food was somewhat cold, he felt well enough to eat some of the turkey, ham, mashed potatoes, cranberries, pickles and mince pie. After picking over this feast on the menu, he decided oranges was the very best diet. He and the others in sick bay discovered there was a crate of oranges in the hallway at all times. All you needed to get one was to feel well enough to crawl forth to get yourself one or several.

Back in his barracks, he cleaned up in the communal shower and shave-room to find he was still very weak. In spite of how he felt, there was a lot of catching up to do. His washing was the worst task. With perspiration pouring from him he finally managed it. Before his sweat dried, or his knees felt strong enough to hold him, Company 53 had a 12-hour liberty. He was struck by an urge to take advantage of this chance. He needed to burst out the door and get away from the strict confinement of the Service and his recent illness. The laundry had taken the last ounce of his strength; but maybe he could hold out until he reached Grandpa and Grandma Parker's in Coeur d'Alene. Afterall, Coeur d'Alene was only twenty-five miles north of Farragut. Liberty buses ran there five minutes after the hour, day and night, with extra buses during the peak hours. The fare was a shocking 35¢ one way, 70¢ round trip. Then there were also the liberty trains between Farragut and Spokane, which ran three times daily, coming in directly to the Naval Base on a spurline from Athol. The round trip fare only $1.10. Or maybe he could just coax a ride from one of the workers on the base before they left for whatever town they made their home in.

Maybe Willie Wiley would let him jump aboard his Model T. "Take me wherever you're going," he'd say to Willie, "I can't take anymore confinement. I can't do another wash. God, Willie, I was born in the mountains, and it's going to take more than the Navy to take them out of me! I was born *free!*"

Willie would understand; for Willie was born free, too, a back-to-nature advocate. Though a lot of the recruits laughed and called him eccentric, Wilbur always came to his defense, "He's just living his life Nature's way and what he believes. He isn't hurting anyone. Someone told me he's a victim of T.B. I'll be willing to bet he'll live longer than healthy us."

"Yeah, he sure as Hell won't die under gunfire in the war," sneered a recruit. "I'll bet his back-to-nature act is just a cover up."

"Then that makes him smarter than you or me... you know being a naturalist is no draft dodge." Wilbur smiled at the image he carried of Willie, his thin body, clothed only in a pair of shorts

and a pair of shoes, as he bent to sawing boards
or pounding nails. Wilbur often wondered how
Willie kept from being all scratched up by the
rough lumber. Fearing he may step on nails or
slivers, it was strict Company rules that demanded
Willie wear shoes. Off the job, shorts was his
only garb.
    Willie had a companion very unlike himself.
Wilbur often wondered why they teamed up. He was
a tall, black-headed, good-looking man. Wilbur
never learned his name. Someone remarked, "He's
a good joe." Thus, the recruits always referred
to him as "Good Joe".
    When Joe and his companion, Willie Wiley,
came to work, September 1942, on the street construction of Farragut Naval Base, the whole 4,160-
acre site was fenced in. Camp Bennion, only, of
the six proposed camps was finished and already
alive with recruits. Twenty feet outside the
fence were the nurses' quarters. Although Joe's
job was the street outlay, one-half the streets
were already in. Joe's profession definitely was
not carpentery. He was temporarily out of a job...
more likely to say he was waiting between jobs
and hoped to be transferred soon, In the mean-
time, he was making much more in Farragut than he
ever made on the railroad. His draft card classified him in 11A, which meant he was exempt from
military duty because of holding an important
job or being in an important industry; besides,
he was a family man with two small children.
    At one time he though he'd like to join some
branch of the Service...sort of mob psychology,
he concluded, all able-bodied men were joining
and feeling guilty if they didn't. Now, as he
watched the drilling mass of recruits, he didn't
envy them. Men in collective herds, he thought
cease to be individuals. These, young, smooth-
faced, men with the crew-cut hair, and wrapped
in their uniforms, all looked the same. At
night when Joe and his co-workers started to go
home, dozens of recruits swarmed their cars,

clamoring for a ride into Athol or to any other town...<u>anywhere</u> they'd say just to get away. They all seemed to be seeking the same thing...a short repreive from the confining headquarters of Camp. He knew each recruit must long to be his own person again doing his own thing, leading a life of his own choosing. He'd invite them to climb aboard as many as could hang on. However, of all the passengers they hauled into town, he never learned any of their names...nondescript, their individual faces merged into one likeness.

    Wilbur day-dreamed until his opportunity to catch a ride into Athol with Willie or Joe passed. Heck, the Station's Central Auditorium right here in Farragut very likely had some good entertainment going on if entertainment was what he wanted. Most every night there were all sorts of entertainment on base, movies, dances, swimming, some of the sailors fished in Clark Fork River east of Pend Oreille Lake. Noon dances were often provided for Ship's Company in the Recreation Building. Civilian employees as well as the Waves participated in these pleasant interludes.

    Wilbur wasn't seeking entertainment. He wanted to be free; he wanted to be alone. When most of the boys left for liberty, he was glad he stayed. With everyone gone, he could rest here, right in his own home-stanchion better than most anyplace he could go.

    The next day found him feeling a bit stronger. Before starting the studies he had at hand, he decided he must find out how he came out on his test. Taking himself firmly in hand he went forth to seek out the Selective Officer. His knees were even weaker than he thought, and he felt a slight trembling in them as he waited for the officer to look up his grades. It seemed long moments before the uniformed bulk of the officer turned from the file, papers in hand. He peered over them at Wilbur, his heavy brows coming together in a dark V. "Well," he said, "You certainly should have no trouble getting into school on

these grades!"
All of a sudden Wilbur's knees felt stronger. He was so surprised by the answer, he said a quick, "Thank you, Sir," saluted, and left.
"What were your grades?" he was asked when he returned to Company 53. With something akin to shock,he realized he'd been so relieved by what the officer told him, he'd forgotten to ask! Well, he wasn't going back to bother that gloom, bushy-browed, officer again!
"Lord," he stammered, I forgot to ask. I passed, but I scarcely think it could be more than 70 or 72 average, which doesn't seen to me to be very good."
As the days went by he felt comfortable just to know he made it. Also, when someone asked his grades, he could be honest and say he didn't know. This way there was no grade-comparing. Many of his buddies revealed they received a grade as low as 25-50. One recruit announced, "I only got a 15 in one subject." Wilbur could not understand why he told this on himself.
Thus, by not knowing his grade, Wilbur couldn't put himself down, nor could he brag. Somehow it all seemed to put himself on an even keel with his buddies. Some of the recruits did make bragging grades. He learned several men came up with a grade of 90 or better. One man got 100 in the hardest subject.
Nevertheless, Wilbur went along content. If he'd flunked the whole test, he wouldn't have been surprised. What did surprise him was that he *passed* with a fever of 104 burning up his marrow. The morning after the test his fever rose to 105, and the darned thermometer didn't go higher than 108.
All that mattered at the present, he'd get to go to school. The question rose in his mind would he try for Aircraft, Metalsmith, or Aircraft Mechanics? By going to school very likely he he wouldn't get to go home after he was through at Camp Ward. The way he understood the rules, no

one got leave until he was ready to go on sea duty, or was sent aboard, or was sent to any place outside the United States, Alaska, or any territory. Well, then how long would it be before he merited a leave? Schools in aviation subjects were 6 months courses. He might get out of trainby Dcember 1943. In this case , he would be lucky if he got home on leave for the 4th of July, 1943.
"Ha," he thought, "If they'll only let me do the figuring!"
He continued to write to his sister, Ruby, regularly. She poured over his letters seeking answers to calm her fears for him. Where would Wilbur be placed after he finished his schooling? Would he really go into *active*? "Of course, he will, you fool," she answered herself, "Why else are they training him?" Then she'd shudder at the thought of her gifted brother being mere gun fodder. He could better serve his country in so many other ways, for he was a talented person. He wrote beautiful poetry; he did perfect sculptoring; he could draw and paint. The list of his abilities went on and on; but best of all he was a compassionate, honest,and sensitive person.
It seemed he had the very ingredients that would be a detriment to him when he faced enemy fire. Maybe, being the humanitarian that he was, he'd hesitate too long before he fired into the face of an opposing man.

W. A. Parker, A.S.
Co. 53, U.S.N.T.S.
Farragut, Idaho
December 6, 1942

Dear Ruby,
It doesn't seem our "training" has amounted to very much. About all we've learned so far is how to march,(Thought I'd get out of that when I joined the Navy!) and we've still got plenty of room for improvement. Learned the names of highranking Naval Officers, how to tie a number of

knots, a variety of Naval names, terms, and definitions, the alphabet in signal code, and how to swim. (I took the swim test and easily passed, so, of course, I didn't have to bother any more with that).

We all have a book, "Blue Jacket's Manuel", of about 800 pages that we are supposed to know from cover to cover. We had a test on the forepart of it the other day. The majority passed easily, but some had pretty poor grades...24 was the worst...poor guy must not be able to read! By the way I made a 97...pat, pat...I'll forget it all inside of a week!

I think the main object of our training must be to teach us patience. By gosh, we spend hours standing in line waiting every day. We wait for chow, for lectures (which we have about every day) then we have to stand guard for 4 hours about every other day.

They found out I can carve so they have me whittling out wooden guns and swords we are to use in drill later on. By gosh, it sure looks dumb wasting time during war to whittle *wooden* fire arms! One thing is to be said for it...it's SAFE!

I seem to have gotten over the effects of the measles pretty well, but had to stand guard last night and I caught a little more cold.

Snows a little about every day, and is gradually piling up until there must be 10 or 12 inches on the ground. Write soon, Wilbur

News of Camp Ward and Wilbur's wood-carving expertise made news in *THE SPOKESMAN REVIEW,* December 27, 1942, Spokane, Washington

Navy Recruits at Farragut Station Are Wood Carving Experts

The rifle held by Roy E. Dryer, San Francisco recruit at the naval training station at Farragut, Idaho, and Mrs. Dorothy Starr, station receptionist, is one gun that will never go off. It is carved entirely of wood and is but one of the many models of guns, planes and ships that have been created by recruits as visual aids for lectures and have been on display at Camp Ward.

By December 18, 1942, Wilbur and Company 53, were working eight hours a day. An American submarine sunk the Japanese Cruiser TENRYU in the Bismark sea.

"What are you working at today, Hank?" Wilbur's buddy from the next "stanchion" asked.

"I'm *sewing*,what're you doing?" Wilbur grinned widely.

"You're *what?*"

"Well, I guess I'm really braiding rope mostly. Oh, Hell, I really don't know what I'm doing. It doesn't make sense. Part of the time I'm fashioning a wooden sword for the Regimental Commander. I made one for the Company Commander. He showed it to the Reg. Commander who liked it so well, I have to make one for him now. Then I made two for display, so that's where all my spare time goes. For entertainment I get to wash my clothes."

"Yeh, we're into full-time war production," exclaimed Wilbur's buddy, "Hell, man, we're supposed to be fighting a real war, not playing toys!"

"The Company Commander says we'll be in the melee soon enough. Guess we'd better take time to play while we can." Wilbur wasn't laughing anymore. "These wooden guns maybe our country and family's only inheritance."

"You say the truth,Man. I think we'll graduate from our training pretty soon. We probably won't be here much longer. Six of the boys have already left."

"I hope we don't leave until after Christmas," said Wilbur, "It's begun to seem a bit like home here. At least, I feel acquainted. If we're here it won't be like having Christmas among total strangers."

There was a mad scramble amid Company 53, when the next day Wilbur received a big box of cookies from Ruby. He thought he may lose all his Christmas goodies before he could get the lid back on the box. He hung on to it yelling, "Good, Lord, you guys have some manners!"

"Who wants manners? We want cookies. Don't be

so darned stingy." Another lunge was made for him and the box.

"It's too damned cold outside or I'd fix you guys," Wilbur growled as he hung onto the box. "Stop, They'll be nothing but crumbs!"

"We'll eat crumbs."

"Tell your sister to send more cookies!"

"Is this fantastic cookie-maker married?"

Someone was always wanting to know if Ruby was married. He got so he ignored the question.

Back in Wyoming, Ruby was undergoing her own special misery. While her husband, Bill Goodwin, was busy riding and covering twenty miles of the Standoline Pipe Line by horseback, she and her three-year old son, Stanley, hovered in a small, two-room cabin, situated on the Standoline Pipe Line, two miles or so from Wendover, Wyoming. Wendover was a railway junction, boasting a population of perhaps, six people...three adults, and three children. Guernsey, the closest town, was 38 miles away.

With the war ravaging and threatening the entire world, Ruby was isolated out on Wyoming prairie land...the nearest neighbor being two miles from her. Here she was forced to bury herself when she wanted to help *the cause* so much it was sheer agony to be tied. In towns and cities her cousins became active in so many war-time industries. If they had children they hired baby sitters. Everyone was jumping in to do his bit.

Ruby soon learned that sitting, waiting, and worrying, was a much more difficult task that working, or fighting, or doing. She chafed the long hours aways. "I'm young," she thought, "I'm healthy, I'm *able* if I was given a chance!" Then in a frenzy of frustration, she cried to the walls, "And I am *buried!*" *It was like standing by and watching her brother shot with no effort to help him.*

Sometimes she buried her head in her arms and wept, and her son would start crying, too. "This is no way to raise a child," she cautioned her-

35

self. "I've got to straighten up and do what's right." Only she found there's no such thing as *right* during a war.

Bill's job was classified as an important war-industry work, so here they must stay. She crammed this fact down her lane of muddled thinking each day. The railroad was her companion. It split the prairie with its black rails that ran through sagebrush and across sands. The loud whistle of an engine often split the somber silence of the flat lands before it crossed the roadway that ran to Wendover. Its rumble shook the tiny cabin which stood, perhaps, 300 yards from the rails. "Choo, choo!" piped Stanley who ran to look as fast as his chubbly legs could carry him so as to see the train puffing by in its gray swirl of smoke and steam. If it were winter, he'd crawl upon the bed to look out the window. In the summer, Ruby had difficulty keeping him from going to stand on the tracks. "Wait, Choo-Choo," he cried as she carried him home.

It was on a December day, Ruby settled in the one rocker the cabin afforded gathering Stanley upon her lap, "If you'll sit still," she told him, "I'll read to you about Aunt Dorothy." Immediately he settled down, for he always liked for her to read to him whether he understood what she read or not. Wilbur sent her the letter he'd recieved from Dorothy Parker, sister-in-law..."You wrote you hadn't heard from Les for sometime, so I thought you may like to read this letter."

593 No. Grevillea Ave.
Hawthorne, California
December 17, 1942

Dear Wilbur,
     The North wind doth blow and we have some rain along with all of this cold weather that we have been having; so wait a second while I hitch up closer to the fire and shake the ice out of my fingers. Now there...let's see what's new around

here? As usual very little...here are a few choice bits which are quite old and stale, but still the best I have to offer.

Les got a raise this last week. That makes him a dollar an hr. now. And we're still expecting the general raise which should be about fifteen cents. I think that I told you before that he is going to that J.I.T. school again. Tonight is his last night of that. Guess that he had done pretty good with it. Heavens, he should as long as this is his second time at it. They told him he was to go to another school sometime in January. That is supposed to be some kind of thing that teaches you about the different parts of the ship and the jobs that go with it. His foremen told him the other night that he would be over all the line of riveting just as soon as they break the experimental department up into several departments. Leslie will have four of five group-leaders and about one-hundred other men. In one respect it might be some easier, but there will be more book-keeping etc. to it. Leslie says that he would still rather go back and just rivet. Well, I guess that is just about the line-up on the job situation, so now what shall I talk about?

How about a bit of Trojan, S. Dak. scandal...?

The Marvin Anderson's have a new son. They say it looks like the big apple himself, only it has red hair....

Mr. Lord quit the Navy yard and is back in Denver. He got a ninety-day objection to being employed in any defense job out of the bay area when he quit the yard.

Ellis Lord is in San Francisco. They're teaching him carpentering, so he no doubt will be there quite a while.

Donald Johnson is to be sent overseas. Bob Benda is in Texas.

I believe that I told you before the Cattles and McCoys both went to their ranches.

Harley and Louise DeWitt were over for a couple

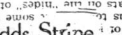

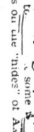

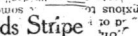

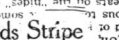

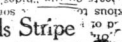

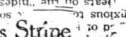

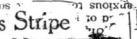

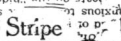

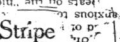

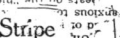

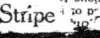

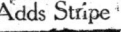

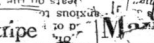

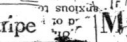

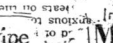

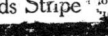

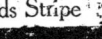

"FARRAGUT NEWS"

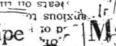

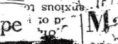

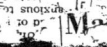

FARRAGUT NEWS

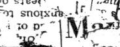

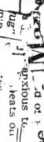

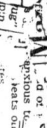

VOLUME 1   UNITED STATES NAVAL TRAINING STATION, FARRAGUT, IDAHO, DECEMBER 24, 1942   NUMBER 3

Camp Waldron Boxing Draws Large Crowd

No holding of punches and plenty of fast fistic action was the bill-of-fare last Friday night at the Camp Waldron drill hall. The boxing events were topped by the light-heavyweight bout between Lampkie of Co. 148 and Bastas of Co. 126.

Lampke, who was declared the winner after a fight where punches were flying faster than recruits legs on the grinder, tipped the scales at 165 pounds and Bastas weighed in at 163 pounds.

In the featherweight division, Corea of Co. 74 won a decision over Romera of Co. 107. Moore of 126 took a decision in the lightweight division over Blye of the same company, and McIntosh was awarded a close decision over Maw in the middleweight division McIntosh is a member of Co. 78 and Maw is from Co. 95.

A new style of footwork brought

MERRY CHRISTMAS

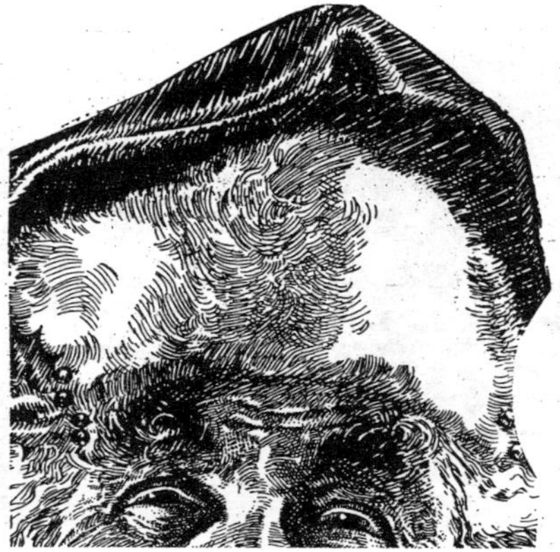

Recruits Will Celebrate Holiday at Xmas Programs

When recruits write home about Christmas at Farragut, many a father and mother will wish they could have been present at the festivities. With the holiday on a Sunday, the bluejackets will be able to have time to open packages from home, eat an enormous Christmas dinner with all the trimmings and enjoy the special events.

All five camps are decorating huge Christmas trees erected in front of the mess halls and a program which will see all the recruits in attendance will be held around the tree.

Funds from Welfare and Recreation Department have been allotted to each regiment for the preparation of programs that will appeal to the men in training. Up to now those in charge have managed to keep most of the details from interested news reporters.

Camp Bennion probably has the most elaborate plan for the occasion and recruits will be treated to a double feature movie, party on the drill field in front of the mess hall, singing of carols by a chorus of 60 voices and many other features.

SEAL BENEFIT GIVES ADDITIONAL FUNDS

The Christmas Seal Benefit at all four theaters on the Station proved entertaining for the personnel and profitable for the seal fund. It gave everybody an excellent opportunity to contribute toward the Anti-Tuberculosis Association and at the same time see a good show.

A complete report on the drive throughout the Station will be made in the next issue of the "Farragut News." Rumors from the

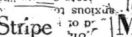

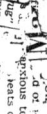

BEDTIME STORY

"Sense" comes the Bureau of Aeronautics

PAGE FOUR "FARRAGUT NEWS" THURSDAY, DECEMBER 24, 1942

Regimental Review....

Entertainment is free and plentiful in the barracks of Co. 81, where B. Brown and C. Rist, plus a few other talented guitarists have been providing their shipmates with lots of music.

* * *

The departure of Roland Mickelson from his home in Milwaukee on December 7 for training at Farragut, raised to six the number of sons Mr. and Mrs. Peter Mickelson have seen off to the service. Roland, 31, is now at Camp Hill, training in Co. 151. He has three brothers in the Navy and two in the Army.

* * *

There is one Navy mother who is certainly making sure, her son John Francis Patterson, Co. 137, does not go hungry at Christmas time while in the service. John has received a "small" gift package which was equally welcomed by his shipmates. Its contents included two pounds of mints, five pounds of Christmas candy, two pound box of cherry chocolates, two pounds of mixed nuts, three cartons of candy bars, one fruit cake, one carton of gum, one carton of cigarettes, ten cigars, eight dates and figs, two pound packages each of dates and figs, two pound mixed cookies, a five pound fruit cake, one carton of gum, one carton of cigarettes, ten cigars, and of course a copy of the following issue of the home town newspaper.

No wonder John is such a popular man!

* * *

Another lucky man in Co. 137 is George Blessinger, who received four Christmas cards in one day, each containing a $5 bill. There's nothing like the Christmas Spirit.

* * *

Arthur Lee Schwartz, Co. 113, has had plenty of experience in photography. He attended Sullivan High School, Chicago, where he was editor of a year book that won an "A" rating in that city for an exquisite photograph. Y-u photo for for?

Items are on the priority list but still they hope. . . . .

Members of Co. 102 took it on the chin in a recent bowling match with Co. 40, thanks to Adams, Sullivan and Peters of the winning company. "Porky" Nelin, Co. 102 continued his high standard of play matching top score for the boxing situation is getting well in hand with Liepe, Bunfill, Leathers, and Carpenter to represent Co. 102.

* * *

Bond sales looked up this week when Ed Handley, Co. 102 put over $700 into War Bonds last week. According to Ed it was the best thing he has done since his arrival here. Gives you a good feeling, doesn't it Ed?

* * *

There is certainly an unusual recruit in Camp Hill. He doesn't mind it in the least if his shipmates look at him shoulder while he writes a letter to his girl. Reason: Silk Guey Hom knows how to correspond in Chinese.

* * *

In answer to a letter a recruit from Co. 116 sent home recently concerning his work on the grinder his mother sent the following advice: "Dear Son: Don't get your fingers caught in that grinding machine." Well, sometimes you do put your foot in it.

* * *

Co. 119 has discovered its share of song birds when tryouts for the Camp Ward Glee Club were announced. The musical team of "Sim and Duncan" are planned to be presentation of the Christmas program.

* * *

Bert Palmer, Co. 132, is doing his love-making by mail and his result has been satisfactory. At least he got the girl, for Virginia Herd has promised to tie the knot anytime it's convenient for Bert.

* * *

Co. 41 has made a perfect record

Quick! Doctor, Watch Those Teeth

Small, But Mighty Recruit Has No Trouble Lifting

John De Marco, Co. 144, may be small but is he mighty! Pound for pound he is probably the strongest man on the Station, and is plenty willing and able to prove it as can be seen by the accompanying picture.

Just for morning exercise, De Marco does such things as lifting 200 pound sacks with his teeth and throwing them on tables and lifting 175 pound men above his head. It's a hobby with him to constantly test and improve his strength.

His extremely well-developed back and neck muscles enabled him to save a man's life once in a Bethlehem shipyard where he was employed as a driller and reamer. During a launching the bench-ing ceremony when he observed a 900-pound steel plate leaning against an upright begin to slip. A man watching the ship slide down the ways stood beneath the slipping steel. Realizing that only quick action would save the man's life, De Marco hastily ran under the plate, braced it with his back and shouted a warning to the man. The plate had slipped completely away from the upright.

Although not very tall, and only weighing 152, De Marco's strength lies in huge chest, big arms and 17-inch neck.

Praise Given Men Trained at Farragut

A whole-hearted and spontaneous tribute to the training which is given men at Farragut came this week via letter from H. P. Thompson, passenger rep-

Training Aids in Navy Career

Technical training and experienced leadership mean a great deal everywhere, but in the United States Navy they are two assets which are hard to beat. James Wren Hale, Co. 151, enlisting as Moulder, 2nd Class, has just such an enviable combination of talents.

Hale hails from Milwaukee, Wisconsin where he held the position of Acting Lieutenant of the Milwaukee Fire Department.

Hale's nine years' experience in the Milwaukee Fire Department (one of the best in the world) has run the gamut of engine companies, truck companies, rescue squad work, fireboat details, the instruction of auxiliary firemen, and the inspection of industrial buildings and defense plants.

Although Hale has had extensive training and experience in the field of fighting fires, he has enlisted in the Navy as a Moulder, 2nd Class. He has had over 10 years' experience as a moulder at various plants in the State of Wisconsin. He has done a certain amount of shipwork, including the production of four foot propeller blades.

Hale has a good cause to distinguish himself. Although Hale is somewhat annoyed when someone mentions the fact, he is a descendant, on his mother's side, of the famous English architect, Sir Christopher Wren.

Outgoing Unit Puts on Train

Want to see a pretty sight? Of course you'll have to be disdainful of mud because it's kind of "squishy" down in Area E. But if you're about to send your "blues" to the cleaners, and when you have a little time on your hands, make a landing some night at the drill hall in Area E when a sea draft is show-

Mother Appreciates Training Given Son At Farragut Base

Sunday Services
December 27, 1942

CAMP BENNION:
0700—Holy Mass
    Chaplain Monckton
0830—Holy Mass
    Chaplain Lynch
0945—Protestant Service
    Chaplain Tindall
1030—Bible Discussion
    Chaplain Tindall

* * *

CAMP WARD:
0600—Holy Mass
    Chaplain Lynch
0700—Holy Mass
    Chaplain Lynch
0945—Protestant Service
    Chaplain Miller
1030—Bible Discussion
    Chaplain Miller

* * *

CAMP WALDRON:
0600—Holy Mass
    Chaplain Kelley
0700—Holy Mass
    Chaplain Kelley
0830—Holy Mass
    Chaplain Monckton
0945—Protestant Service
    Chaplain Ayers
1030—Bible Discussion
    Chaplain Ayers

CAMP HILL:
0600—Holy Mass
    Chaplain Monckton
0700—Protestant Episcopal
    Chaplain Holiday
0945—Protestant Service
    Chaplain Holiday

Recruit Acts, Band Entertain at Waldron Show

Music and laughter were rampant at Camp Waldron Friday night when the recruit smoker presented talent of all types, including the First Regiment dance band, instrumental and vocal solos and comedy acts.

Under the direction of S. F. Vincent Reel, CSp, members of the various companies gave their shipmates a well-rounded and excellently prepared show.

The Camp Waldron dance band sparked the performance with lively numbers. Composed of Al Bryan, Co. 126, Jerry Capanero, Co. 69, Blair Sconeld, Co 57, Roland Roberts, Co. 85, Byron Jolivette, Co 85, George Boynton, Co. 103, trumpets; Gerald Newby, Co. 76, trombone; Bob Smith Co. 75, electric guitar; Dick Reimer, Co. 100, drums; and Jake Brownlow, Co. 100, piano; the organization has been entertaining at various Waldron shows.

Individual acts were presented by Roland Roberts, Co. 85, trumpet solo; Honley Lucas, Co. 80, vocal solo with guitar; Clarence Fowler and William Murray, Co. 95, harmonica duet; Charles Graziano, Co. 142; Bob Smith, Co. 75, banjo solos; Sam Silver, Co. 129, baritone solos; and a jam session by Reimer, Capanero, Brownlow, Roberts, Smith and Bryan.

Exerpt from:
"THE FARRAGUT NEWS"
December 27, 1942

of hours two Sundays ago....Then Wauna and Jack were over to see his draft board. He has been reclassified to 1A. So it looks like he will be going before too long unless he gets a deferment from Douglas Aircraft. I guess they're a little better than they used to be about that. They lost about all their good men before they took time to wake up. Jack was in the army three years before he was married that is why they're setting him up.

We were out to Sears last week. It doesn't look like the same place as it did last Xmas. They don't have any selections at all. In fact, any and everything that you start to buy now, you either have to change to something else or you just can't get it at all. It's almost disgusting at times. Today there was a limit on canned milk. Just three cans, and in some stores they say it is just one. We haven't had any meat for so long that we have forgotten what it tastes like. We just don't get up early enough to get in on it.

Write when you can, and try to keep us posted on the latest happenings as long as you can.

Night now...Dorothy

As Wilbur and Company 53 were being graduated from Camp Ward, December 28, 1942, American patrols on Guadacanal were trying to pick out the weak points in the Japanese Gifu strongpoint on Mount Austen. New Guinea fighting continued around Buna Mission where the Allies were trying to surround the Japanese defenders.

At O.G.U. Barracks #1, Wilbur and his buddies waited to be called. There was nothing entertaining about the waiting. One just had to calm himself and do the little things at hand A number of the fellows had already left. Some went on leave before going out on sea duty.

Even the weather was not interesting...no disturbing storms, no glistening sunshines. It remained ever the same. It was snow a few days, then a warm up, and a thaw...just enough to keep it

38

sloppy under foot at all times. Wilbur busied himself with the little things. Of course, the washing, like the weather, was always there.

"Good Lord," he grumbled to himself, "I'm beginning to believe washing is one of the biggest jobs in the Navy!"

He recalled his mother bending over a washboard back home only she was washing for *six* not just for herself! He'd really never given it much thought until now. It was just something mothers did. "By Gosh," he promised,"The minute I get out of the Navy, Mother is going to have a washing machine!" He bent his own back to the present chore, thankful as he worked that he didn't have to iron, too, as his mother did. There was no ironing in the Navy, everything but dress clothes was rolled.

In the Service you never knew what you were going to do or when you were going to do it. You knew more what the service men in other parts of the world were doing better than you knew what you, yourself, were doing! On January 5, 1943, the Americans were receiving large reinforcements on Guadacanal in preparation for a big offensive.

The Neutral Swiss reported that the Germans regarded the Eastern front as very serious and on the New Guinea front, the American 127th Infrantry Regiment was moving along the northwest coast towards Tarakena.

Disasters in appalling magnitude was the story of the United States' first year at war. As 1942 ended one found himself searching for hope and encouragement. Production and progress on the assembly lines sometimes exceeded all expectations. The U.S.S. Montpelier, a 10,000 ton cruiser, was completed six months ahead of schedule, and launched at Cambridge, New Jersey. Almost simultaneously two new destroyers were launched at the nearby Philadelphia Navy Yard. Thus, the homefront was performing exceedingly well. It was the overseas progress that was found short in victories...

U. S. NAVAL TRAINING STATION
FARRAGUT, IDAHO

O. G. U. Betricks 1
Jan. 1, 1943.

Dear Sister,

Since I my self start to new year I thought to scratching you a line. I was moved to a different camp, a Co. 127, and havent got any mail since to amount to any size here the news was more disastrous than promising.

"SHIP OUT!" Company 53, Farragut, Idaho CAMP WARD

The order was received January 5, 1953. Wilbur and his companions were jubilant as they boarded train to leave Camp Ward, and they remained that way the entire trip to Camp Mayhon,U.S.N.S.,San Diego, California .

A trainload of 500 sailors can make quite an uproar. "Just so you keep the train on the track," their company commander spoke, "That's an order."

Of course, there were only recruits on board, still they kept themselves curtailed before they reached the destructive level. Every little incident provoked a lot of laughter,and talking, and kidding. Each city they passed through turned into a big debate. What city was it? Where were they going? and what time would they get there? When the trip ended they all came to the agreement they had come by the way of Spokane, Portland, Oakland, and Los Angeles, to finally end up in San Diego.

Enroute, they didn't stop in any of the main places long enough to get off the train. The young men, all exuberant that they were moving at last, made a big to-do over the slightest incident. During a particular rowdy time, the train stopped at a small town unnoticed except by Wilbur who quietly slipped out without being noticed. As he went down the steps of the train he could see he was in luck. He was close enough uptown to see he could soon get into some store while the train took on water or whatever it was going to do. Wilbur was an oddity as a sailor, due to the fact he always headed for an icecream bar instead of a beer parlor. Just as the train started pulling out, he struggled up the steps with a box of icecream bars. He was greeted by a chorus of voices, "Hey, Hank, where the hell have you been? What cha got in that box anyway?"

They stood up as he came down the aisle,blocking his passage.

"Good God, Man, NO beer! Then by God, give us those bars!"

"Hands off, you guys," Wilbur ordered,"You know you don't care for ice cream."

He yelled to no avail. He was nudged, and wheedled and threatened from all sides until he relented.

"You're a glutton and a skinflint,"they said, "so we'll pay you for them by damn."

Wilbur found he couldn't even glean a bar for himself. They stripped him clean even to the box he carried the ice bars in. "Oh, what the heck," he laughed to himself, "I made a profit of $1.75, which is more than I've spent on the trip so far."

This was one thing about the Navy, you didn't make much, but there was no chance to spend your pittance either, unless of course, you gambled and Wilbur hadn't got onto that yet.

The night of January 8, 1943, found Wilbur in Camp Mayhon, Barracks #18. When he arose the next morning to see the sun, he exclaimed to himself, "Dear Lord, it's good to see the green and feel the warmth of the California sunshine again!" Yes, the flowers bloomed, the sun shone, and it was so good to put your feet down without bracing yourself to keep from slipping and falling on your face, or splashing your trousers with mud and slush.

Yes, the weather was great, but the station was lousy. There were too many gosh-blamed sailors. They waited in line by the thousands. There were ten thousand for chow, the shows, or wherever he wished to go. Wherever he went he stood in line.

Then one day someone from those ten-thousand sailors stole his wallet. With it went all his money. It was a sneaky, clever act that happened in the time it took to change his clothes. Some of the guys never missed a chance to steal. He made the mistake of turning his back as he lay his soiled pants down to don clean ones...a quick-seeing eye, a hand reached down and slipped his billfold from his pocket. "I'm kicking myself all around the barracks," he wrote his sister, "for being so careless. Am I going to be this careless at sea? I'm too trusting for war." His sister had known this all along. Uncle Sam was going to experience some difficulties in training all its good, honest, citizens to become criminals. What measures would the Navy have to take in order to persaude her compassionate brother to murder, steal, and rape?

According to the radio reports the war was still vicious on all fronts.

On February 20,21, 1943, the Russians retook Pavlograd and Krasnograd on the Eastern front in south and southwest of Kharkov. They were continuing to close in on Orel from the east, south, and southwest, repulsing fierce German counter-attacks.

In Tunisia, Axis forces regrouped. General Messe took command of the Italian 1st Army,and it was the 25th anniversary of the creation of the Red Army. A sword of Honour was presented to the city of Stalingrad.

It was taking Wilbur this time to study and wash.

W.A. Parker S 2/C
Group III, Class 16-43
U.S.N.T.S. San Diego, Calif.
February 21, 1943

Dear Ruby,

Not much to tell about...shop practice 5 days, and a half day on Saturday or Sunday,and Wednesday evenings. I never take the mid-week liberty. It doesn't seem I find time. I have a lot of notebook work and studying to do in the evenings.

They issued us gas masks last Wed. I haven't got around to trying it on yet. It's a clumsy looking contraption, and I hope I never have to use it. Take care, Wilbur

Another letter on March 4, 1943:

    I should be studying for tomorrow's tests. We have 2 tests a week. However, I have to write and *wash* sometimes. Maybe I should try making the grade the way most of them do...copy off the other guy. Seems like they get the best grades anyhow. Sure don't know what they'll do when everyone starts it though! A lot of these brain pickers sit around me to copy my paper, so on second thought, I doubt if I'd get much of a grade copying from *my* neighbor! One guy was mad at me this evening because I didn't show him anything but the answers to the problems in Math. He said they wouldn't give him a good grade if he didn't have some work to show, too, so they'd know how he worked them...ha,ha!

    So, Ruby most of the time is spent studying, and washing...don't ever forget the *washing*. I saw "Camel Caravan" on the stage at one of the theaters here in camp. And, Gosh, we have radios by the dozens...maybe this isn't something to contend with when you're trying to study! Even so, I missed President Roosevelt's speech. I suppose the guys had all the radios turned on the *Barn Dance!*   As ever, Wilbur

DONATE THE DRAWERS OUT OF YOUR LOCKERS
TO THE SCRAP METAL DRIVE

    The order above was received from Headquarters, March 17, 1943. At the same time Berlin admitted that, as a result of RAF raids, over 20,000 were homeless in Munich, and over 100,000 in Essen, Duisberg, Bottrop and Stuttgart.

    "Considering the great loss of homes, think of this as a mere loss of drawers," Wilbur said to his group as they cleared out their belongings to dump them in a heap at the bottom of their locker, "After all we could be living in Munich."

"Oh, you and your damned optimism," growled one man, "I want my drawers and my home, too. That's the American way."

Wilbur was busy rummaging in the bottom of his locker. "What a God-awful mess!" he exclaimed in disgust, "Oh, well, such is a home without drawers!"

As was his custom, Wilbur waited until the last minute to fill out his income tax. When he finally got it done, he found he owed the Government $159.00.

He pondered this situation which, indeed, was quite a chunk viewing the pittance he received monthly from the Navy. "Maybe I should get a deferment in paying it until after the war," he pondered, "On the other hand it may be as hard to pay then as it is now. Yes, I believe I'll scrape up the money someway and pay *now*. This way I can cry around a week or so and forget it, which may be better than crying and worrying in earnest the length of the war!"

While he was busy scrounging around, and raking up funds to pay his tax, someone stole one of his hats. "Good Lord, that hat cost me 65¢." He chuckled when he told one of his buddies about it, "Even at that since income tax I don't have the 65¢ to buy another one."

"Do plenty of *griping*," advised his buddy, "That's what you better learn to do in the service I'm told...*gripe*. When you've learned to be a bitch of a griper, then you'll become a true-seasoned and qualified soldier, sailor, or whatever."

"Really, I'm so used to losing things I don't think much about it anymore," Wilbur said, "But you know, they caught the hat thief with it in his locker, and he's in the brig now for that measly 65-cent bonnet! I wish to heck, they'd look after the big thieves and let the petty ones go! I'm about to give up catching the man who stole my wallet."

"keep *griping*," said his buddy, "Never let them

forget it."

"If it's the guy I think it is, he left A.W.O.L. about a week ago. They're just waiting until he gets back so they can catch him."

"There you are...get in there and wallet-holler at the same time." The two men were laughing as they left the barracks.

Warm California *was good* to be in again after the penetrating chill of Farragut, Idaho. As Wilbur sat studying he looked up to stare out the window a moment, his eyes taking in the sunshine spreading its gold across a green land. The blue, green, gold, of the out-of-doors seemed to beckon, "Come away, come away." A queer feeling of nostalgia surged over him to throw him back into the yesteryears. Yes, only yesterday, he was in grammar school sitting at a small, wooden, school-desk, which boasted of black-iron legs, and an open ink-well in its sanded, wood, top...his text book spread unread before him. His memory brought the full scene back like it had happened yesterday. He saw the low wash shelf in the back of the small room. A tin cup hung on a nail pounded into the brown log wall above the three-gallon, galvanized bucket, which held cool, fresh, spring water. On the homemade washstand was the white-enameled wash pan, its interior ringed by dirty finger prints. The pot-bellied, wood heater squatted aside the center of the school-room, which required numerous wood stuffings during the winter months.

Wilbur looked up to stare out the four-paned window in that old, log, school his father, Samuel M. Parker, constructed..."Cottonwood School". It was registered with the Wyoming State Superintendent, in Laramie, Wyoming, by that name.

It was a warm spring day and the whole world was coming to life in the draw of Cottonwood Creek where the school house sat. Even inside, he could hear the sighing of the pines on the hillsides that bordered the valley. The creek gurgled full and energetic from the spring thaw, green grass was appearing on the hillsides.

And this voice called to him, "Come away, Come away!" There was such urgency about the sound, he wanted to cast the tedious studies aside and heed the call, for well he knew what joys the out-of-doors held in that mountain valley...the mountains to climb, the mountain breeze blowing your hair, the babbling stream to leap, and the forest to hunt all the many living things there were to marvel about. There were so many plant and animal creatures one shared the joys of the universe with. Together, somehow, he and these creatures made a compatible whole as they sang the variables of life together.

"Wilbur! Get to work!" A quiet, yet stern voice came from the head of the room. He'd forgotten the teacher in his reverie.

As from a trance, Wilbur leaped back to the NOW. He stared at the Navy uniform that clothed him. How come he was wearing this garb? He'd had the *dream* back in his boyhood school. Today he was experiencing the *Nightmare!* Soon he'd be placed in a spot where he'd kill or be killed. The beautiful wild life and its habitat would be scorched and left burning...a flaming pier lit by man's greed and rage.

"Thou shalt not kill!" God's voice sounded like a thunderclap in his muddled mind. Dear God, what was man thinking of to raze the human race...to knowingly and deliberately obliterate his habitat...his own god-given world, his very home! THIS IS WAR! You murdered a serene day at the very *thought* of it!

Yes, on this very day, March 23, 1943, there was a bitter and bloody war going on in Tunisia making it look as if a counter-offensive by the Italians may result in the recapture of the positions taken by the Allies on the Mareth Line.

War and sunshine were totally incongruous, but even under war's shadow there must be some reason for the sun. Ah, that was it! He'd been dreading washing his whites. Of course, the sun was shining so he could get them dry. He could

get back to pondering the war while on mess
duty. The next nine weeks would give him plenty
of time to contemplate as he stirred beans and
peeled potatoes. Anyway, it didn't do you any
good to *think* in the Navy. It was true when
people said the Service does your thinking for
you. However, this didn't keep you from doing
a heap of *wondering* on your own. For instance,
there were a lot of married men thirty-seven
and older here in his group. "By gosh! I don't
know what's going to become of the home front
if the Service starts taking men like these!"

   There were three weeks of school left as
Wilbur sat writing to his sister, Ruby, April
11, 1943. At the same time Goering was writing
notes in his diary, one being:"The Fuhrer told
me that in these four days the Duce fully under-
stands that he has no alternative but to con-
quer or die with us...."

   Wilbur bent over his tablet, trying in vain
to shut out the noise of the men around him
who were whooping it up over a game of cards;
besides the radios were going full blast. "Well,"
he wrote, "It won't be much longer until I'll
be leaving this place. I wonder where to from
here? It looks like we're going to get a leave
of 9 or 10 days. I hope so, but I don't think
I'll try to make it home to the Barncastle,
much as I'd like to. The way transportation is
now I wouldn't be able to stay more than three
days. It seems the cost is too great for such
a short visit. After all it has been but a few
months since the folks and I had a really swell
visit.

   "Oh, we're practising on the milling machines
now, and we'll be cutting gears this coming
week."

   Two weeks later, Wilbur was unaware that a
squadron of three American cruisers and six
destroyers commanded by Rear-Admiral C.H. McMorris
were moving in to shell the Japanese installa-
ions on Attu in the Aleutian Islands as he sought

48

out a quieter place to write letters than he had last time.

W. A. Parker S2/C
Army & Navy
Young Men's Christian Association
"The Home Away from Home"
San Diego, California
April 25, 1943

Dear Sister,
    Find myself downtown with not much to do so will write you a line. Am at the Army & Navy Y. It's really quite nice...restful and quiet you know...good seats, and writing tables. I don't know why, unless it's farther out of town, but it's never nearly as crowded as the U.S.O. The buildings, and U.S.O.s aren't nearly as nice. They have a show here in the evenings, too, and they serve cake and lemonade about 2 o'clock (I get my share). There are two ladies on the stage now, playing some soft music on violins and another at the piano. It makes me sleepy.
    Well, there's only a week of school left. We had our final exams last week so I've sort of relaxed.
    Sort of hate to leave and yet I'll be glad to go, too. I only hope some of the boys I've become acquainted with will be sent the same place as I. Of course, I know there are always good people to meet wherever we go; but one enjoys the old acquaintances the most...especially in the darker moments. I'll try to keep you posted.
                      As ever, Wilbur

    On May 2nd, 1943, as Wilbur was graduated, the Americans in Tunisia had taken "Hill 609" but could advance no farther against the dogged resistance of the Germans.
    Wilbur was in a quandry. He got but 10 days leave, and he had to report in San Francisco in 9 days, and they hadn't left the base yet. After much worry, he made up his mind he wouldn't try going home. He was luckier than some of the boys

Army & Navy
YOUNG MEN'S CHRISTIAN ASSOCIATION
SAN DIEGO · CALIFORNIA
"The Home Away from Home"

April 25, 1943

Dear Sister,

Just myself downtown with not much to does Wis write you a line. I'm at the Army & Navy Y. It's really quite nice. Sheffield and who didn't get any leave at all, so he'd make the most of the few days he had. If he worked it right he should get about a week to stay with Les, for Les lived in Hawthorne, California, which was right on the way.

He wrote to Ruby, "I'm a little better off now than when I joined the Navy. I got promoted to Fireman First Class, and I'll make about $25 extra pay now, which will mean about twice as much for me. After $6.00 a month comes out for insurance, and then the allotment for Mother, I've only made about $25.00 a month. Still, it's more than I would spend, for there's not much one needs that isn't furnished. Buying new clothes will be an item when the ones I have begin to wear out, and they will soon. I've had to buy quite a few already.

"There's not much more to say. I'll send you my new address as soon as I know it myself. You might drop me a line at Leslie's place. I hope to be there from this coming Tues. until the next Tues. I'm sure having a deuce of a time trying to write with this old pen. I lost the little red pen that you gave me in town the other day...must have lost it in the Y where I wrote you my last letter. When I think of you, it's sure been hard to make up my mind that I'm *not* going home. After more mulling it over, I'll visit Les instead. Of course, I do want to see him, and I'm so lucky to have someone close to go see. Will write you from Los Angeles. W.A.P.

Three weeks went by. Ruby waited in her tiny, two-room cabin at Wendover, Wyoming, ever anxious to know where her brother would go now that he was through school. Then, too, she looked for movement and adventure in the outside world by the way of her brother's letters. She and Bill listened to the progress of the war by the way of the little radio on the shelf above the small breakfast set. Sometimes, Ruby stopped to listen more closely, and invariably, it seemed as she did so, the coffee would boil over onto the gas burner of the stove. Bill turned the radio knob to "loud" this morning to omit coffee disaster, she supposed. Amid a splattering of static she heard, "Good morning, it's May 28, 1943. The Japanese have squeezed into the Chicago Harbour area of the Aleutian Islands, while the Americans are dropping leaflets inviting them to surrender. Over Italy more than 100 US Fortress bombers made a devastating daylight raid on Leghorn. While other heavy attacks on Italian targets continue."

Ruby's thoughts wondered as she lifted the pyrex coffee pot from the gas burner just in time. Was Wilbur already on his way overseas? His short leave would have ended over a week ago. The day before yesterday the news said the Joint Committee for War Planning in the U.S.A. was asked to work out the requirements in men and materials, and to suggest possible dates, for invasion of the Marshall Islands in the Pacific. With Wilbur's Naval training over, surely he'd be assigned sea duty. WHERE? was the big question in her mind.

Stanley came up to the stove and leaned against her, at the same time pulling on her skirt, "No, Cooties," she said, "I'm frying bacon. The grease might splatter on you. Go over to Daddy. Go on!" Whimpering he moved away. "Come over here." Bill held out his arms from where he sat in the rather flimsy, straight-backed chair at the table awaiting breakfast. He'd already fed Old Chic, his horse. While he was eating his horse ate also, then together they'd be ready for the twenty-mile ride to Ft. Laramie. Tomorrow he'd ride back to Wendover, and the day after he'd ride the twenty miles to Glendo. He rode every two days to one of the towns checking for possible oil leaks along the Standoline Pipeline. Near Ft. Laramie he rode past a farm house where a little boy always ran out to meet him. "Hi, Linerider," he'd call.

As Stanley was safely ensconced on his father's

lap, Ruby thought, "He'll be four years old tomorrow. If this war lasts as long as the first World War, he'll be ten or twelve years old before Wilbur comes home." Ruby never allowed herself the thought, "What IF he doesn't come home?"

Tales of heroic men sometimes plastered the local papers with gory details. What were newspapermen trying to prove? Were they possibly trying to bolster the moral of the people by printing the agony and gallantry of the wounded? Whatever, the purpose, Ruby found it only served to make her despair deeper. It was like shouting, "Be prepared! This may happen to your son, or brother, or other loved ones." Enevitably she thought of the dead one's families and of their grief. "THE WOUNDED DON'T CRY"...proclaimed a head line. Then the paper proceeded to show a picture of Ralph J. Theis of Ionia, Iowa, on a hospital bed with both legs gone above the knees. He was a private in the 2nd Marines stationed in the Soloman Islands when it happened. His story ran like this:

"It's hard to talk to anybody about it...who hasn't been there. When one of the other guys comes along, we start remembering things.

"Well, we were advancing along a hill. The Japs had started firing mortars. Something knocked me off my feet. I tried to get up and start on, but my feet wouldn't move. I looked down, and I didn't have any feet.

"I didn't feel anything then; the corpsman came and got me. I couldn't look at my feet, because I wouldn't believe I didn't have any. One was still hanging, but they cut that off at the dressing station. It's all right; I get low sometimes, but I feel better today. This morning a fellow came in from the next ward. He is just learning to walk on two new legs. He hasn't any arms, or any legs, either. He's perfectly cheerful. I thought if he can feel that way I shouldn't worry. I'll be glad when I can get up and do things for myself."

All this "War Glory" merely tended to terrify Ruby. "Sure, they don't cry," she thought, "but does that make their pain and grief any less deep?"

Seems she was always feeling heartsick for families she didn't even know. What of the families of the four heroic chaplains, Rev. George Fox, Rabbi Alexander Goode, Rev. Clark Poling, and Rev. John Washington, who sacrificed their lives (so four soldiers could live) when they gave up their life preservers on the American transport, the Dorchester, moments before the ship sank in the North Atlantic?

"Thank God my brother's still in the States." Her hands shook as she opened his letter. Swiftly she slit the envelope with a paring knife, always careful to never cut the contents. "I'm going to save all his letters," was her silent vow. "If I can do so, perhaps someday they may be valuable history." Right now she could scarcely wait to read:

W.A.Parker F 1/C
Barracks J. - Sect. 29
Receiving Ship
Treasure Island, California
May 28, 1943

Dear Ruby,

I'm going to get Stanley something for his birthday, but it's going to be a little late. There just isn't anything for a kid on this station.

I had a nice long letter from Grandma Parker yesterday, and I was sure glad to know Grandpa is so much better. What Mother wrote sort of worried me, Grandpa is getting so old and all. (85 years)

Well, I'm doing very nice here. In fact, I should get quite fat, for all I do is sweep one small room three times a day, and I have a man help me do that. (Ha) At least, I got in on the soft end of things for once.

I worked a few days at the Navy Warehouse in Oakland and two days at the Federal Building in San Francisco making sandwichs for the Ladies'

Aid (or something) before I got the sweeping job. That was a little more work, but it also, was more fun.

It makes me a little peeved when I think of all this busywork foolishness when they could as well have given me all this time on leave, too, so I could have gotten home and seen you all. Of course, I had a good time in Los Angeles, but on that much extra time I could have visited home and Les, too!

I still don't know when or where I'll go from here. Most of the ones that went to school and came up here with me have gone out, so I suspect it won't be long now.

I like it here better than in San Diego or Los Angeles. Maybe it's because of the time of year. The weather has been lovely. People are so friendly, too, and there are lots of places to go. I still only go skating and sometimes to the U.S.O. dances, so guess the place I'm at shouldn't make all that much difference!

Write soon to your loving brother (most abused in the Service!)   Wilbur

The next two weeks was a long wait for Ruby. It seemed a letter would never come. She knew there was no other alternative now for her brother...he would be shipped into a war zone some place. With the fighting so heavy in the Aleutian Islands, it could be he'd be sent there. If so, why was he at the Receiving Station way south on the coast at Treasure Island?

What of the Soloman Island in the South Pacific? During the middle of May a squadron of American cruisers and destroyers commanded by Rear-Admiral W.L. Ainsworth shelled the Japanese positions on Munda and Vila, and a group of mine-layers mined the Gulf of Kula, a narrow arm of the sea between Kolombangara and New Georgia.

Then on June 7, Japanese aircraft began a series of heavy raids on Guadalcanal, the assembly and communications centre of the American troops preparing for the offensive, Allied fighters intercepted and destroyed 23 aircraft. In the Mediterranean, after intense bombing and naval bombardment, June 12, Lampedusa surrendered unconditionally to the Allied forces.

"Perhaps," mused Ruby, "It wouldn't be good for the morale of the Allies at home should they be told how many of ourselves and our aircraft are lost in each battle."

It was hot in the cabin this sunny June day; nevertheless, she felt cold shivers running up and down her spine as she recalled Irma Holcomb's pinched , white face, and her hollow-eyed stare. She and her husband, Ernie, were notified that their son was "missing in action". This could mean one of two things, he was taken a prisoner, or he was dead, which would be the worst?

The Holcombs were the Goodwin's neighbors who lived at the small store and Post Office at Wendover about two miles from Bill and Ruby's cabin on the Burlington-Northern Railroad. The store was handy. When you picked up your mail you could also buy milk or a loaf of bread. Then again, you could hang to the news pouring from Ernie Holcomb's radio he kept turned on back of the grocery counter. All Ruby had to do was look at Irma's drawn face to know there'd been no good news for them. Nor was Ruby so naive as to think tragedy couldn't strike any day, any time, to any family, even her own.

There were already some *sung* war heroes like Captain Colin P. Kelly Jr. killed while scoring three direct bomb hits that sank the Jap battleship *HARUNA* off the Luzon coast; but more often than not the dead were nondescript to be replaced as soon as possible by new recruits.

Alan Harvie, a British seaman, was one of the luckier ones, who was commended for his bravery while yet alive. He had been on ships that had four times been sunk by enemy submarines in the Atlantic. A newspaper showed him sitting in a New York library, reading a book entitled,"How To Live."

As the summer of 1943 advanced, most of Wilbur and Ruby's cousins of eligible age were in some branch of the service. Frank Hill was in southern Florida where he was flying big fortress bombers. He said flying one of these could be compared to driving a truck after driving a small car. George McCullough was sent for training,while his older brother, Floyd, Jr. was in Cedar Rapids, Iowa. Floyd Jr. had been thrown into the Service before he could finish his college year. Then there were Aunt Maude Sornberger's sons, Wayne, Sterling, and Parker, they, too, were out of the m aternal home and into a branch of the service.

At last the letter for which Ruby awaited for untold, anxious hours, arrived. It gave no clue as to Wilbur's where-abouts. This she knew, he had to be somewhere in a war zone to have the stamp of the Naval Censor upon the envelope:

N.O.B. Navy 131
Care of Fleet Post Master
San Francisco, California
June 14, 1943

My dear Sister,
 I suppose you will be wondering why I haven't written, but of course, I couldn't write on the way across. I think I wrote you just before I left San Francisco. I wrote to Mother yesterday, but that was all I found time for.
 Have a tent here to live in and must say it's a very poor one at that. I got my bed wet the first night...got out and stretched it a little tighter yesterday, but suppose the next time it rains, I'll have to swim again (ha).
 I have a lamp I made from a tin can filled with kerosene and a rag for a wick. It's kinda crude

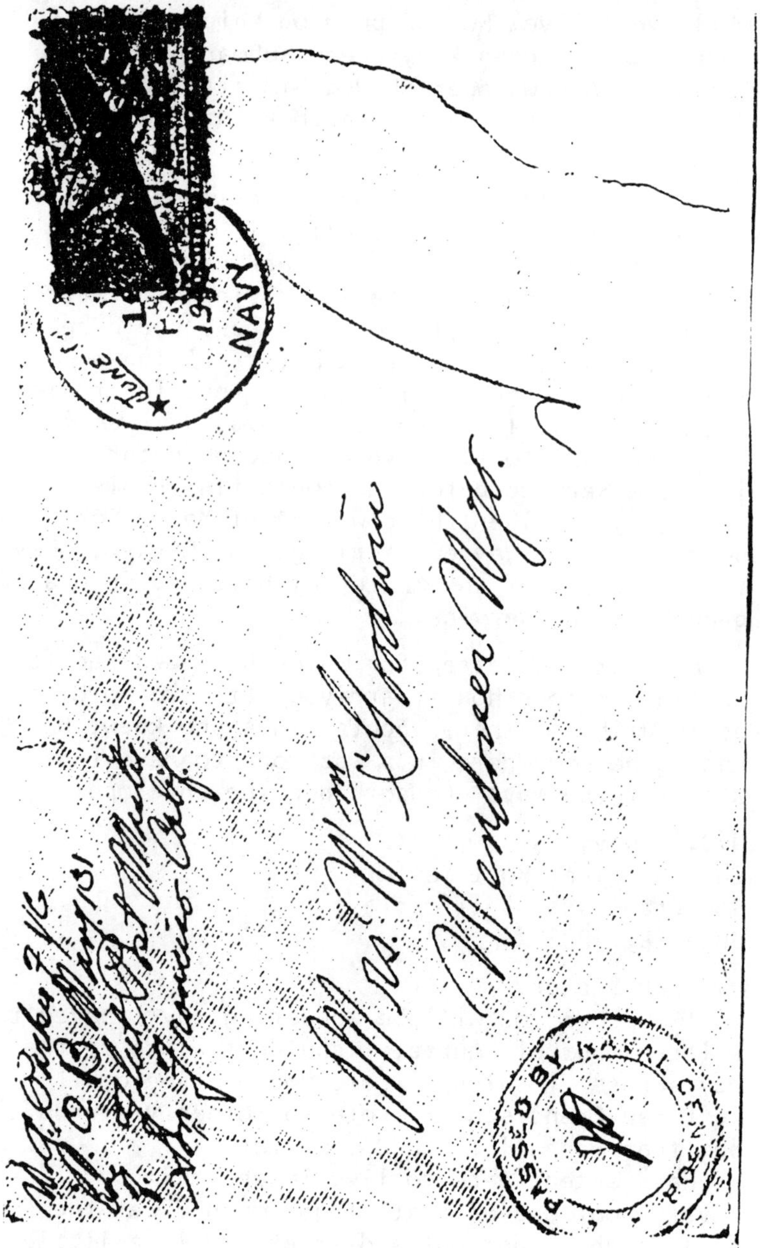
NAVY

M E Bellamy 131
co of Fleet Post Master.
San Francisco Calif
June 14, 1943

My Dear Sister.

I supose you will be wondering why I havent written but of course I couldent write on the way across. I think I wrote you just before I left San Francisco. I wrote to Mother yesterday but that was all I found time for.

Have a tent here to live in and must say it's a very poor one at that. I got my bed wet the first night. got out and staked it a little tighter yesterday but supose the next time it rains I'll have to swim again (Ha.)

Have a lamp I made from a tin can, filled with kerosine and a rag for a wick. It's kidd of crude but I can see a little.

Worked from 7:30 this morning until about five and got so ̶ ̶ ̶ d dirty I thot I never would get clean in our cold water shower. Have been letting my beard grow since I left the states and am sure getting a crop. I thot I'd never get the dirt out of it.

We didn't have a bit of trouble on the way over. And I never got sea sick though there were sure a lot that did. We were terribly crowded or so it seemed to me and it got pretty tiresome before we got here. It was awfully hot too for a few days before and after we crossed the equator.

Well Ruby there are a lot of things I could write that would probably interest you but they would probably be censored. I think they should give us a better idea of what we can and cannot say. They shouldent object to this foo-ey-le Poll but if its half crossed off at least you'll still know I'm O.K.
    Love   Wilbur

but I can see a little.

    I worked from 7:30 this morning until 5:00, and I got so d----d dirty I thought I never would get clean in our cold water shower.

    I've been letting my beard grow since I left the States, and I'm sure getting a crop. I thought I'd never get the dirt out of it.

    We didn't have a bit of trouble on the way over, and I didn't get seasick, though there were sure a lot that did. We were terribly crowded or so it seemed to me, and it got pretty tiresome before we got here. It was awfully hot, too, for a few days before and after we crossed the equater.

    Well, Ruby, there are a lot of things I could write that would interest you, but they would probably be censored. I think they should give us a better idea of what we can and can't say. They shouldn't object to this fol-de-rol though. However, if it's half-crossed off, at least, you'll still know I'm O.K.   Love, Wilbur

    "*Where?*I wonder, is he?" Ruby read the letter many times hunting for possible clues. If he were on a ship, he wouldn't be living in a *tent.* Did the Navy put Naval First Class Firemen on *land?* Or what *did* the Navy do? If one could out-guess it, perhaps, the enemy could too.

    On the Wyoming prairie at Wendover, Wyoming, Ruby lived most of her hours in anxiety and restlessness. "I can't wring my hands," she laughed almost in hysteria, "They're *tied.*"

    She received a letter that very day asking, "WHAT are YOU doing to aid your country? Uncle Sam needs *you!* Yes, YOU, a civilian." She gave thought of answering it, "I'm raising a four-year old for your next gun fodder." As it was a tear fell onto the page when she dropped it to the kitchen waste.Thus, she waited for one of Uncle Sam's sailors to send another letter. "Just let there be a *next* letter,dear God," she prayed.

As she waited she watched the progress of the war, especially did she watch were she thought big ships may be stationed. Kisha Island in the Aleutian Islands was bombed and shelled from sea and air a number of times. During the past months the aircraft of the U.S. Air Force had dropped over 1200 tons of bombs. July 22, 1943, two battleships, five cruisers, and nine destroyers again bombarded Japanese installation of Kiska Island, which the Japanese Imperial Staff had already decided to evacuate.

In the Solomon Islands, in New Georgia, the Japanese put up a stubborn resistance against the 161st Infrantry on the Munda Pass.

News came of the fall of Mussolini, and Pietro Dadoglio, Marshall of Itlay, became the new head of Fascist Government.

THE *letter* arrived at last. *U.S.S.COLORADO* leaped out at Ruby from Wilbur's return on the envelope...*U.S.S. COLORADO*, the mighty battleship, or, perhaps, she should say,*ONE* of the mightiest battleships...this was to be the arena of her brother's war activity.

W.A.Parker F 1/C
U.S.S.COLORADO
c/o Fleet Post Office, Box 11
San Francisco, California
July 24, 1943

My dear Sister:

I know you will want to know that I finally got assigned to a ship, and to have my address. I sure was getting tired of hossing that sea bag from one place to the next, and I hope it's over for a while at least. I slept on my hammock last night for the first time after carrying it around all these months. It doesn't sleep so bad, and I guess I may as well get used to it as it looks like I might have to use it all the time here.

I'm going to start out here in the Electrician's Division. Isn't that dumb after studying to be a machinest? (Ha!) Well, they gave me a chance to learn to be an Electrician and I took them up on it. I don't figure a person can go wrong as long as he is learning something. They selected eight of us altogether, mostly firemen like myself.

 Would sure like to get some mail, and maybe I will soon, now that I am stationed. Haven't had any in nearly two months now. When you write send it Air Mail or V Mail, it will get here fairly quick that way, I think; whereas, it might take months by sea.

 Just got acquainted with a fellow from Wyoming by the name of Wood. He's been in the Navy three years.

 It's chow time and I've run out of anything to say - also ink. With love, Wilbur

 (Later Wilbur told his mother, his ship, the U.S.S.Colorado was as large as a small town with several thousand people on board. There were stores of various kinds, including a barber shop, to accomodate those thousands.)

 "*Somewhere in the ocean,* is rather a broad statement", thought Ruby reluctant to lay the letter aside, hoping it would relent and give her a clue to his whereabouts. She couldn't help him *if* she knew. "I'm going to guess the Pacific." Surely, in the *PACIFIC* or his Fleet Post Office wouldn't be San Francisco. But no doubt about it, whereever he was, the scene would be a position of WAR. Not to mention, a *battleship* was a major fighting ship of any fleet. In fact, the most complex fighting machine ever divised.

 The U.S.S. COLORADO (U.S.1921) was being refitted on the West Coast at the time of Pearl Harbor. An old battleship, her displacement was 35,500 tons, her dimensions 624' x 97'6" draft.

Complement:1,443. Horsepower and speed: 27,300, 21 knots. Armor: 16"-14" Belt, 8' (Aft.), 3" deck (ends), 3½" Upper Deck, 2½" Lower Deck. Guns:8-16 inch, 45 cal.: 8-5 inch A.A.: 2-6 pdr. (aluting); 2-M.G.: 11-M.G. A.A.: 3.CATAPULTS: 1 on Turret, 1 on quarter deck.

  The U.S.S. COLORADO *was* magnificent. She was one of the mightiest battleships afloat. But, though she was old as she took her place amid the rest of the fleet, her sea worthiness was unquestionable. The most awesome thing about her, to Ruby Goodwin, was the fact that aboard this ponderous vessel, among thousands of other sailors, there was the one and only sailor by the name of Wilbur Allen Parker.

  Ruby could not devine the ship's location as she perused Wilbur's letters...all passed by the U.S. Naval Censor. There was absolutely no reading between the lines to even remotely guess his whereabouts. She was merely grateful that the simple, tell-nothing, letters kept coming. He sent her a little one-star flag, which she tacked to the cabin wall and hung his picture beneath it. Everyone who had some one in the service was now sporting pins and flags, each star upon them representing family members who were in the service. While in Guernsey one day, Ruby found a round, varnished, wooden pin with a blue star atop the center, which she displayed proudly on her coat.

W.A.Parker
U.S.S.COLORADO, Box 11
c/o Fleet Post Office
San Francisco, California
August 17, 1943

Dear Ruby,
  It keeps me pretty busy studying electricity and keeping up on my Math course besides my letter writing. Of course, there is a certain amount of

deck swabbing to be done, and other things I could most happily eliminate.

I found time to go to the last show last night. Gosh, I've forgotten the name of it, but it was a skating picture and made me homesick for the States. I went on liberty day before yesterday and went swimming on the beach and hunting for sea shells. I want to find some nice ones to take back home for souvenirs.

I bought me an ice cream and two beers, too, something we don't get aboard ship. Though there is a canteen where we can get ice cream, I've never found time to stand in line and wait. Anyway, the ice cream was mighty good, but I didn't get to taste the beer. A sailor stepped up and offered me two dollars for it so I figured he must be a lot thirstier than I! By gosh, Tom Pickeril should be here, shouldn't he?

It's getting close to time to get to work again, and my paper is about gone. I don't dare use another sheet because this is about all I have and there is NONE to be had at the ship's store. Tell Stanley Uncle Wilbur says *hello*. I'll bet he's getting to be a big boy.

Your loving brother, Wilbur

Ruby continued to closely watch the war going on in the Pacific. Perhaps, Wilbur was in the Soloman Islands. During July 1943, the fighting in New Georgia continued. General Griswold asked for reinforcements to follow up the attack on Munda. The Americans were advancing very slowly, and the Japanese exacted a high price for every yard of ground gained, when the first of August, in New Georgia, the Americans surprisingly advanced to the edge of Munda Airfield with little resistance. The Japanese Imperial Staff realizing that New Georgia was no longer defensible, decided to concentrate all available men and materials on Kolombangara Island, northeast of New Georgia.

Subsequently, in August of 1943, the Americans mopped up the airfield area at Munda. It turned into a 12-day siege of bludgeoning and blood, but the Americans triumphed in taking their main objective, Munda Airfield, and they began mopping up the whole island of New Georgia.

Thus, Ruby kept guessing Wilbur to be in the Soloman Islands. It seemed to be the concentrated spot of the war in the South Pacific. Of, course, when she heard from him, there was the censor's stamp, and his words could give no clue. This time he wrote via V-MAIL.

After the V-MAIL letter, his next letter had a big hunk torn from it, supposedly by the Censor. She could only wonder at the word or words that had been torn from the sentence..."I went on liberty again yesterday, but I am getting tired of hunting sea shells, picking ---------,---------, and swimming, too." Would those words have revealed the spot where he was?...the island he was on? He went on to say, "I'm sorry you were disappointed on the job change, but maybe it will come through afterall. I imagine the folks would sort of hate to see you leave, and I would too, in a way. It seems we are getting so scattered out that we never will all get together again.

"I wrote a letter to Doris, but you'll probably be home before the time it reaches there.

"Did I thank you for the picture? If I did I'll thank you again. I sure would like to have one of Doris and the folks, too. If they get down to your place sometime maybe you could coax them into having one taken. It sure would make a nice birthday or Xmas gift...small ones wouldn't cost very much and could be carried easily.

"Things get pretty dull here, and I'm glad for my work and studies to keep me too busy to notice."

Not until way past the middle of September did Ruby receive another letter, and each time that it was so long between letters, she poured over the news wondering IF during the thick of the fighting he may be one of the casualties. She didn't

WAR & NAVY DEPARTMENTS
V—MAIL SERVICE

OFFICIAL BUSINESS

SAN FRANCISCO, CALIF.
SEP 9 11:30PM 1943

PENALTY FOR PRIVATE USE TO AVOID PAYMENT OF POSTAGE $300

BUY DEFENSE SAVINGS BONDS AND STAMPS

To: Mrs Wm Goodwin
Wendover
Wyoming

From: W. A. Packer
Hdqt. Guard Co.
Flt. Post Office
San Francisco Cal.

Aug 25 1943

Dear Sister,

Got your letter of the sixteenth. Am glad to know that Bill got the job he applied for, and know you both will enjoy a change.

Every day here seems the same and it gets truly monotonous. I manage to keep too busy to think the dull time passes fast.

One of the boys found a phonograph and the music helps but the few records are beginning to get tiresome. Our laundry broke down so I spent most of today washing — D--- I wish I had a table. Maybe you could need this anyhow you know I'm O.K. as long as I can scratch.

It's getting late, so will stick my haversack.

Your Loving Brother
Wilbur

V---MAIL

kid herself, for well she knew there was always
that possibility. Japanese fighters and anti-
aircraft guns were causing heavy losses in the
Aleutian Islands, while in the Solomans, the
Americans were trying to capture Arundel Island,
and they were asking for reinforcements. Some
ships had luck, others went down. There was the
story about Captain Arthur G. Robinson, of Washington, D.C., and Commander Nicholas V. Van Bergen of San Francisco, only this wasn't just a
quiet little tale, it was a fantastic, for-real,
war event. Anyway, after sailing half way around
the world with a vessel badly battered by Japanese bombs in a battle in Macassar Straits off
Java, the nation listened in admiration to the
story of their daring exploit. They told how
the cruiser, Marblehead, underwent three hours
of constant bombing by thirty-seven Jap planes.
The Marblehead's steering apparatus was gone,
and there were gaping holes in the vessel as
Captain Robinson and Commander Ban Bergen made a
perilous voyage and, unbelievably, survived to
tell of it.

W.A.PARKER F1/C
U.S.S.COLORADO, Box 11
c/o Fleet Post Office
San Francisco, Calif.
Sept. 19, 1943

Dear Sister,
    Well, at last I'm in a position where I can
write to you again. It has seemed like a long
time to me too, for when we are in such a position
that we are unable to send mail, of course, we
don't get any either. I have your cute birthday
wish now, also several letters. Yes, the typing
is all right.
    I put off writing to you and went in on lib-
erty and bought you a little souvenir that I won't
be able to send. That makes sense, doesn't it?

I didn't get much sleep last night, but had a fair time today, anyhow. And I bought a good dinner. I had some small pictures taken but they were pretty bad and the guys talked me into giving them each one until there were none left. Maybe I'll get some more.

We get liberty every other day here, but we have to wear whites, and is the *washing* ever a job! One wearing is all they are good for.

Say, Ruby, do you know Mary Delle's address? The last letter I wrote her came back, and I haven't heard from her since she wrote first.

Hope you make good on your hunting license this year. Gosh, how I'd like to be there to help you out!

I'm studying, but I don't find nearly the time I'd like to have for it. Have only two more lessons on my Math course and that will help when it's in. Though I would like to take some more higher math, I'm afraid I won't find time. I want to go up for a rate this time but if I don't get down to studying I'll never make the exam.

Thanks again for the clever birthday greeting. I am sorry I have to leave all the interesting things out, but the censor requires it. It's getting pretty late, so I'll close. Tell Little Stanley that Uncle Wilbur would like to see him. And I'll try to write another line before too long. Ever my love, Wilbur

Why was Wilbur too busy to study or write? Wilbur knew she'd figure it out...he was in WAR... he was fighting, of course! True to his word, he did write again in less than a week. His letters didn't have to reveal where he was. Just knowing he was well enough to keep writing was all that was necessary.

September 24, 1943

Dear Sister,

I have another letter from you, so I'll write

a line though there is little to say.

   I went into town yesterday and had a nice time looking around, I bought some more souvenirs. They will probably have to do as Xmas presents, too, and even then I won't be able to send them now; but hope to later on. If not you'll just have to wait. I got me a new razorstrop, and I just about walked my legs off to get it. Sure've had   a time trying to shave since I lost the other strop. Oh, yes, I cut the moustache off and have a duece of a time twisting my lip to shave it now. (Ha)

   I got your nice stationery;but haven't got it here now as you can see - also, please excuse the red ink. I hung the soap you sent up in my locker. It makes it smell good. We rented a camera while in town; haven't got the pictures back yet, and probably they won't be able to send them when we do; but they will be something to keep and show someday. Goodbye now, Love,Wilbur

Within a week he wrote again:

September 29, 1943

Dear Sister,

   I received you V-MAIL today and your Air Mail the day before yesterday. There doesn't seem to be any difference in the time it takes for them to come. You said you liked the V-Mail. Would you rather I write by V-Mail? It's so tiny and my writing is so poor is the reason I don't use it. Now if I had a typewriter!...Oh, well! I'm sure glad Bill is feeling better, and you, too. I had a letter from Myrna and she said you were looking much better.

   Oh, yes, I had a letter from Aunt Alta, too. She said it was the first she'd written in over a year. Can you imagine? She sure wrote a nice letter though, and I sure enjoyed it. I got another letter from Mary Delle too, but it was

addressed to Treasure Island and pretty old.
Like most everyone does, she says I make her
think of you so "Uncle" Wilbur feels pretty proud.
Have you heard from Dot and Les yet? I rec'd a
letter from Clara today, and everyone is well and
working even Mrs. Parr. I think Dot makes nearly
a dollar an hour. Pretty soon Les can stay home
and cook. (Ha)
   Buck and Ellen fell out, I guess. Clara said
they weren't living together...guess they've
always had a time of it. Please don't mention
it though, for I'm not sure she meant for me to
tell. Guess that's about enough gossip, so I'll
see what there is to say about things here.
Nothing as usual, that I can tell. I had liberty
today, but stayed in to study, and I wrote letters
instead. Yes, writing letters keeps me pretty
busy, but I can't expect to get them if I don't
write, and I do so enjoy hearing.
   On my last liberty I went with a fellow who
is a Mormon, so we went to see the Mormon Temple.
It sure is swell. We saw some wonderful scenery,
too.
   A poor letter, but guess it about covers everything. Anyhow, you know I'm O.K. Write soon,Wilbur

   As September, 1943, ended, the Japanese began
to evacuate Kolombangara Island in the Solomons,
for their bases had become useless as a result
of the American-island-hopping strategy.
   Through October Wilbur's letters kept going
through to reach the welcoming hands of his family
in the States:
Wilbur A. Parker F 1/C
U.S.S. COLORADO, Box 11
c/o Fleet P.O.
SanFrancisco, California
October 12, 1943

Dear Sister,
   Things haven't changed much here, and there is

little to say, but anyhow I'll try. I think the censorship rules are more strict for the Navy than for the Army. Also, ships have to be more strict than land bases, so I'll just have to leave such things unsaid until such a time it's all over, and we can get together again. I did get the souvenirs censored and off on the mail several days ago. We are not allowed to put our return on things that are marked that way, and I only hope they get through.

I received Mother's letter that she wrote from your place. I'm so glad she got out of the mountains to see the doctor. I worry about her and Dad being so far from a doctor sometimes. They must have decided the car would be more bother than it would be worth. Maybe they are right. I probably would have sold it before I left if I hadn't have wanted it to run around in. I don't care though because I got enough good out of it in that month I was home to more than make up for any loss, even if it has to be given away now or scrapped.

October 13, 1943

The light went out on me last night so I'll try to finish this now. When I got back from liberty today your letter was waiting for me. Maybe you'll be up home when this arrives, but then you can read Mother's letter. I sure do hope that her ankle gets better. She should go to the doctor more often.

I didn't do much in town today, but a lot of walking and looking in shop windows. I spent a good deal of time hunting Xmas cards, and I bought myself a larger photo album as the little one you gave me is nearly full, and I have so many more pictures to paste. I had the most delicious banana split, too. I only wish you could have enjoyed it with me.

Gosh, this is the last sheet of this tablet!

I have what you gave me and I like it fine, but it's pretty hard to lay paper on your knee to write. I sure have got a lot of good out of that set you gave me when I left. It sure has taken a lot of punishment but it's standing up good.

I haven't heard from Les for a while but got a letter from Clara Mae today, and she said that she was keeping the canary while they were away so they must be on their vacation. I think they planned on going to the mountains near Bear Lake.

Tell Stanley, Uncle Wilbur says "hello".

Always your brother and Pal, Wilbur

October 20, 1943
Sister Dear,

Things are always so nearly the same that it's a little hard to write, but must thank you for the swell Xmas package that came in yesterday afternoon's mail. You sure are a good guesser; I needed a shave kit and it's just right to fit my locker drawer, too. All the other items will come in mighty handy, but won't attempt to thank you for each separately. I thought I never would get them all out and unwrapped. I sure had fun. Seems sort of queer to be getting Xmas things so early, but I guess it seems about as much like Christmas now as it will later on.

It's been nearly a year now since I joined the Navy, and it seems like a century already!

I sure would like to be there for the hunting season again this year...get a big buck for me, will you? I sure do hope you'll get one at least.

Believe that I told you before that I sent the souvenirs and they should be there by the time you get this. I sure hope they get through O.K. as they may have to be your Xmas, too.

I haven't heard from Leslie and Dorothy for a while but Clara Mae said in her last letter that they were back from their vacation. Buck finally got his call and joined the Sea Bees, but I don't

think he's left yet.
  I got a letter from Biffer (Lee Parker). They are at Estes Park,Colorado, and Uncle Waverly is working on a tunnel or something. Guess he makes more money there, and they like it better than at Sunrise. (Wyo.)
  Sure hope Mother's ankle is better. I hardly know whether to write her at your place or home, so guess I'll just write to Doris and to you until she is back home...that way everyone will hear.
  I've been pretty busy and it keeps me going to get time to answer all my letters.
  Thanks a lot for the Xmas things.
  <u>Write soon</u>, Love always, Wilbur

  Wilbur's family would receive one letter and then start anxiously awaiting the next one.
  "I don't know what I'd do if he weren't so good to write whenever he gets a chance," his mother, Ursa Parker, remarked. "And yet, when there's a long time between letters I can't help but worry that something has happened." Tears glistened in her blue-gray eyes as she spoke.

Wilbur A. Parker F 1/C
U.S.S. COLORADO, Box 11
c/o Fleet P.O.
San Francisco, Calif.
Nov. 5, 1943

  Just a line that you may know I'm O.K.
  It seems a long time since I've got any mail and no doubt seems as long to you since I've written. There isn't much to say anyhow. I've been working pretty hard but have found some time to study. We are permitted to study our courses on watch though we can't read magazines, etc. I guess it's a good thing they'll let me study then, for I don't know what other time I'd find.
  I didn't pass the test the last time, but I

don't feel bad about it because none of the
others that went up with me passed either. It
sort of come unexpected like, and we had all
been too interested in going on liberty to study,
I guess. Well, anyhow I managed to get a little
shopping done and though it wasn't much everyone won't think I entirely forgot them at Xmas.
 I sure have got a lot of good out of the
shave things already. It sure was what I needed.
I loaned the cards, and I guess they are about
worn out now. I doubt I'd ever found time to
use them, so I know you'll be glad to hear that
someone got some good out of them.

Saturday, Nov. 6, 1943
 Have yours of the 17th. Gosh, it sure seems
good to hear again! and to know that Mother is
feeling so much better. I sure would like to be
there to help out what I could and go hunting
with Bill. Also, I hope Bill's sister is better.
 I scarcely know where to send this. Wendover
will probably be the wrong place but will send
it there anyhow just in *case* because you can
always read Doris' if you are up home...provid-
ing I get it written, ha!
 I had a swell letter from Leslie and Dorothy,
and one from Clara Mae that I simply must answer,
so as I have a feeling you will be up home, I'll
close. Tell Stanley Uncle Wilbur said, "Hello"

 Ruby was "up home"...in the mountains, in the
Barncastle, Fletcher Park, Wyoming. Fletcher Park
in 1943 boasted of one family, the Samuel M.
Parker family, who lived in a long, low, log,
house built by Sam. It was dubbed the "Barncastle"
by his daughter, Ruby, for when Sam laid up the
first log he was planning to build a log shelter
for his sheep. Then as it grew fresh log by fresh
log, Ursa said it was too good for dirty sheep, it'd
make a better house. "We need a house more than

76

the sheep do," she told her husband. Thus, to Ruby it turned from a barn to a castle. And Ursa got her house with all the rooms she needed. She was sick and tired of living in a one-room log cabin; for this meant Sam, Wilbur, and Leslie slept in the shed, while Ruby occupied the sheep wagon, and she and Doris the cabin.

At the present Ursa was having a long siege of trying to heal a massive, running, varicose ulcer on her left ankle and leg. The doctor's orders were to keep off her feet, and elevate her leg. While doing so, she needed help to do the cooking, cleaning, and other household chores, Here was where Ruby fit in.

During those long winter months in the Barn-castle with snow piling up in the valley, the Parkers, as they read and re-read letters from Wilbur, speculated on his location. Before the winter was over they all were in agreement Wilbur was somewhere in the South Pacific. Ruby abandoned all thought of his being in the Aleutian Islands as the news shifted almost entirely from that point of battle to the Gilbert Islands in the South Pacific.

Wilbur's letters of November 5 & 6, 1943, were forwarded by Bill Goodwin from Wendover where Bill continued to ride the Standoline Pipeline.

"Whenever Wilbur can't answer mail or receive any mail," surmised his father, Sam, "Then we can be pretty certain he's in the midst of a battle."

A letter and Christmas card followed the November 6th letter:

Dear Sister;

Just a note in answer to the lovely letter I received last evening. I'm glad to know that the gifts came through O.K. and I'm glad you liked them. (Shame on you for wearing Stanley's little necklace.)

I can hardly wait to see the pictures, especially of Stanley. I bet he sure has changed. I'll have to write him a letter, just for him someday if I ever find time.

Gosh, if the old car will bring anyways near what you think, you better figure out a way to get rid of it for me in a hurry. I suppose you'd have to dig the title out of my strong box and send for me to sign. I think I could sign it over to you and then you could sign it to the buyer.

Well, there isn't much to say since I last wrote. I thought a nightmare had caught up with me last night. It's pretty hot where I sleep, and so, I have a fan blowing on me. It was stirring up a nice breeze, and I was right in the middle of a swell nap, when something happened, and I thought the darn thing had me. Boy, I really came to! I stumbled down to sick bay in the dark and had the doc sew up a big gash in my arm! Now I've been hiding all day to keep the boys from asking questions. (Ha!)

I guess the ugly cut is doing pretty good because it doesn't hurt a bit only when I bend my arm. (Just label it:*Wounded in Nightmare Action!*)

"Down the Road of Remembrance
   I'll journey today
Toward the things that my heart holds
    so dear---
Down the road where I know
    every step of the way---
Where my thoughts lead so often all year;
And I'll have as companions the sweet
    things you say,
The kind, thoughtful things that you do,
And my heart will be glad as I journey today
Down the Road of Remembrance with you."

MERRY CHRISTMAS to: My Dear Sister and her Family on Christmas Day 1943, With Love, Wilbur

THE BARNCASTLE

SAMUEL M. PARKER

His folks may not know where he was or what he was doing. However, Wilbur was alert and very much aware that soon all Hell would break out on Tarawa.

Everyone read the Orders for the day. Today, he'd slip a copy in his locker, for they may well spell history in the making:

ORDERS FOR THE DAY, SUNDAY, 21 NOVEMBER 1943:
(RESTRICTED)

INFORMATION:

1. SECOND Section has 00-04 watch.
2. SECOND Section is duty section.
3. WORKING division - division FOUR.
4. Tactical Watch:
   00-04 - Lt. BYWATER   16-20 - Comdr.REITHER.
   04-08 - COMDR.REITHER   20-24 - Lt.FINAYSON.

GENERAL:

1. Underway
2. Condition of Readiness III, maintained by Battle Cruising Watch. Material Condition of Readiness YOKE, maintained day and night except when General Quarters is sounded, five minutes after which Condition ZEBRA will be set.

ROUTINE EXCEPT:

---- - Uniform of the day will be dungarees, blue-dyed white hats.

---- - Call cooks and bakers of the watch.

0440 - REVEILLE. (Including Officers and CPO's).
0445 - Serve out coffee.
0510 - General Quarters.

0611 - Secure from General Quarters. Mess Gear.

0630 - Breakfast.

0800 - Muster on Stations.

0815 - Flight Quarters. Prepare to launch both planes for anti-submarine Patrol.
0845 - Launch both planes.
1130 - Flight Quarters. Prepare to recover both planes.
1200 - Recover both planes.
NOTICE: 1. Be prepared to transfer 750 5"/38 charges and shells to landing boat sometime after sunrise.

Commander, W.A. BOWERS U.S. Navy

After reading ORDERS, Wilbur scanned the COLORADO DISPATCH to tear "Undated Pacific War" from it and place it with other papers he had in his stationery shut in his locker. He liked these souvenirs that took up so little room.

-: COLORADO DISPATCH :-

23 November 1943

UNDATED PACIFIC WAR:

A communique of Admiral Nimitz disclosed today that US Marines have landed on Apamama Atoll 8Ø miles southeast of Tarawa in the Northern Gilberts and that US forces have improved their positions on both Tarawa and Makin atolls, but are still encountering considerable enemy resistance. The Communique said, "We have landed on Apamama Atoll." Liberators heavily bombed the airdrome area at Nauru Island November 20th and continued diversionary attacks in the Marshalls. The Central Pacific operations are being directed by Vice Admiral Raymond A. Aprauance US Navy. The Amphibious forces are under the command of Rear Admiral Richmond K. Turner US Navy. Landings were made at Tarawa by the second Marine Division in command of Maj. Gen. Julian C.Smith USMC. Those at Makin by Maj. Gen. Holland Smith USMC in command of the 27th Infantry Division and Maj. Gen Ralph Smith USA in command of the landing forces. It was learned that Marine Lt. Col. James Roosevelt had landed with the Infantry on Makin. He was second in command when Lt. Col. Evans Carson's Marine Raiders landed on Makin Aug. 17 and 18th 1942.

General MacArthur's communique reported that Australians have punched through stiff resistance to within half a mile of Japanese entrenched plateau positions at Sattleberg on the Huon Peninsula of Northeastern New Guinea. The Communique also reported that Aussies killed fifty Japanese in patrol actions to the east of the coast above the harbor of Finschhafen. The communique reported the destruction or damage of 19,000 tons of merchant shipping including the sinking of a 4000 ton ship off dutch New Guinea and the probable sinking of an 8000 ton ship off Kavieng New Ireland. The attacks on shipping were made by liberators. On the West central coast of Sougainville where the Japs are opposing an extension of the American Beach head at Empress Augusta Bay American dive bombers and torpedo bombers have dropped 62 tons of explosives on the Japs. Liberators for the second day delivered a heavy attack on the Gasmata Air Base area on the South central coast of New Britian hitting supply dumps with 49 tons more than dropped in the previous attack. The Jap airforce got in some more blows at Empress Augusta Bay on Bougainville raiding shipping and ground positions and inflicting minor damage and some casualties.

WASHINGTON:

The Senate passed and sent to the White House Monday legislation which would delay drafting of pre-Pearl Harbor fathers into the armed forces until after the nations supply of available singlemen had been exhausted. The measure would strip war manpower commissioner McNutt of all authority over selective Service. There have been reports that McNutt would ask a Presidential veto.

****

The U.S.S.COLORADO made its laborious way from the Hawaiian Islands to the Gilbert Islands that November 1943, Tarawa its goal. Someone labeled the battle of Tarawa a *FLAMING HELL*. However, to begin with, it was called the start of "Operation Galvanic". Actually, more than 100 warships, transports, and landing crafts of all kinds...the U.S.S. COLORADO among them, had approached the atolls of Tarawa and Maken during the night.

On Tarawa, the Japanese had been building up fortifications for some time.

It was the first big battle that Wilbur was to witness. Afterwards, he thought,"It was like being initiated into HELL."

With the huge guns of the U.S.S.COLORADO and the other American warships raining shells on the island, blowing up Japanese amunition and fuel stores as it did so, Wilbur watched the ships' Marine Detachments march into the flaming jaws, for the loading craft could get only to the end of the pier, unable to go farther because of the coral reef. Thus, the marines waded to the Tarawa beachhead, unprotected, and under fire all the way. Wilbur was stunned into a sense of unreality and misbelief as he watched...stunned with horror...man did not do this to the most insensitive animals. Was man brought to life only to be exterminated by his own hand? He felt the huge steel deck of the U.S.S.COLORADO fairly leap beneneath his feet as the ship's guns pouredforth their murderous, chaotic ruin far ahead of the marching marines. The belching fire and black smoke soon arose as smoke screen.

Tarawa was comprised of a series of islets on a reef about 22 miles in length. It's native population was almost wholly Micronesian. Tarawa was a port of entry and the main centre of this group of islands. The lagoon had one entrance. Here at Tarawa were the Government Central Hospital, the leper station, the lunatic asylum, the King George V School for Native Boys, and a colony gaol. However, war could and would not be stopped in consideration of any form of institution, which one would think would be the humane thing to do. But no one could afford to be human. To be human would only mean annihilation, so each and all turned into hellish demons. Friend or foe, no one was spared, unless it was the heads of state back in the government strongholds. The survivors of one battle were the ones cursed to meet yet another demonical battle to follow. The thought of facing another battle made Wilbur think, "The ones who lose their lives instantaniously are the lucky ones."

On November 23, 1943, Tarawa and Makin atolls fell to the Americans, It cost them dearly. About 3,500 Americans were killed and wounded. In contrast, of the Japanese, 5,000 were dead. The Americans almost completely wiped them out. It was the side who could deal the most Hell, kill the most men, raze the most land and buildings who was considered the *best*...by necessity the motto was, "kill or be killed." The whole of humankind turned into the Devil's advocates. The bigger hell-hole one could burn, the bigger his glory. Satan could be proud of the Americans at Tarawa where the 17 Japanese survivors were taken prisoners, while 129 Koreans surrendered, and little Tarawa atoll was turned from a lush,

THANKSGIVING
25th November, 1943

U.S.S. COLORADO
AT SEA IN THE CENTRAL PACIFIC

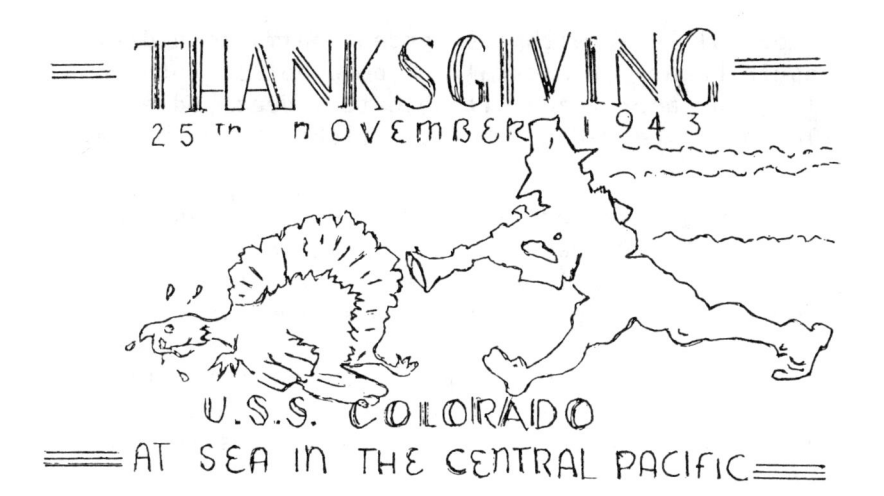

W. GRANAT
Captain U.S. Navy
Commanding

W. A. BOWERS
Commander, U.S. Navy
Executive Officer

H. P. KNOWLES, Jr.
Lieut. Comdr. (SC) U.S. Navy
Supply Officer

H. O. BURNS
Chief Commissary Steward
U. S. Navy

MENU

TOMATO MADRILENE
RIPE OLIVES   CELERY EN BRANCH   SWEET PICKLES
ROAST YOUNG TOM TURKEY
OYSTER STUFFING   GIBLET GRAVY   CRANBERRY SAUCE
BAKED VIRGINIA HAM
PEAS PARSISENNE   FRANCAISED POTATOES   ASPARAGUS TIPS
PUMPKIN PIE   PARKERHOUSE ROLLS   PLUM PUDDING
MIXED NUTS   ASSORTED FRUITS   ASSORTED CANDIES
CIGARS   CIGARETTES
ICED FRUIT JUICE

tropical islet with its verdant palms to a dark ashen heap. It was full of deep holes, torn up terrain, and strewn with bloated, dead bodies. The palms reared as charred sticks above the devastation.

It was November 29, 1943. For ten days the U.S.S.COLORADO had been at combat in the area of Tarawa. At last, it was time to turn from this concentrated destruction to make the 2,000-mile voyage back to the Hawaiian Islands, and so on into the port of Los Angeles for necessary repairs, and to give the war-weary crew necessary leave and liberty to restore themselves insofar as they were able.

Once again Wilbur was free to write letters, and mail them out. Also, he received most-welcome mail. Now he could write and tell his sister "there isn't much to say". He found himself relieved that there was no way to tell her of Tarawa. No writing could portray what he saw, and if it could, there was no way to tell it in the words of a gentleman. Instead he'd send her a Thanksgiving menu. The ship and crew were still in the Gilbert Islands Thanksgiving November 25th. It was a good dinner. He worked on search light shutters that had been damaged during battle..."not much to say, Dear Sister."

He did wish he could send her THE COLORADO DISPATCH of November 24;but even that might be a harsh way to to say, "This is what I'm doing."

-: THE COLORADO DISPATCH :-

U.S.S.COLORADO   NOVEMBER 24 '43

ALLIED HQ ALGIERS:
Charging before a backdrop of burning towns and and villages,German troops struck sharply at Canadian units of the Eighth Army North-west of

85

Agnone in the Central Italian sector, but were repulsed after a hard two hour battle, the Allied Command said Tuesday. Throughout the mountainous inland sector the enemy was firing and dynamiting everthing he could not carry with him to this powerful new gun-studded defense line. Smoke shrouded the horizon as the sizable cities of Castel Di Sangro and Alfedean burned through the long day. Yesterday's counterattack east of those cities was designed to give the Nazi demolition squad time to complete the thrust toward Agnone taken by Montgomery's veterans three days ago. Other units cleared the enemy from additional heights overlooking Alfedina from the southeast. American troops wiped out a German machine gun nest northwest of Montaqsila on the right wing of the fifth army front without suffering a single loss.

WASHINGTON D.C.:

President Roosevelt sent Congress a formal request Tuesday that it do something now about providing unemployment allowances and Social Security credits for men and women in uniform. In addition he urged the legislators in a message to enact without delay, a measure setting up an unemployment insurance system for the merchant marine. "Though Congress will agree I am sure", Mr. Roosevelt said,"that this time we must have plans and legislation ready for our returning veterans instead of waiting until the last moment. It will give notice to our Armed Forces that the people back home do not propose to let them down."

WASHINGTON:

The Allied leadership is preparing tremendous psychological and military blows at the Nazis which can be expected, also to have profound repercussions in Tokyo. This became increasingly clear Tuesday as a welter of rumors and reports flew here and in London of possible great actions designed to hasten the war's end. Word out of the British Capital was the President Roosevelt, Prime Minister Churchill, and Premier Stalin may map final military plans and then tell the German people in effect that they must throw off the Nazi yoke or be smashed.

LONDON:

The heaviest aerial bombardment in history poured more than 2300 long tons of explosives and incendiaries upon Berlin Monday night and Tuesday night. German radio stations shut down in a possible indication that Allied Forces were attacking again in a campaign to force the Nazis to their knees through airpower. One-thousand RAF bombers participated in Monday night's attack on the worlds fourth largest city in an assaut which exceeded even the 2300 ton bombardment which knocked out Hamburg.

WASHINGTON:

The Navy announced Tuesday Award of the Legion of Merit to Rear Admiral Olaf M. Hustvedt, Chief of Staff to the Commander in CHIEF of The United States Atlantic Fleet for services in organizing the fleet and its bases.

UNDATED PACIFIC WAR:

Capture of one atoll in the Gilberts and impending capture of two others was announced today on the fourth day of the American Mid-Pacific Invasion. This virtual completion of the first critical phases achievement of air base from which to rout the Japs from the rest of the Gilberts and pound the Marshalls incessantly, stamped the drive as the fastest moving one yet unleashed against Jap's outpost defense. Only a few hours after Secretary of the Navy Knox defined the strategic objectives as ouster of Japan from the Mandated Islands and shortening of American supply lines to the Southwest Pacific,

Admiral Nimitz announced these developments; Makin has been captured, Tarawa site of the bloodiest enemy resistance is certain to be captured, Ademamas situation is well in hand. American aircraft carriers continue to pour out their planes in a teamwork assault with Army land-based planes on the Marshalls. Tokyo radio told the Japanese that the invasion approaches a real decisive battle of the fleet. Secretary Knox in characterizing the drive as the beginning of a new campaign against Japan from the Central Pacific on a much more direct route toward Japan...said at Washington no elements of the enemy fleet have been seen. The attack has not as yet pulled the Japs out of their shelter. In the sectors of Admiral Ahlsey and General MacArthur to the Southwest of the Gilberts where other enemy outposts are being crumbled in the Northern Solomons and on Northeastern New Guinea war advices today mold of aerial assaults on eleven Japanese points with the heaviest directed at Gasnata, New Britain. One-hundred-forty-two tons of explosives were dumped on Gasnata. Within three days upwards of 300 tons of bombs have hit that air base guarding the back door approach to the enemy's pivotal air and naval base of Rabaul. Fifty-two tons of bombs were dropped at the Cape Clou Estep Airdrome on New Britans..
....
    There was more of The COLORADO DISPATCH. He'd put it in his locker when he got out his writing paper. He'd better be writing letters.

Wilbur A. Parker F 1/C
c/o Fleet P.O.
San Francisco, Calif.
Dec. 12, 1943

My dear Sister,
    Received the Xmas box yesterday and your lovely

card and the pictures. Maybe the pics weren't as good as they could be, but I surely am tickled over them. I think the one of Stanley is good, and it's just the size to fit in my nice birthday wallet.

Gosh, Clara Mae sent me another shave outfit. It really is swell, but I don't know what I'll do with two, and anyhow, it's too nice to use, so guess, I'll send it home. Think I'll send the cute little pin that Doris sent, too. We aren't allowed to wear pins on our uniforms, and besides, I might lose it.

Leslie sent me an Eversharp fountain pen and his old watch, which I asked him for, because I couldn't get one and they come in so handy. Parrs sent a sewing kit, and Buck and his wife, candy. I got a box from some folks I know in S. Dakota, too, so I've had quite an Xmas. Maybe I should have waited to open the presents, but scarcely have room to lay them aside, even though they were not perishable.

I intended to put my Thanksgiving menu in Mother's letter, but will put it in here if I can remember it when I send this out so you can see what we had for Thanksgiving. It looks good, and it was, but I'd much rather have eaten at home with you.

I had liberty yesterday, but I didn't do much but look the same things over and buy some more souvenirs and Xmas cards. Went bowling and had a good time until time to return, then stood in line for a bus...stood in line for the ferry...stood in line for the ship's boat...stood in line for chow...stood in line for the wash room....Heck,if you think this doesn't get tiresome you should try it! Ha!

I don't know why I'm starting a new page for I'm all run down. This is Sun. but I worked all day trying to get caught up so I can go on liberty tomorrow, but find myself about as far behind now as this morning. Gosh, I did get one break, I haven't had a watch in Port this time

so get every night to sleep.
   Ina Lee Hall sent me some of her Senior pictures. She sure must have grown up...bet she and Glen are go-getters.
   At Christmas I'll think of you and all the good times we used to have. Must close for lack of news.
   As Ever Your Old Pal, & Loving Brother, Wilbur

   Ruby stared at the Thanksgiving Menu that came in Wilbur's letter, the words "At Sea in the Central Pacific" on the tan, rough paper glued her attention . Perhaps, the words were so general the censor didn't mind, for "Central Pacific" could mean a lot of area! However, for Ruby it meant a great deal. This meant Wilbur wasn't in the NORTH pacific, nor was he in the SOUTH Pacific. CENTRAL had to mean the U.S.S.COLORADO was involved in the on-going wars either North or South of the equator.
   Wilbur must have emerged from a recent battle to be free to write. When she received his next letter she was overjoyed to find he'd been back in the States.

   As Wilbur set his tired feet on the California shore, up from his numb,war-torn, inner being, he thought of but one thing, he was free to go see his girl. He felt soiled when he thought of her, she was so young and so innocent. Good, wholesome, fun, right now, seemed her only aim in life. Afterall, she wasn't out of highschool. Yes, he'd let his heart go out to a girl much too young for him. To be sure, she seemed to like him well enough. Very likely she was the little school girl flattered by an older man's attention,charmed and excited while playing her first game of love. However, it was too late for him to back out of the game, for he'd already lost his heart.
   Even when he wrote to his sister he had the

feeling that maybe some of the war-taint may somehow rub off in his writing.

W.A.Parker, EM 3/C
U.S.S.COLORADO, Box 11
San Francisco, Calif.
Jan. 14, 1944

Dear Ruby & All,
   Received your letter of the 3rd. It was a swell letter and I sure enjoyed it. I know I've neglected my writing something awful, but will try to catch up now. The worst of it is I've sort of forgotten just who I owe.
   Well, I did have a swell time and a grand start for the New Year. I think I just about played Leslie and Dorothy out and almost felt ashamed. Because they have to work and I know how it is to have to work after being up all night. I got out several times and they generally brought me back. It's so terribly far that we would never get any sleep all night long. We had a lot of fun though, and we took some pictures. Rather we had some taken one night. I think Leslie is going to send you one, but if he doesn't maybe I can later on. Clara Mae wanted some and I gave her some money to get me some, too. They are pretty good I think.
   I got to go through the place where Dorothy works and saw all the machines and things. One of the fellows explained it all to me. The same night we went out to where George Parr works and he showed us through the machine shop.
   One night we saw one of the fellows that used to work at Trojan, and we went to his home for a while. Yes, we went to quite a few places, and we had lots of fun, but I never did get over to the De Witt's and I feel sort of guilty, but gosh, the time was so short.

January 18, 1944 - Tues.
   I haven't had an opportunity to send this out

yet so I'll add a line more.
   I worked all day yesterday on a stainless steel cabinet for our coffee pot, etc.,and still have a good deal of work to do to complete it. The day before that being Sunday, I worked on a knife I am making for myself.
   I caught a terrible cold on my last liberty, and was nearly down for several days. It's much better now, and I am gradually catching up on my neglected work. Even found time for a little study this morn. Gosh, if I don't do a little better I'll forget what little I learned. (Ha) I bought a good book on practical electricity, and I have the course they give us but the big job is *learning* it.
   Your telling about the snow makes me homesick, Ruby; but I like to think about it. It seems so long since I've been free to walk in the snow...to feel the peace and quiet, and the calm, beautiful, loneness of a great, white world. I know I've lost much of the finer feelings of life. The emotions and elusions have melted, leaving the stark, naked, truth, and unlike the snow covering a dark earth, cannot return; but I like to think of the snow as a promise, ever new and pure, as the beginning of life in an old world.
   The water is a little rough today. Can you imagine trying to write with the room swinging from side to side, or the table moving along the floor? It's not bad really but a little aggravating!
   I'll close and hope to get it off before too long. As Ever and Always, Wilbur

   THE U.S.S.COLORADO having repaired, refueled, and rearmed, steamed a steady course towards its next destination...the Marshall Islands with Kwajalein being first on its itenerary. The Marshall Islands are a double chain of coral atolls,

32 islands, and 167 reefs. Kawajalein consists of 38 islets. These islands had been under Japanese mandate for a quarter of a century. The U.S.S.COLORDO spent 7 days at Kwajalein and during that time the island was literally cut to pieces with the fire-preparations for landings. Some 15,000 tons of high explosives were used during the destruction of Kwajalein. The Naval Task Force shelled the atoll for 48 hours, and still Kwajalein had to be taken foot by foot.

   Preparation for battle had been a great and powerful production aboard the U.S.S.COLORADO. The song of World War I, "Just Before the Battle Mother," echoed in Wilbur's mind. Did all sons think of their mother just before entering combat? When a warrior faced death was the vision of his mother his last mental image?
   In the grey hours before Revielle sounded or the hour of General Quarters , Wilbur sought his pen. He knew it was foolish, and it would never reach her hand; but he started to write:

January 31, 1944
Dear Mother,
   The days have slowly passed since we left the states, and the lights and life of Long Beach.
   Slowly, the COLORADO, the MEXICO, and the TEXAS,together with a score of Tr. destroyers, and cruisers, have nosed their way Southwest toward the land and peoples of the Rising Sun.
   Day by day the chill and fog of the more Northern waters have been left farther in the past, and now the sun, directly overhead at noon, blazes hot and long, transforming iron deck and hold into a sweltering Hell of torment as hatch and ventilation are shut in preparation for battle.
   G.Q sounded half an hour ago, and the men sit or stand, waiting!...sweating in their iron box.
   Few seem nervous though the zero hour is at hand...Kwajalen Atol scarcely out of sight.

Some read or play pinochle on the deck, while others joke performing their duties, checking water valves and hatches vital to the integrity of the ship and crew.

"Open fire in ten minutes!" comes the order from Sky Control. The men at Watch repeat the word sent over the ear phones...uncomfortable contrivances but necessary. There is no response from the men receiving the word nor from the next..."Portside is the engaged side 1500 yards!" No one moves from Port to Starboard.

It's nearly seven by the clock, and on top it must be nearly full light as one watchstander gets the report that the big crane on the island is visible. "Stand by to fire!", and the ship vibrates to the single shot, close followed by two others, and others, as the main battery forward opens up. The ship rolls and trembles. Dust and paint chip from the overhead. Still no return fire, and one wonders???

"The Americans shall find a surprise waiting at the Marshalls'," was the radioed word from Tokyo picked up as the fleet steamed Southward, and someone in jest said, "Nipons surrendering without fight could be the *only* surprise", but there was less of humor and more of irony in the joke, especially when one looks back to December 1st at Tarawa. Firing ceased. There is word of a fire on the beach. On the bridge the Chaplin sends the word of the fire over the loud speaker to the men in compartments below. There is one large cargo ship and several other smaller vessels in the harbor.

So far we've launched only one of our planes, and we can fire only with the main battery forward. Thus, the day wears on, and still no rousing word, no roll of thundering guns from the beach, only occassional A.A. fire. Two dive bombers are lost in a clash, The major outlying islands of the Atol are taken one by one with scarce any resistance, and a huge pall of smoke obliterates the island as the ships pull out to open water for the night, and men come out of their holes like rats drenched in their own sweat.

    Quietly the night slips by, and the morning finds the men again at their stations ere the last shades of darkness lift over the island, or the sun pokes its head above the sea. The ship steams back toward the island. On the morning of February 1st, 1944, the firing begins to increase steadily to its hottest about 10 o'clock with no answering shots from coastal artillery. The Marines begin to nose their landing barges toward the beach of Camouflage and Burlesque.

    About noon the COLORADO moves farther out to sea, firing ceases, and at this time men are secured into groups to drink or go out top for a breath of air. At this time, as I look over the smoke and haze of Camouflage Island at the group of our dive bombers pealing off and deciding to drop their missles of destruction, there occurs a terrific explosion sending a great pall of smoke and flame even above the clouds, and on to the heavens covering completely the southern portion of the island, and obscuring the bombers in their descent. Many may have been lost. Even the flame reaching hundreds of feet skyward must have seared them. To the Northern tip of Camouflage just out of the great black cloud, I distinctly saw two fall in a graceful dive. Just what this explosion was, I think, is not quite known aboard. Some say it was barges loaded with dynamite our Marines sent in ahead to clear the beach, but this seems doubtful in view of the damage to our planes, though it is accepted that dynamite barges were sent in.

    The Marines nearly succeeded in taking the whole of the Islands before nightfall. The visibility has been low all day with occassional showers, and the sky has looked so sullen, the air so damp. As I step to the quarter deck with my blanket, I hesitate, and decide to go below again, but the heat has driven me out and I've ascended the mast, together with my partner. Thus, we lay beside on the screen and slept, only to awaken early during a heavy shower. Though it must have sprinkled nearly all night, we did not suffer, but now, as the rain lessens, we make our way below. Our clothes are sodden and clinging. However, we are more refreshed than had we bathed in our own sweat below.

FEBRUARY 2, 1944
    G.Q. lasted only an hour, and the rest of the day has slipped by quietly. The hatches below the second deck have been kept closed. It is reported firing has nearly ceased on the Islands, and the loss in personel has been slight. The Island has not been in sight since morning, and we seem to be underway for "somewhere", but the fire on Burlesque can be seen again. We pulled right up into the lagoon as I stood watch (6-8) and watched the Marines in their amphibious tanks advancing on a small island directly abeam. We weighed anchor only a short way out from this Island, (80 miles) and could see the tanks advancing along the reef that streaks from one island to the other. There was considerable firing from the tanks that was answered from the beach by machine gun fire, but the tanks advanced steadily, and soon overcame all resistance, making their way along the reef to the next island. There, after dark, we could see a blaze of tracer bullets streaking the sky. It was too dark to tell if they were drawing return fire or if they were firing from both ends of the island.

FEBRUARY 4th, 1944
    It's been reported that out of the 2500 Japs on the island, 75% were killed by the concentrated

fire of Naval guns. Captain_____ _____
was on the Island and said the COLORADO covered
its target very well; only one small A.A. gun remains in possible firing condition.

If any prisoners were taken, no word has been announced. It seems incredible, almost merciless, in view of the overwhelming odds....And what of the women and children on the Islands!

****

By February 4, 1944, after fairly blowing Kwajalein off the continent, Japanese-organized resistance ceased. Then after its capture the Infrantry made 42 amphibious landings, seizing one islet after another. By February 7, the mopping-up proceedure of the tiny isles had been completed and the U.S.S.COLORADO was ready to move on to the next operation.

After this second horrendous battle came to an end, Wilbur was a well-seasoned warrior. When word was out aboard ship that they were moving to a new war zone, he knew just what it was all about. It was really not the "War Operation" the folks back home would think it to be, but a hellish destruction of everything. Nothing was spared whether moving or immobile, flesh or vegetation, buildings or ground, everything was cut down,bludgeoned into Lucifer's Hell Holes rimmed with blood, death, and stench.

Wilbur was certain he, nor any other man, had never been "one of God's children" as Amie had proclaimed of all mankind. Here was a world of men without humor or the sanction of God. Man of his own volition had turned himself into a demon... merciless, cruel, branding himself a follower of Satan . If one ever entertained any lofty thoughts or principles they'd better be scrapped, for they were the swords that drew your life's blood as certain as the bombs that burst over head. *Kill, destroy, fight, or get yourself blown right off the map!*

THE COLORADO DISPATCH

Vol. 2 No. 6   U.S.S. COLORADO   6 February 1944

Undated Pacific War:-

American invasion forces have established firm control over the vital sections of Kwajalein atoll in the mid Pacific Marshalls with the complete conquest of three more islands and Navy planes have struck at possible bases of Japs counteraction. In two communiques late today Admiral Nimitz announced the capture of Kwajalein, Ebye, and Roi Islands on the world's largest atoll, and aerial strikes at Wake Island, Eniwetok, Mile, and Jaluit atolls. United States forces now hold 19 out of 32 islands in the Kwajalein atoll including the most strategic points. In less than a week our offensive forces have gained two airfields on Roi and Kwajalein islands, a seaplane base at Ebeye, and a harbor big enough to shelter the entire American fleet all living within Japanese outer ring of Pacific island defenses with the Southern tip of the atoll securely in their hands by capture of the three atolls announced today. Seventh Division Army troops concentrated their attack on Gugegwe, commanding the Eastern entrance of the lagoon. Its fall is expected momentarily. The Northern end of Kwajalein atoll including Roi, islands one excellent airfield is of the triangular shaped atoll remains under enemy control. Attempting to cut off help for this corner or any of the bomb shattered and bypassed Marshall atolls carrier based planes dumped many tons of bombs on Eniwetok, most Northwestern point of the Marshall group and relay point for Japanese planes. For the same reason bombers of fleet air wing two made a round trip flight of more 2,000 miles to make the eleventh raid on Wake 620 miles north of Kwajalein.

The Army Airforce hit the Southern Marshalls from the Gilbert Islands. Fighters raided Mili atoll and bombers sank a small freighter in Jaluit Lagoon. "It's too early to tell whether the enemy's navy will elect to fight", said Rear Admiral Richard L. Connolly who led the Northern Task Force against Kwajalein but he added significantly, "Where the Marines have landed, there the Americans will stay."

General MacArthur's communique today reported that twenty to twenty-six Jap planes were shot down in new raids on Raboul, New Britain and Wewak, New Guinea. More than 100 tons of explosives blasted revetment and installations at Wewak where in two days 300 tons of bombs have raised havoc with four airfields and 88 enemy planes have been destroyed. In the latest raid heavy bombers started fires visible for 50 miles. Jap airfields were attacked from Amboina in the Dutch East Indies to Kavieng, New Ireland. Heaviest toll of enemy interceptors was taken at Rabaul.

There at least thirteen and possibly nineteen were brought down in renewed strikes at Tobers and Lakunai fighter strips. Other bombers concentrated on Madang and Alexishafen, New Guinea. Australians advanced another mile and a half up the New Guinea coast against Japanese ground forces trapped between the Aussies and Americans near Saidor. American destroyers ruling the seas around the Solomon islands turned their guns against Jap installations on the Northwest coast of Bougainville Island.

LONDON:
　　The Church of England Newspaper praised President Roosevelt's International leadership Saturday, and declared that Governor Thomas Dewey of New York, "Ceased being isolationist only when events made it ridiculous." "It is going to make the difference of life and death for future generations whether next November the American people elect as President the statesman who feels in his very bones the necessity for International community and cooperation or a stateman whose belief in International solidarity is the grudging concession to the pressure of events," the editorial said.

HOLLYWOOD, CALIF:
　　Bandleader Harry James said Saturday he has been classified 1-A by his draft board in Texas, and will take a pre-induction examination there next week.

LOS ANGELES, CALIF:
　　Vice President Henry W. Wallace told some 40,000 shipyard workers here today that finding jobs for returning servicemen and war workers should be the Government's first Post War objective.

LONDON:
　　Eighteen persons were believed killed and 20 hurt by an explsion of an ammunition dump near a northern England Railway Yard, Friday. The blast wrecked the station and scattered debris for miles around.

RALEIGH, NORTH CAROLINA:
　　Frank T. Davis, 51, of Oxford N.C. former Major League Baseball pitcher died Friday in an ambulance which was taking him to the hospital.

He was a veteran of twenty years in organized baseball and was with the St. Louis Browns seven years.

U.S.S.S COLORADO

* COLORADO DISPATCH *8 February 1944

UNDATED PACIFIC WAR:-

American Naval forces shelled Paramushiro Island only twelve hundred miles from Tokyo in a possible prelude to invasion of the home Islands of Japan while American task forces were wiping out 8,122 Japs on Kwajalein Atoll to establish an offensive base in the mid-Pacific Marshall Islands. In contrast to the heavy toll taken of the enemy the U.S. forces lost 286 killed, 82 missing and 1,148 wounded in the Marshalls invasion the Navy Department announced today. In addition they took 264 shell-shocked and terrified Japs prisoners. The American losses were one-fourth of those killed in the Gilbert Island invasion last November while Japanese losses were doubled. Both testify to the terrific bombardment which ripped up the Kwajalein Island like a giant plow. At Kwajalein, Americans are only eleven hundred miles by flying-fortress to Tokyo. The Tokyo radio warned simultaniously of the Kurile Islands. Vichy radio quoted a Japanese communique as saying the invasion of the Kuriles was already underway, but Vichy has so often gargled reports of Pacific war action that it should not be taken too seriously. More significant was the report from associated press war correspondent, Norman Bell, that the American task force carried as an observer Brig. General E.D. Post, Chief of Staff for Lt. General Simon B. Buckner, whose troops of the Alaska Department were at that moment engaged in assault maneuvers.

The bombardment of Paramushiro last Friday night was the first attack by American sea forces on Nippon's home islands. It seemed so easy Bell wrote that none disagreed with the sailor who said, "Why, we ought to go ahead and take that place." The Japanese defenders were so taken by surprise and so confused that they fired along their own shoreline at imaginary landing barges, into the air, to the east, into the Pacific, and to the west into the sea of Okhotsk. They did not hit a ship in the American force which included cruisers, destroyers, and possibly battleships. Brilliant star-shell illuminated the blacked-out snow-covered island as the task force moved in under bright moonlight to bombard the harbor at the southern end of Paramushiro for twenty minutes. The only Jap ship sighted was left beached and an ammunition dump or fuel storage tank was left blazing so brightly that departing ships could see it until it disappeared below the horizon. The sea raid was teamed with bombings by the Navy's Aleutian-based air wing Four on Paramushiro and on Shimusion which lies in the narrow stretch of water between Paramushiro and Siberia Kamchatks Peninsula.

SAN FRANCISCO, CALIF.

Vice PRESIDENT WALLACE told leaders of San Francisco Latin-American Colony Monday that "our enemies now are convinced with the desperation born of their military position". But he declared, "We have the two-handed weapons of Truth and Faith, and we must continue to fight with both hands." On a visit to the San Francisco Bay area Wallace told the Latin-American breakfast meeting that in the post war world years, "The essentials of life, food, clothing, shelter, education, must be within the reach of all. There must be peace without poverty."

In an address here Sunday Vice President outlined a general program for a busy and happy post war United States through an increased ational income.

LONDON:

The Polish telegraph agency said Monday that 177 hostages were shot by the Germans in Warsaw the last two weeks in October. Details of the shootings have just come from Poland the agency of the Polish government in exile said, listing Miss Jania Aszkenacy, daughter of Dr. Simeon Aszkenacy, Polish Historian and delegate to the League of Nations as among those executed.

-:-

ENIWETOK in the MARSHALL ISLANDS was next on the agenda for the U.S.S.COLORADO.
None of the Marshall Islands rise more than a few feet above sea level, Eniwetok included. Eniwetok, its alternative name of "Brown" was discovered in 1790 by Captain T. Butler, its number of islets is 40. All natives in the Marshall Islands are of the Polynesian type with a distinct Asiatic ُmixture -(Micronesian).Wilbur thought these natives a good-looking lot. Their coloring was a light olive, and they had a pleasant, peaceful, hospitable disposition. Like most Polynesians they were intelligent and clever, and, Wilbur learned they were notable sailors. In old times they made long voyages in their outrigger canoes which had large sails made of native mats.

The fleet was in position February 17, 1944. The landing force, commanded by Rear-Admiral Hill, included the battleships PENNSYLVANIA, and the TENNESSEE besides the COLORADO. All ships landed army troops and Marines on some of the islets of Eniwetok atoll after a powerful preparation by aircraft and naval gunfire.

U.S.S. COLORADO

* COLORADO DISPATCH * 17 Feb. 1944

UNDATED PACIFIC WAR:

   Two weeks after they completed the capture of Kwajalein Atoll in the Marshall Islands, U.S. Army forces put their new gains to active use by springing a fleet of heavy bombers to pound the important Jap Island base of Ponape in the Caroline Islands. The Raid announced by Admiral Nimitz today marked the farthest land based aerial invasion of Jap territory in the Central Pacific. Ponape is only four-hundred-ten miles east of the Jap base of Truk. The bombing target served as a main supply and defensive base for the entire Jap defense line to the east extending thru the Marshall Islands. No enemy aircraft was encountered and all our planes returned. One Jap ship was sunk in the harbor and land fortifications were plastered with fifty-five tons of bombs. While the Ponape Raid and other lesser attacks against remaining enemy forces in the Marshall Islands kept the Japs busy in the Central Pacific. Allied airmen in the South Pacific ripped Kavieng, New Ireland with a heavy assault but lost eight planes in the raid. One heroic pilot landed his Catalina flying boat in the Kavieng Harbor during the battle and calmly picked up fifteen downed American airmen then took off without damage. General MacArthur announced that American and New Zealand troops which landed on the Green Islands east of New Ireland Monday have consolidated their positions without incident. Other American fliers roared in over Wewak, main Jap supply and air base in New Guinea, destroyed or damaged twenty-seven planes on the ground, and shot down seven zeros out of an intercepter force.MacArthur made one of his infrequent press conferences the occasion for an attack on the belief that Japan can be brought to her knees by air power and blockade. We must defeat Japan's *army* he said, and for that purpose our strategy must devise ways and means to bring our ground forces into contact with his at decisive points.

WASHINGTON:

In twin moves to assure future oil supplies despite dwindling underground petroleum reserves the House voted a thirty million dollar program Wednesday to develop synthetic fuels and the Senates Truman committee suggested that United States oil interest expand abroad. The house sent to the Senate legislation authorizing the Bureau of Mines to build experimental plants for producing motor and aviation gasoline from coal oil shale agricultural and particularly the British be asked to turn over to the U.S. a compensation volume of proven reserves.

-:- -:- -:-

On February 18, 1944, the American warships opened up at dawn on their target, Eniwetok. February 23, saw their mission won.

It was on February 21, that Wilbur, on night watch, found time to write to his sister to tell her how *dull* things were.Actually,he'd been running his tail off fixing searchlights and shutters during the bombardment.All this afternoon they'd been firing the 5 in. Then he got the word the mail ship just may come in, so could he get some letters written just maybe they would go out in a day or so.He wished he could send her the scrap he tore from The COLORADO DISPATCH and put in his stationery yesterday. It would explain a little to her just what was going on in his "neck of the woods."

THE COLORADO DISPATCH

Vol 2 No. 20   U.S.S COLORADO   20 February 1944

U.S. PACIFIC FLEET HEADQUARTERS, PEARL HARBOR:-

   Leap frogging American amphibious forces fighting on Eniwetok atoll in the Marshall islands have unleashed a threat against Truk which rivals the audacious carrier raids on that mighty Jap stronghold. Progress of the twin strikes in the lighting offensive through the Central Pacific remained obscured by radio silence. Security reasons prevented disclosure of whether the airborne attacks on Truk started Wednesday were still underway, likewise there was no immediate report of the progress at Eniwetok. Prizes of the Eniwetok battle are air bases from which continuing raids could be made on Truk, Japan's own Pearl Harbor 750 miles to the South.

-:-   -:-   -:-

W.A. Parker
U.S.S. COLORADO, Box 11
c/o Fleet P.O.
San Francisco, Calif.
Feb. 21, 1944

Dear Ruby,

   It hasn't been but a few days since I wrote, and there isn't much to say, but thought I'd drop a line as the mail may go out tomorrow.

   It sure did seem good to get your letters the other day, and I'd like to be able to write a great fat letter in return, but gosh, I don't know what I'd say. Most of what little I can think up would probably be cut out by the censorship rules.

   You can imagine how dull things become when you don't get off the ship for so long.

Some of the fellows went swimming a time or two, but somehow, I never got around to it. Some were fishing too, but don't think they had much luck with the lines, though one of them did catch a four-foot shark, and they had to shoot it to get it aboard.

I don't quite remember what I told you on my card I wrote it so hurriedly to get it off. Did I tell you I was offered $50 for the knife I made? I guess I'm crazy not to sell it but money doesn't mean much here.

I haven't found much time to study though I should. It's too hot below and too windy on top, and besides I haven't found much time.

I'm so glad you're feeling better, Ruby. I sure wish we could take one of our good old strolls like we used to. There'd be so much to say then.

I have a number of other letters I should write, and I know you will understand how hard it is to think of anything to say here.

Hope to hear again soon, Love, Wilbur

As Wilbur wrote, Japanese resistance had ceased on Eniwetok. IF things stayed with any measure of calm, maybe, the U.S.S.COLORADO might return to the States for repairs and reprieve. He had torn the information of Japanese defeat at Eniwetok Atoll from the COLORADO DISPATCH, folded it, and stuck it in his stationery:

THE COLORADO DISPATCH

U.S.S.COLORADO   23 February 1944

U.S. PACIFIC FLEET HEADQUARTERS, PEARL HARBOR:

Conquest of Eniwetok Atoll in the Western Marshall Islands within bombing range of Truk neared completion Tuesday with American forces engaged in clearing the Japanese from Parry Island. Eniwetok, at the southern end of the atoll, is in United States hands, Admiral Chester W. Nimitz announced Monday night and American Air and Naval forces have Parry under heavy attack. The important island of Engebi, which has an airfield, was captured last week within a few hours after the invasion of the atoll.

WASHINGTON: USS COLORADO PRESS NEWS - Page TWO

Prime Minister Churchill's reluctance even to hint at an Allied victory over Germany this year is shared in military and naval circles here. A strong belief has grown up that the European war could go into 1945. The clue to what will happen is an utterly immeasurable factor, German moral.

-:-   -:-   -:-

ORDERS FOR THE DAY, SUNDAY, 20 FEBRUARY 1944:
(RESTRICTED)
INFORMATION:

1. THIRD Section has 00-04 Watch.
2. THIRD Section is duty section.
3. Working Division - Division TWO.
4. Tactical Watch:

00-04 - Comdr. HENKEL.   16-20 - Comdr.REITHER.
04-08 - Comdr. REITHER.   20-24 - LT.CDR.HOLLOWAY.

GENERAL:
1. At anchor. The ship is ready to get underway on 30 minutes notice.
2. Condition of Readiness III, Material Condition of Readiness YOKE, maintained day and night except when General Quarters is sounded, five minutes after which Condition ZEBRA will be set.

ROUTINE EXCEPT:
---- - Uniform of the day will be dungarees.

108

---- - Call cooks and bakers of the watch.
0535 - MAAs call leading division POs
0545 - REVEILLE. Make preparations for getting underway at 0630.
0555 - Leading division POs report to MAAs that men sleeping in their spaces are turned out.
0600 - Station anchoring and piloting detail.
0645 - Breakfast.
0700 - (About) Anchor.
0800 - Muster on stations.
0830 - Rig Church in "M" division compartment.
0855 - Sound Church call.
0900 - Protestant Divine Service in "M" division compartment.
1025 - Sound Church call.
1030 - Catholic Mass in "M" division compartment. (Chaplain NEE officiating).
1530 - Swimming call. Carry out Executive Officer's Memorandum No. 2-44.
1545 - Commence firing.
1635 - Cease firing.

NOTICES:

1. The following dispatch from Commander Task Group 51.11 is quoted:

    "WELL DONE ON FIRE SUPPORT. YOU DID A MAGNIFICENT JOB."

                           W. A. BOWERS,
                      Commander, U.S. Navy
                         Executive Officer.

20 FEBRUARY 1944

ORDERS FOR THE DAY, FRIDAY, 25 FEBRUARY 1944;
(RESTRICTED)

INFORMATION:
1. SECOND Section has 00-04 Watch.
2. SECOND Section is duty section.
3. Working division - Division 6A.
4. Tactical Watch.

00-04 - Lieut. B.Water   16-20 - Comdr.REITHER
04-08 - Comdr. REITHER   20-24 - Comdr.HENKEL

GENERAL:
1. Underway.
2. Condition of Readiness III, Material Condition of Readiness YOKE, maintained day and night except when General Quarters is sounded, five minutes after which Condition ZEBRA will be set.

ROUTINE EXCEPTY:
---- - Uniform of the day will be dungarees.
---- - Call cooks and bakers of the watch.
0520 - REVEILLE for all hands (including officers and CPOs).
0535 - Serve out coffee.
0550   DAWN General Quarters. Make preparations for entering port.
0700 - (a) Flight Quarters.
       (b) Breakfast.
0730 - Launch one plane for anti-submarine patrol. Plane will be recovered after anchoring.
0830 - Quarters for muster.
1000 - (About) Will anchor at Majuro Lagoon.

NOTICES:
1. EXAMING BOARDS are directed to submit rough 624's of men successfully completing examinations by 1600 today.

W.A. BOWERS
Commander, U.S. Navy
25 Feb. 1944   Executive Officer.   110

True to his hopes, the second week in March the big, battered, ship lay in dock at Bremmerton, Washington. It seemed he couldn't wait to set his feet on the good, old, U.S.A.! Oh, God, just good home soil that was still in tact...no burning heaps, no littered streets! Wilbur could well-understand, men going to their knees to kiss the dear homeland!

W.A.Parker, EM 3/C
United States Navy
March 16, 1944

Dear Sister,
    Received your swell letter of the 29th, so I will try to scratch out a line or two in answer.
    Bremerton doesn't seem so cold though it is foggy a good deal. On my first liberty (the 13th) I only went to Bremerton and did some shopping, and saw a show which I thought was good. Maybe one reason I enjoyed it was because I'd not seen one for so long. I came in about one o'clock and there was so much racket here that I didn't get much sleep so consequently, was a bit dead the next day. That didn't keep me from going out again last night (15th) though!
    I intended to go to Seattle last evening, and thought I'd call down to Los Angeles but did neither. Bill and I only did a bit more shopping and went to another show. Haven't got much more dope on the leave. I think I'll get it all right, but it's going to be terribly short.
    Your letters sure give me itchy feet, but the weather reports we've been getting don't sound so good.
I got a nice, long letter from Dorothy and Leslie today. Guess they keep mighty busy. His classification has been changed and he thinks he'll soon be going. Harley De Witt is in 1A now, and he started before Les, and has worked up pretty well. I was in hopes this would be over before Leslie

would have to go, but guess it just won't. I'd like to get around to seeing them again but guess I should be thankful that it hasn't been so long since I did.

Buck Parr got home on a 21-day leave a short while back, but he had to go a long way, too, so didn't get long at home.

I have the watch and must close. It just seems I never find time to sit down and write the kind of letter that I'd like to. Will try to write again before long.

As Ever, Your Old Pal & Bro.   Wilbur

Sunday, March 19, 1944

Well, Ruby, I didn't get this off so I'll add a line.

Friday, I had liberty so another fellow and I took the ferry over to Seattle. It's about a 90-minute ride. I only wish that you could have been along because I know you would have enjoyed it so much.

We went bowling first, but it was crowded so we went to a show, then out to the ice rink. We had a lot of fun but when the skating was over it was too late to catch the ferry, so we had to wait and catch the 5:45 one in the morning. We looked around a while then decided to go to another show. It was good but we were most too sleepy to enjoy it. We got in just in time for breakfast after which we managed a nap. You can imagine we needed it! (Ha)

That's about all there is to say so I'll close for this time. Yours Always, Wilbur

Wilbur continued to work aboard ship, writing letters, and waiting for his leave, wondering how many days he'd get. You learned patience in the Navy, nevertheless, he found himself most impatient now. He wanted to see his girl. Was she *still his girl*? Was she ever his girl? Why would a young, pretty girl who has everything going for her want an old, ship-worn, man with the stench of war upon his brow? Guess this leave would give him a chance to find out. He wired her a dozen roses and waited.

Then during his leave, a miracle unfolded... this tender, sweet, girl really did love him. There was so doubt in his mind that he loved her. Yes, she would wait for him. When the war was over he would come back to her. They dated, and planned, and talked those glorious days of his leave from April 4th through April 14th, 1944. Heaven came to an abrupt end on April 15th when it came time to catch the plane back to his ship. All that day they held one another while Brother Les did the work, even prepared their dinner. The painful time came to board the plane, and his brave Sweetheart shed not one tear at parting.

April 17th found Wilbur back aboard the U.S.S. COLORADO at 7:36. The war must go on, and now *he* had something to go on for...the anticipation of a woman whom he loved and who loved him. Ah, maybe any war would be worth such a prize!

He quickly got back into routine, changed his clothes and worked on the searchlights, finding time in the evening to write to Ruby.

W.A. Parker, EM 3/C
United States Navy
April 17, 1944

Dear Sister,
 I must sit down and write you a line tonight. I certainly have had a time finding a place to do it though. Lord, but things are torn up! We have fifteen new men in the division so we are really crowded. Believe me it was bad enough before, but

I don't know what we will do for places to sleep now when everyone gets back from leave.

I sent you a card from Seattle yesterday, but it may be sort of slow getting there. I took the plane back from Los Angeles at 5:30 on Saturday evening (15th) and got into Seattle at 2:30 in the morning of the 16th, so had plenty of time to fool around, and I almost wished that I had waited and spent another day in Los Angeles.
    It was a wonderful trip back. Believe me they sure do give you service on those air lines! They served dinner soon after we left L.A. It was a delicious meal and it was sort of heavenly eating with a few fleecy clouds drifting between the plane and Earth.
    We stayed at San Francisco and again at Oakland to change planes. Also, made a couple other stops before reaching Seattle, but it became dark about the time we left Oakland and I slept most of the rest of the trip, so couldn't say where we did stop. Took a cab from the airfield to the swellest hotel in town. There was but one place open...a swell suite for 12 bucks...special to service men; but there were four of us and two beds so we took it as it seemed the last chance, and was it nice! The other fellows had to get out early so I had it the rest of the day to myself. I got up about 10:30...took a nice bath, shaved, and cleaned my suit up, then went out and had a nice turkey dinner, and strawberry shortcake.
    I've been having trouble with pains in my neck for sometime so I decided to go to a chiropractor. I went to one in San Francisco but he didn't help me much so I had an X-ray taken this time and it showed my neck to be about $\frac{1}{4}$ inch out of line. This chiropractor seems to know what he's doing and I hope to get several treatments before I leave here.
    I fooled around Seattle all day yesterday... stayed at the Y.M.C.A. and came back on the 5:30 ferry this morning.
    I wanted to do a little washing, and sort of

get my things together again today, but, by Gosh, they put me right to work, and I've been at it all day. What a life! If only (ha) leaves could last!...sigh,sigh!

I certainly did have a good time on my leave while it lasted even if I didn't feel so good. Gosh, what rotten luck having to have a bum leg at a time like that! If I hadn't kept hot packs on it a good deal, I guess it might have gotten plenty bad. About all there is left of it now is a hard lump and a small sore spot.

Maybe it was about as well that I didn't catch a plane to Cheyenne that day. If I'd gotten to Wheatland in a snow storm and had to walk to get the rest of the way I'd just have been stranded. Anyhow, with the weather reports and the way I felt, I didn't have much heart to tackle it. On the other hand, I guess I was a fool to try to go by L.A. when I wanted to get home, but I promised Clara Mae...and I guess every man is a fool sometimes. Also, I wanted to see if Leslie couldn't get away, too.

This sounds a bit like a bunch of excuses, but it was just one of those decisions a man can't quite make up his mind to. If I'd started around the other way I'd probably never gotten to Los Angeles.

The Sunday that I didn't catch the plane, we went on a picnic, Les, Dot, Clara Mae, and I. Then I stayed two days at Les and Dot's and we just rested and didn't go anywhere. Stayed at Parr's the next night and we went to a show. So I sort of went back and forth most of the time but everyone is working and Clara Mae is in school, so we didn't do a great deal but I had a swell time.

I felt so homesick yesterday...the first time in a long time...seemed sort as if I'd missed something I might have had, and I sure would like to see you, Ruby, all of you folks! I think you know that though...I'm so glad you are coming nicely with your studies. I had a nice bunch of letters waitin' when I got in and I sure enjoyed them. With Love as Always, Wilbur

It was while on this furlough that Wilbur mailed his mother a special, little map of the Pacific Ocean with specific instructions how to use it so she'd know where he was at all times. When she received a letter from him, somewhere in it she'd find a dot within a tiny circle. She was to put this page of his letter within certain boundary lines on the map. Wherever the dot fell on the map that was where he'd be. "I'm sending one to Ruby, too," he wrote.

-: THE COLORADO DISPATCH :-

Vol.2,No.25   U.S.S. COLORADO   April 25, 1943

-: THE WAR IN THE PACIFIC :-

-:-

UNDATED:-
The Navy disclosed today in a communique that American forces have occupied islands of the strategic Ellice Group about four hundred miles south of the Japanese occupied Gilbert Islands in the South Pacific. The communique reported an enemy bombing attack on Japanese installations there, but said the occupation was unopposed although a communique in October 1942 had told of a surface engagement in adjacent waters and it was presumed then that the Japanese had moved in. The island group of nine palm-covered atolls lies eleven-hundred miles east of the Solomon Islands, athwart

Allied supply routes to Australia.

Allied headquarters in Australia meanwhile, in a communique dated Saturday, April 24, made the first mention of ground activity in New Guinea since March 23, telling of Allied........

Washington:-

British First Army has seized all intitial objectives in Bou Arada sector and our gains on Eighth Army front are "firmly held", a communique from North African Allied headquarters today reported. Air patrol in Gulf of Tunis encountered formation of enemy transport aircraft escorted by fighters and during battle twenty transports and ten escorting planes were shot down. Heavy and continuous attacks on enemy troops and positions were carried out. During course of which seven enemy airfields in Tunisia and shipping and harbor installations at Carloforte, Sardinia, covering both targets with bomb bursts and starting fires at Carloforte, the communique added. One enemy plane was destroyed during these raids while five of our aircraft are missing from all operations.

New York:-

Earlier in the week Rome radio communiqued that "violent" artillery fire on the entire Tunisian front continued. Our air force bombed enemy supply columns in a day and night attack during which time thirteen enemy planes were shot down by German fighters. Eight civilians were killed and fifty wounded during an enemy raid on Spezia. After a long chase, an enemy submararine was sunk in the Tyrrenian Sea.

-:- -:- -:-

THE U.S.S. COLORADO had been in dock for 6 weeks. Her repairs completed, she was ready to move back into the conflict. She was moving out when Wilbur wrote to Ruby. He mailed his letter in Burlingame, California, in the San Francisco Bay area. This was to tell her he was on his way back "across".

May 2, 1944
My dearest Sister,
   Received your two letters of 18th and 25th, also Mother's of the 20th. Have been mighty anxious to hear from you since I got back and I sure was glad to get them.
   You must have had some pretty rough weather. If I had tried to come it would have taken all my time on the road. Although it seemed like kind of a tough break at the time, maybe it was as well that I didn't try to come. I like the winter and I love the snow, but a snow storm is a poor time to make a rush visit. I envy you sitting by the fire in the evenings free to work or muse over your studies unobstructed by a world definitely mad...free to walk at your leisure through the snow that adds silence, and grateful distance between you and the disturbances of restless men. I guess, it will always be the habit of the mind to bask where the body is not, and man will travel fruitlessly in an effort to re-unite the two. So I ask myself, "If I were there would I be content?" This question helps some for a time, but soon I find my feet in the snow or walking the old trails with you.
   I wonder if you are still up home? I hope... but then, I guess Mother can send this on if not. It hasn't been so long since I wrote and there isn't a lot to say. I made several liberties in Seattle, and on the last one I came in an hour late. I thought the ferry ran at 10:30, and it

left at 10:20 so I missed it and was an hour late. They didn't do anything but call me to mast and give me a warning. I hated to spoil my good record, but there were about 80 others at mast for nearly the same reason, so I didn't feel so bad.

We'll be in San Francisco in the morning and I rate liberty, and I can get this sent off. Don't think that I'll be in Frisco more than a few days, but hope I'll have another letter waiting me there. I haven't heard from Leslie since I returned. Clara Mae has written several times, and she says they are planning on moving closer to Dorothy's work, so they may be plenty busy.

I've found no time to study for a long while. We have been very busy, and then I've gone on liberty a lot too.

Wish you could be with me tomorrow, then I could really enjoy it

I've been wondering if you got the package that I sent. I can't tell you how much I'd like to have heard you sing "Whispering Hope". It's sort of a part of me that song--a part that burns in my breast and makes tears come to my eyes--a promise given on a yesterday and carried through each tomorrow.

I noticed that you used 8¢. You really only need 6¢ for oversea addresses...think I'll go to bed now as I'm about run down anyhow.

    Ever, Your old Pal, Wilbur

Ruby received the package Wilbur mentioned in this letter. It contained a superb photo of Clara Mae Parr, Wilbur, Leslie and Dorothy Parker, taken as they were all seated together around a table in the Zamboanga South Sea Cafe and Nite Club, at 3828 Slauson Ave., Los Angeles, a meeting place of Hollywood stars and celebrities. With the picture was a beautiful, colorful, abalone pearl necklace with the message, "Happy Easter! Happy Birthday!"

May 10, 1944
Dear Sister,
 Just a line as I wrote to Mother today. I haven't heard for sometime, and you may be back home by now so just to play sure I'll write and maybe Bill will like to read it anyhow. I've been having some cold, but I think I'm about to get the best of it.
 There has been a terrible lot of work, and I've been on the go continually. We are beginning to get caught up now, but some will get liberty again tomorrow, and we will probably get behind again.
 We held a big field day today and tried to get the shop cleaned up. It looks a lot better, but we still have a way to go.
 I *washed* clothes, ironed my whites, and showered after chow tonight, an I'm trying to catch up a bit on some of my neglected letter writing.
 I haven't found time to study for so long I think that I've nearly forgotten all that I learned. I wish I could be there to study with you. That really would be fun...hope that you are still coming O.K. and are enjoying it.
 They have a movie tonight on the quarterdeck, but I knew I couldn't get any ahead on my writing out there. After having a little leave and liberty,things seem pretty dull again, and there is really very little to say. I don't look forward much to going over tomorrow, but there are a few little things I want to buy. Then, too, it's a change and I can get some milk to drink. Gosh, I don't guess I'll ever get over missing milk!   As Always, Wilbur

 "It *works!* He's in Honolulu!" Ruby called to Bill who had just come in and was washing his face after his hot, eight-hour ride on the pipeline. "Uncca Wibber, Uncca Wibber," Stanley joined in with his mother's excitement.

"Well, you might tell me what the excitement is all about", said Bill as he took the towel from its hook and started wiping his face.

"The *ringed dot!*" cried Ruby, "See, Wilbur has a ringed dot on this sheet of his letter, and you place it over the map like this," she said as she demonstrated, "and the dot falls right on Honolulu!"

Someway the knowledge of his whereabouts seemed to give more meaning to his letter:

W.A. PARKER EM 3/C
U.S.S. COLORADO, Bo 11
c/o Fleet P.O.
San Francisco, Calif.
May 18, 1944

Dear Sister,

I dare say that I'm scarcely in the mood for answering your nice long letter of the 7th tonight.

It came in yesterday's mail, but somehow, I didn't find time to answer last night. Maybe it was because I went to the show...ha...the show wasn't worth much either, and I wished afterward I'd gone back to my turret and wrote instead. It has been several months since I went to a show aboard ship. I manage a seat last night so I stayed, and enjoyed the fresh air out-of-doors on the main deck, if not the show.

I envy your time to study, and I'm sure glad that you are so nearly through your course. I just haven't found any time at all for study for a long while. What little time I get in the evenings, I take to *wash* and write letters. How glad I would be to get away from it all! But, now, I am building air castles.

Sometimes your letters make me homesick, or

maybe, it's just the mood they catch me in. I also envy David his long talk with you and wonder if someday there will be a time when we may have a good long chat as we used to. Somehow, our thoughts always seem to run so close together. I doubt we've either changed very much inside, though probably, we have outwardly. (I know I have.) Perhaps, our greatest trouble was in expecting too much out of life and giving it too little confidence. I've often thought of that; of how much we had in our understanding and how much I've missed it.

It is nearly twelve so I think I'll quit and maybe add a line tomorrow. Goodnight....

May 19, 1944

Will add a bit now and try to get it off in the morning.

I hardly know where to send it, but I wrote to Mother the other day, so I guess, I'll send this to Wendover, then you'll hear either way.

I went on liberty again today, and I like to wore my poor pups out. I wanted to rent a camera and get some film, but the shops had let them all out before we (Bill and I) got in. We were sort of slow, I guess, and it was about noon before we got down town, though we got off at nine. We didn't do a great lot or have too much fun, but the sun was nice and I enjoyed myself. The getting ready and doing the *wash* afterwards is always the bad part. Those crazy whites just won't stand more than one liberty no matter how careful one is!

Have you found much time to write with all of your studying? You said you're going to will your writings to me. Cripes! you better let another party in on that, too. I'm older than you. Really, I do appreciate the thought a lot, and I'm sure no one else could treasure them more.

I've scarcely tried to write a bit since I

joined the service. It's like trying to write in a mad house, and even my letters are lurid.

I never did quite finish my Math correspondence course that I started when I got out of Machinist school. I doubt I ever will get to it now.

Believe I'm about run down. I did have a poem that I was going to send you, but guess I'll have to look it up some other time.

Seems the mail has been awfully slow. I didn't get any mail again today.

As Ever Your Old Pal, & Brother, Wilbur

Thereafter, the ringed dot always spelled excitement, and a lot of times, it was a source of fear and torment because it would fall upon a port of fiercely, raging, war. On May 28, 1944, however, the dot revealed he was still in the Hawaiian Islands.

Dear Sister,

Guess it's about time to answer that nice letter. You do write the best letters, though, sometimes they make me a little homesick.

Little we knew ten years ago as we carved our names in the rock atop Laramie Peak, or walked the familiar paths together, where the world would find us today, or what our lives would be like. It makes me think of these lines from a poem I learned while looking out over those familiar, home-hills:

"So widened ways which once unbroken love did
    link and span,
So diverged the paths which once ran close up-
    on the better plan,
So drifted far apart the barges, which on
    Life's sunlit sea
Saw not the current's course or separations
    yet to be."

Anyhow, those days will always be ones to look back upon with joy and pleasant memory.

I had a letter from L.A. today, and Leslie has another six month deferment. I'm certainly glad. The kids were so worked up and unsettled. I rec'd a letter from Buster (Burnett) too, and he hardly thinks that he will be called. They are pretty busy on the 10 Ranch...help is hard to get and Fred (Prager) isn't so very well.

I sent little Stanley a birthday gift the other day, but suppose it will be late. It isn't much, but perhaps, he will enjoy something more grownup now. I got it at one of the canteens here on the base.

It's so crowded down town that I've not gone off the base on any liberty lately. That sure saves washing those whites!

They have a swell swimming pool on the base, and athletic gear such as baseballs, boxing gloves, etc. I sure do feel a lot better since I've been getting out in the sun and exercising a little. I got a good burn yesterday, but guess it will wear off, though it sure doesn't feel like it now.

Jack's wife sent him the pictures we took when we were there that day. She included a full set for me, and I guess that I can spare you one.

Gosh, I meant to put some gum in that package I sent Stanley. I bought three cartons the other day. They have the best pineapple juice at the canteens, too...15¢ for a big can, nice and cool, and is it good! They have beer, too, but I never buy it. There is always a line about a mile long, and I'd rather have pineapple juice, anyhow.

I'm about run down and I want to write a few other letters so will close. Hoping to hear again soon, With Love, Your Old Pal, Wilbur

The dot in his next letter of June 8, 1944, shouted "MARSHALL ISLANDS!" And Ruby's heart quaked.
    The U.S.S.COLORADO was back in a war zone. Why had the ship been so long in the Hawaiian Islands? In his last letter of May 28, Wilbur spoke of "being on base". She interpreted this as meaning the ship was in dock at the time. He'd sent her six snapshots that Jack MacDonald took while in Honolulu. According to the pictures, Wilbur's face had filled out, and he looked better than he had in years.

June 8, 1944
Dear Sister,
    I have only a few moments, and five letters to write so please excuse this short, hurried note, I must get all letters in the mail right away, or they won't go out. There isn't much to tell, anyhow. Just a "Hello", and a word to let you know I'm feeling O.K., and too busy to be bored.
    I do miss the liberty every few days, the swimming and baseball, and I'm losing my tan. I've only been out in the sun for a bath once in over a week, and one does fade out awful quick. It's so darn hot below deck.
    I haven't had any mail for some time and I'm beginning to fear we will get none today. Well, I must hurry along with those other letters. You know I'll be thinking of you and will write when I can. As Ever, Wilbur

    To Ruby, his whole letter sounded as though he were hurrying into battle. He may not be able to write to his friends and family again. This could be the last time for everything or anything!
    True, THE U.S.S.COLORADO was making its toilsome and determined way from the Hawaiian Islands to the Marianas some 3,4000 miles west. Its goal being, little, mountainous Saipan. Saipan,

14 miles in length, crescent-moon in shape, was an isle with many sharks in its water, the white shark among them. Sharks were purely incidental compared to the threat of the Japanese commander on Saipan, Lieutenant General Saito with some 30,000 Japanese troops. Trying to anticipate where the Allies would strike next, the Japanese attempted to guess. They began to pour troops, equipment and supplies into the Marianas and western Carolines.

The bombardment of Saipan didn't begin until June 14, 1944, when the U.S.S.COLORADO took its place with the other battleships and cruisers. At 5:45 A.M. June 15, the fleet opened with covering fire, and after violent bombing by aircraft, the first of the 700 amphibious craft of the Marines went ashore at 8:40 A.M. on the west coast of Saipan. Accurate Japanese fire left large gaps among the men as they barely reached the beaches. The Marines defense was made easier by the continued firing of flares. No one seemed to be progressing. It was a melee where no one had control. Still the Japanese failed to drive the Marines back into the sea. Slaughter by both sides...the American and the Japanese...was indefineable, unpredictible, with the mingled and mangled bodies of both sides strewn in whip cord fashion.

However, by June the 18th, U.S. landing craft prevented the Japanese from bringing reinforcements up Tanpag Harbour Beach. An American destroyer was sunk by Japanese costal batteries, and two U.S. tankers were sunk by bombers, while the escort carrier "Fanshaw Bay" was also hit by bombers off shore.

Nonetheless, in the end, little Saipan was taken by the Allies. Their "victory", a bare, crisp, waste, and stinking human flesh. The only thing left alive on the tiny isle after the shelling was the do-do bird which Wilbur had believed was extinct. "How ironic", he thought, "that out of all the beautiful, lush green things that have been razed, this useless, idiotic creature is spared! On the other hand, it'd take a real do-do to even want to live in this human, war-crazed world!" And so it was, the old do-do, turkey-sized bird, with its rudimentary, functionless wings, lumbered along with a senseless cry, no good to itself, no good for anything, no good for anyone...very appropriate for the world of today.

Saipan's surrender advanced the United States' front line in the Central Pacific to 3,400 miles west of Pearl Harbor, thus coming within long-range bomber range of Japan.
The Japanese set up strongholds in the caves of Mount Tapotchau where the American Infantry made small progress in routing them out. However, this fight dubbed "Death Valley" was no concern of the Naval Fleet, so the U.S.S. COLORADO withdrew and moved on to cover for Marines in the next attempt to take a beach head. First, she must return to her "hide out" to stock up on ammunition, food, and mail. Thousands of pounds of death were gathered to her sides, which wasn't hard to figure when one considered a 14-inch shell for one of her naval guns weighed about 1,200 lbs., a 15-inch shell approximately 1,800 lbs, and a 16-inch shell nearly 2,400 lbs., so the U.S.S. COLORADO "mass loaded" for mass killing.
Ammo, food, mail...these three items seemed of equal importance. They were all correlated into making a workable defense of a ship and a nation. Ammo and food to supply the physical needs; but no need was greater then the spiritual need of the sailors for hearing from home and loved ones.
Detonation, smoke, fire, screams, and stench,

had gone on forever. Sometimes one grew so filled with the sights and sounds and smells of war, he wasn't at all sure but what it was his own dead flesh he was nauseated by, or perhaps, the screams came from his own mouth, and it was his own ship, the U.S.S.COLORADO that was burning. It all became one hellish experience while you lost sight of the "why"...everything about war had no reason.

Here in this hide-a-way, they were extricated from horror for a few days in order to load up for future horror. Besides the loading of ammo and food there was one thread of sanity...that of mail. Also, there'd be a moment to answer those letters..."keep care on the home front, things are dull here...nothing to say...I'm O.K....."

Back in the States, Ruby watched the mail and noted it had been over three weeks since she'd heard from Wilbur. She made daily trips to the P.O. in Wendover, and when at last, his letter of June 27, 1944, arrived, she scanned its pages. This time the little dot with its ring revealed he was somewhere in the Central Pacific north of Saipan.

W.A. Parker, EM 3/C
U.S.S. COLORADO, Box 11
c/o Fleet P.O.
San Francisco, Calif.
June 27, 1944

Dear Sister & All,
    Your last letter is well over a month old, and I sure will be glad if that mail man ever gets around. We have hopes it will be in the next few days, so that's why I'm writing this now. IF the mail does get in, and the office stays open, I will try to get another letter off, and hope for a little more to say, too.
    This is my fourth letter and I've about fought myself blind trying to think up something to say,

but it just isn't any use. Anyhow, I've been mighty well, and that counts a lot.

We have a few Heart or Pinochle games. Then there is the library if one can find the time to read, but in general things are just about as downright boresome as they can get. Maybe that's because there are so many other things I'd like to be doing--walking over the hills with you, for instance. Well, at least I can think, and even as my feet follow the path of this war-crazy world, I can look back and be glad for many pleasant memories.

The exams are coming up again soon, but I've been altogether too busy to do the studying I would have liked to, and I'll just have to wait.

I've abandoned my cot here on the electric deck for my hammock on the top side. Sometimes it rains and that isn't so good, but the fresh air more than makes up for a little soaking.

Well, it's pretty late and reveille comes at 3:30 so I'd better turn in.

Hope to hear very soon, and often. I guess you know I'll write when and IF I can. Goodnight, Ever Your Loving Brother, Wilbur
P.S. be sure to tell Little Stanley, Uncca Wibber says, "Hello"

By July the first, the little dot showed Wilbur back in the Marshall Islands just a ways northeast of Eniwetok. Ruby guessed they must have moved there in order to meet a ship carrying the mail. It was a pure guess, but it seemed logical, for afterall, Eniwetok had come into the possession of the Allies.

July 1, 1944
Dearest Sister:
Have four swell long letters here before me, and as I have a few spare moments I'll see what I can do about that note I promised in my last letter. Of course, you won't expect any news because there just isn't any.

They have been overly busy at the Post Office these last few days, but guess they have the mail about sorted now. I got my share and it sure is good to hear and know you are all well.

I had a line from Dorothy, and she and Les are still hard at it. She says they expect a big lay off at the plant soon, though, and it might even include Leslie. Harley (De Witt) has quit and is working for a garage.

Leslie's deferment will be up again in August the way she talked. Gosh! it doesn't seem that long since he got it! She said that her folks are thinking strongly of returning to S. Dak. I wonder if they may not have left already as I've not heard from any of them, and Clara Mae is usually so prompt at answering.

They had a show out on the quarter-deck last night. It was such a lovely evening I wanted to go, but realizing it may be my last chance to write for awhile, I sat up until about midnight and did quite well on catching up on my writing.

I would sure like to have been there to see Aunt Hazel's and talk with them about Alaska. You know I still have a feeling at times that I'd like to go there sometime.

I'm glad that Stanley liked the horse. I had a box of gum that I was going to send, too, but Gosh only knows if I'll ever get it there now.

Yes, I took several chiropractic treatments, and my neck felt much better. I was wrestling around with one of the fellows yesterday, though, and I wonder if he threw it out again the way it feels now. Maybe it's just the muscles that are sore, I hope.

I'm so glad you can find so much pleasure in your studies. I'd like to be there to review that geometry with you and maybe help a bit.

They have exams for advancement in rating yesterday, but I didn't go up because I just haven't found the time to study.

It doesn't seem possible it can be so close to the Fourth. I wonder what you will be doing? We'll probably have a good dinner, but I know it won't compare with your cakes or pies, so eat a piece for me, will you?

It's time to close now and go back to work.
Love, Wilbur

Scrawled along the margin of his letter were the words: "P.S. Yes, the stationery is for you and not for Stanley. You get the idea, don't you?"

Of course, she *did!* On the eight-inch by eleven-inch, heavy paper pack of airmail was a little map of the Pacific Ocean to replace the thin, paper map he'd made and left with their mother for her. The cardboard left a firm background and so it was much easier to place his position by using it.

His letter of July 9, showed him to be in almost the exact spot in the Marshall Islands as did his letter of July 1.

July 9, 1944, Sun.
Dear Sister,

There are a few moments to spare so I'll drop you a line in answer to yours of the 28th.

I've found time for a little study the last few days, but gosh, I don't know if I'll ever learn enough to do me any good...ha.

I'm sorry to hear Bill is having such a time. It must be pretty tough to feel so bad so much of the time. I suppose if he changes jobs it will mean a cut and I hope it won't be too much.

Friday, we held field day, and about worked our fool heads off getting the place clean for inspection. It's been so long since we held a right good field day the place was plenty tough to get in shape, and I'm sure glad it's over.

Yesterday, we had Captain's Military Inspection, and I was lucky and had the watch so I got out of that.

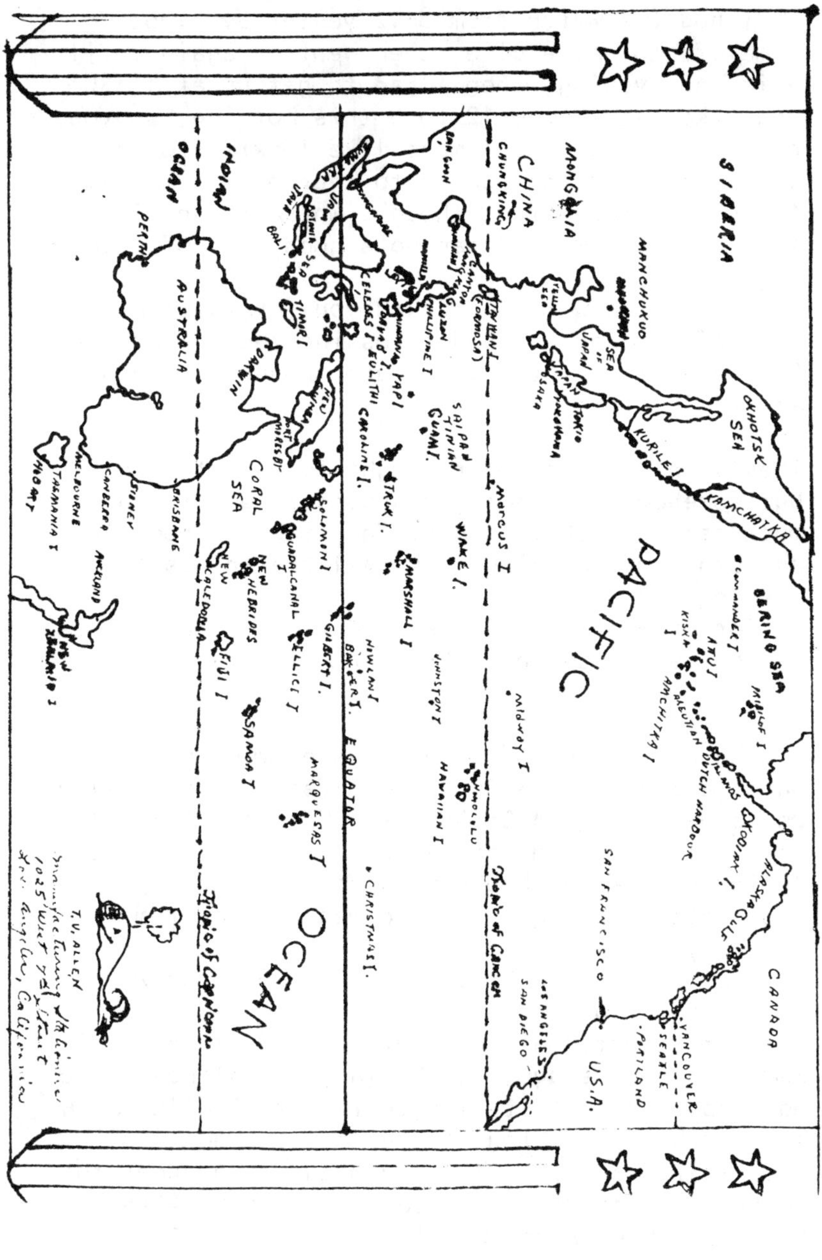
SIBERIA
MANCHUKUO
MONGOLIA
CHINA
CHUNGKING
OKHOTSK SEA
KURILE I
KAMCHATKA
SEA OF JAPAN
JAPAN
TOKIO
YOKOHAMA
OSAKA
PACIFIC
OCEAN
BERING SEA
COMMANDER I
ATTU
KISKA I
ALEUTIAN ISLANDS
AMCHITKA I
DUTCH HARBOUR
KODIAK I.
ALASKA GULF
CANADA
VANCOUVER
SEATTLE
PORTLAND
U.S.A.
SAN FRANCISCO
LOS ANGELES
SAN DIEGO
Tropic of Cancer
MIDWAY I
HONOLULU
HAWAIIAN I
JOHNSTON I
MARCUS I
WAKE I.
SAIPAN
TINIAN
GUAM I.
MARSHALL I
TRUK I.
CAROLINE I.
HOWLAND
BAKER I.
GILBERT I.
ELLICE I
EQUATOR
CHRISTMAS I.
MARQUESAS I
SAMOA I
FIJI I
NEW HEBRIDES
NEW CALEDONIA
GUADALCANAL I
SOLOMON I
CORAL SEA
PORT MORESBY
NEW GUINEA
DARWIN
AUSTRALIA
PERTH
BRISBANE
SIDNEY
CANBERRA
MELBOURNE
TASMANIA I
HOBART
AUCKLAND
NEW ZEALAND I
INDIAN OCEAN
TIMOR
BALI
JAVA SEA
SAIGON
CANTON
HONG KONG
FORMOSA
LUZON
PHILIPPINE I
MINDANAO
CELEBES I
YAP I
ULITHI
Tropic of Capricorn
T.V. ALLEN

I had the watch from 8-12 yesterday...got time off to eat a bite, then went on again until 4 in the evening, then I had to get up at 11:30 and take watch from 12 to 4 this morning, so you can guess that I feel more like looking for a place to sleep than going to church this morning. I have a good, watch, though, where I can sit most of the time and can do a good deal of studying.

I don't know if I thanked you for that snapshot of Stanley and Dad (crossing the dam at the Barncastle) or not, but I sure thought it good and I like it a lot.

They've had a show every night for about a week, but somehow, I've not got around to go. I don't much care for them anyhow. They make me homesick and start me thinking about all the things I'm missing.

For lack of news, space, and time, I must close.

As Ever, Your Pal & Brother, Wilbur

The death orgy of Saipan lasted twenty-five days, and the U.S.S. COLORADO moved on practically unscathed. But, *WATCH OUT!* you "Mightiest Battleship afloat", disaster may well happen to you, too. During battle no ship can expect to be exempt from catastrophe always...no man immune from casualty.

From Saipan the U.S.S. COLORADO got underway for Guam on July 11.

Guam situated at the southern end of the Mariana archipelago, is the largest island of the Marianas, and yet its length is but 32 miles with a breadth of from four to ten miles, the total area of 225 square miles. Guam had been under the control of the United States since 1898. After the Spanish-American War it was ceded by Spain by the Treaty of Paris, while the rest of the

Marianas was sold to Germany by Spain.

Here, in Guam, the natives sought the mountains to avoid the bombing. Wilbur would never forget the giant lizards, eight to ten feet long that crawled the island. They didn't bite but their screams pierced the night.

Tinian, which lies between Saipan and Guam was famous for its natural beauty, and the great herds of wild cattle that roamed its limited area of some twenty square miles. Saipan was the main Japanese base and anchorage in the Marianas while Tinian just below it served as a naval base.

On July 22, 1944, the U.S.S. COLORADO left Guam to move back and bombard Tinian. It was here that the "Mightiest Battleship Afloat" met her "Waterloo".

Off the Northwest Coast of Tinian Island, on July 24, 1944, all hell broke loose for the U.S.S. COLORADO and the destroyer NORMAN SCOTT. In about four minutes the big ship suffered 22 direct hits.

Under the detonation of heavy artillery, the belching flame, and the leaping deck, Wilbur felt the sharp sting of schrapnel and saw some of his buddies blown to bits to slither across the swinging deck.

Forty men were dead and more than that were wounded. Wilbur felt strange that he was spared. He felt his arm, blood seemed to be running down the inside of his shirt. He could see it oozing from a hole in his sleeve. With so many wounded far worse than he, and who urgently needed the busy doctors, he stripped off his shirt, and with his pocket knife extracted the schrapnel from his flesh.

When Wilbur found himself safe on deck of the ship the next day, and he thought of the 40 dead sailors he'd helped pick up the night before to stack like cord wood in the officer's wash room, he thought of all the families that would have to be notified that their loved ones were dead. Maybe he should write a note to his own sweetheart, his mother, and his sister to notify them he was *alive*. His word would have to be brief, for the ship's crew was working like mad in order to repair last night's damage. Poor old Warrior Ship was badly in need of major repairs that couldn't be done while at sea! "We've got to cobble her up somehow," said the captain in charge.

At anchor at Saipan, July 25, the day after the holocaust, found Wilbur working almost in a frenzy trying to get the ship's lighting back to working order. A cable had been cut somewhere, and he tried to trace it down...the circuit numbers were all mixed. The laboring sailors got in each other's way. Not until evening did he find a minute to bring forth his pen and paper.

W.A. Parker EM 3/C
U.S.S.COLORADO, Box 11
c/o Fleet P.O.
San Francisco, Calif.
July 25, 1944

Dear Sister,
    Have a few moments and a chance to get a letter off so I'll see what I can do.
    It's been quite a spell since I wrote I know, but still there is little to say. Everything is about the same here. Am feeling good so have no reason to complain, still I always find something to grumble about and wish I were home...ha.
    Got a couple of letters from Mother, one from Mary Delle, and one from Ina here several days ago, but none from you. Maybe I'll get one on the mail that came in today...<u>I hope</u>. If I do, I'll try to add a bit, though there is absolutely

nothing to say without repeating what I've said so many times before.
   Must close and get back to work now.
                    Love, Wilbur

   As she read this letter, Ruby noted his penmanship was even worse than usual. It looked as though he were having difficulty getting his pen to stay on the page. He wrote over words and his pen seemed to take mad dashs and slashs, and then return to the paper. Was he extra nervous, or was the ship rocking? Could she have known, Wilbur *was* experiencing some trauma. After last night's destruction, he wondered if he'd ever get back to normal.
   While Wilbur was writing a few and possibly his last words to his sister, and hurrying to get back to the repair of his warship, the Marines were busy mopping up on Tinian and following the Japanese as they retired southward. The attacks by the Japanese on Guam were preventing the Americans from joining up their two beachheads on that island.

   By August 2, 1944, all organized resistance by the Japanese on Tinian Island came to an end, and on August 3rd, 1944, the U.S.S.COLORADO pulled out of the Marianas, leaving the mopping-up operation to the Marines.

   The U.S.S.COLORADO had been in the Marianas for 51 days, June 14 to August 3, 1944. During those 51 days when Wilbur wrote, he had absolutely "nothing to say".

W.A.Parker EM 3/C
c/o Fleet P.O.,S.F. Calif.
August 7, 1944
Dear Sister,
   Just a scrawny little note to say that I'm O.K. and a wish that you and Bill are feeling

better.
It sure seems that you have your share of the tough breaks.
    Your last letter is of July 13, so you may have moved but guess you'll get this anyhow.
    Things are the same here except I've changed stations from the Distribution Board to Interior Communications. Only changed Sunday, but I think I'm going to like it.
    Can imagine what a time you have trying to study. I experience about the same feeling here. Am so blamed sleepy when I do get a chance to study I can't concentrate at all.
    Chow call just blew, so guess I'll go get my beans. I know this won't go out for some time, and may add a line then. As ever Your Pal, Wilbur

(over)
August 13, 1944
    There isn't much to add but I'll put it in the mail as it should go out soon and maybe write again when I can find something to say.
        Always yours, Wilbur

    THE U.S.S. COLORADO was badly crippled as she "limped" back to the United States for extensive repairs. She was old, and the 22 hits incurred in Tinian had taken their toll...extensive modernization was anticipated. Overhauling turned into three months before she was ready to return to the war zone.
    As she lay in dock at Bremerton, Washington, being fitted, the time it took for her restoration also gave all her crew a much-needed rest. Everyone would get a leave, and those leaves would be staggered, thus, never letting the sailors all go at once; for the ship, even while undergoing repair, must have a maintenance crew at all times.

W.A. Parker
U.S.N.
Aug. 21, 1944

Dear Sister,
    Have your letter of the 10th before me, and a note already written to Mother, so I'll see what I can do towards answering yours. I don't see how you can find so much to say, but maybe it would not be so hard if you didn't have to keep watch for fear of saying the wrong thing. It sure would seem good to get entirely rid of these old restrictions once again. Believe it or not! I'm back in Bremerton. Can't say for how long...only got in yesterday, and haven't been ashore yet. I rated tonight but thought getting my writing done more important as haven't much to do anyhow. This is kind of a poor liberty town in my estimation... too darn crowded with service men.
    Though there is to be leave I don't plan a trip because the time just isn't long enough. I hardly know what I'll do with those few days, but guess I'll find someway of entertaining myself. There are two Leave Partys;the first of which starts tomorrow. I'm on the second one.
    Haven't found time to study for a long while, but should be able to get quite a bit done now. How much longer do you think it will take you to finish your course? I marvel at your persistence, and pray that you will be really well and back to feeling like studying and working very, very, soon (and Bill, too). It sure seems you two have your share of the bum breaks.
    Have a letter from Mary Delle. She says she has her college degree now. Mighty nice to have, and I guess she has worked for it, but it seems a person has to be a little lucky, too.
Mother said Doris has sort of decided to try high school this winter and I do so hope she will.
    Had a couple of letters from Dorothy but they are pretty old so won't pass any of her news on.

Guess I'd better close and get to some of my
other letters. Will write again soon, though
don't suppose there will be much to say.
  Good-night, Good Luck, Ever,& Always, Wilbur

  About this time Ruby ran onto a queer bit of
history in her daily paper which read: "Sixteen
years ago , August 27, 1928, the Kellogg-Briand
Pact was signed in Paris, outlawing war and providing for the peaceful settlement of disputes."
  Ruby laughed,"The pact must have had as much
value as the paper it's wtitten on!"

Sept. 6, 1944
Dear Sister,
  Have received two letters from you since I
wrote last so guess it's about time I wrote
again. Gosh! I had so many letters to answer
and we've been so busy. Then we rate liberty
every other day which means we never have only
about half a crew and it sure keeps us on the go.
  Haven't taken nearly all my liberties, but I
manage to keep myself played out anyhow.
  Guess from all this you will gather that I'm
still in Bremerton. Think will be here for another month or so. My leave doesn't start until the
12th or 13th.
  There isn't a great lot to do around here on
liberty but to go skating or dancing, and dances
aren't much fun unless you know people. Have
to go clear over to Seattle to skate, and it's
so far I never get in until two or three o'clock.
  Went to the Ship's dance here in Bremerton
last Saturday. There was a pretty good crowd but
the fellows all sat around like a bunch of hicks,
and drank free beer they were handing out. The
girls practically begged them to dance, but they
finally got disgusted, I guess, and a good many
of them went home, so it turned out to be kind
of a flop.

Did have a good time at the ice rink Sunday. Rick,(the fellow I went with) wanted to introduce me to his girl and her girl friend, and we were sort of surprised to find I already knew them...ha. I talk about so many different fellows that I know you'll never be able to keep track of them all. He is one of the fellows I went to school with in San Diego, and he's in the M. Division.

That's about all I ever do...go skating and look in store windows.

Did Stanly get his packages yet? I sure do get a kick out of sending him little things like that. I always remember what a big event it used to be to us kids when a package would come. Expect he has a lot more, though, than we ever did.

Please don't worry about something for my birthday, Ruby. I've got everything I need, and a lot more, too. If I had any more I simply don't know what I'd do with it. Les got me a fountain pen, Uncle Alvin sent me a pencil; besides I already had several pens and pencils of my own. You've really just about sent me all the handy things that I need already. I surely have gotten a lot of good out of this stationery holder you gave me when I left, and the shaving kit, too. You always think of the best things. Right now though, I believe you are about stuck because I can't even think of anything myself. Except pictures and a letter. They are always the best, anyhow, and I'll never, never, complain as long as your letters keep coming.

I'm going to ask everyone not to send any Xmas gifts this year. It's swell to have people remember you, but it's kind of foolish to have them spend money getting things, and then have to bundle them up and send them home for lack of room. So PLEASE! just a letter, and maybe a card this year.

I'm glad you like the necklace. Really it didn't cost anything, and I sent it more for a souvenir than anything else.

Do hope you will get settled before too long. It sure is trying not to know what you're going to do next.

Yes! Ina told me about her and Buster. She writes quite often, and I get such a kick out of her letters. They are so crazy, and yet so natural! I bet she is a lot of fun. She and Buster ought to make a good pair. Maybe I should try to send them a little gift. Have you any ideas?

Sorry you had such a time with your last exam...that isn't a bad grade though, is it? No! it seems I find less time to study when I'm in port than when I'm really busy. Electricity is what I study. Of course, it takes math and so on, too. Must close,   Love, Wilbur

            Wilbur's leave came through.

WOW! September 12 to September 28 was *17 days!* This would give him time to GO HOME!

He and Sailor Reynolds were the first ones to rush to the air port. Reynolds was lucky and got a ride South, but Wilbur couldn't catch one going East. The air lines were all booked days and days ahead. Despondent, he started looking for a job. A job would keep him busy these 17 days. All day he looked, and suddenly at the end of a weary, heart-sick day, he decided he didn't want a job. He wanted to *go home!*

The next morning he scurried to the train depot where he was lucky in getting a ticket to Cheyenne, Wyoming, September 13th, 1944.

Even after he boarded the train, he could hardly believe he was really going *home!* Let's see, it'd take him, perhaps, 3 or 4 days to get to the Barncastle, and 3 or 4 days for the trip back. Heck, that'd still give him at least a

week at home.
   For two days and two nights he rode the train reaching Cheyenne the morning of the 15th.
   It was only 8:00 A.M. as he shouldered his sea bag and struck out. He was surprised how quickly he caught a ride. A lone gentleman stopped for him and picked him up.
   "Where you going Sailor?"
   "I'm hoping to get to Wheatland," Wilbur answered, "I'm on leave and I have folks there."
   "Wheatland is on my way," the well-dressed man said, "I'm going to Casper."
   It wasn't yet noon when they arrived in Wheatland. The congenial man would take no money for fare. He merely wished Wilbur the best, "So glad to be of help to our men in service."

   His grandmother, Jemima Menefee, and his aunt, Dora Menefee, were in for a surprise when they opened the kitchen door at his knock to see a sailor standing on their stoop, a seabag on his uniformed back.
   It took but a minute, however, for them to come from their paralysis. There was a bevy of glad exclamations.
   Wilbur was in luck all right. Over the warm greeting arose the smell of a fresh-cooked, good home meal. While his aunt bustled to set him a place at the table, his uncles, Alvin Menefee and Wayne Pence appeared from the living room. There were more warm greetings, and Wilbur vowed it was the best meal he'd eaten since leaving Wyoming.

   "Sure you can borrow my car to go see Ruby & Bill," Wayne told him, "Your cousin, Betty, lives in Guernsey, too, you know."
   (Bill, Ruby, & Stanley Goodwin had been living in Guernsey, Wyoming, for several months).

Cousin, Myrna Johnson, rode to Guernsey with Wilbur partly to visit with him, partly to show him where her sister, Betty, lived. From there Betty would take them to Ruby's.

Not till he stood on her doorstep, did Ruby know her brother was coming. Just that day, she'd gone to the Post Office hoping there'd be a letter from him telling her he was still safe in Bremerton.

For a moment there was difficulty in believing his sudden appearance was the real thing. She had so often envisioned what it would be like to see him well and whole before her eyes. It was a joyful shock...laughter came and then tears...then suddenly she couldn't talk fast enough, asking him so many things and hardly giving him a chance to answer.

Eventually she became apologetic. It was dinner time and nothing prepared. She'd been canning all day, and in order to finish up, dinner had to wait.

"Let's all go to the cafe and eat," suggested Bill.

The one small cafe in Guernsey was teeming with service men when the six of them, Myrna, Betty, Wilbur, Bill, Ruby, and Stanley, entered its doors.

From then on Ruby saw little of Wilbur; for Betty and her girl-friend confiscated him for the evening.

Ruby went back to her apartment with Bill and Stanley, disappointed, and a bit envious over the turn of events. "It doesn't seem fair that I can't be with him during his short stay," she complained to Bill.

"Well," and she wasn't sure Bill's words were of any comfort, "He's happy; that's all that matters."

"A sister, a married one at that, is truly no competition for his attention." Ruby brushed a tear from an eye, "Betty and her girl friend *are pretty*, and *single*."

Wilbur came in late that night to retire to the bed Ruby made up for him in the apartment's large kitchen.

"After carousing around, we all went to the late-night show," Wilbur explained over breakfast next morning. "Say," he said turning to Ruby, "Why don't you and Stanley pack up some clothes and go back to the Barncastle with me?"

"I can't leave." Ruby answered, "Bill's been sick. His stomach has been hurting him a lot."

"Maybe it's your cooking that's hurting him." reasoned Wilbur,"In that case he'll be lucky to have you leave." He grinned broadly at Bill who was seated across the table from him as he proceeded to spear another pancake with his fork. "It'd sure be nice if we could all be together at home. Of course, we'll miss Les and Dot, but that can't be helped."

"How are you going to get up in the mountains?" Bill asked him.

"I'll find someone to take me...maybe Uncle Wayne; but I was hoping Ruby could go up with me, too."

"I'll tell you what," Bill suggested. "I know Myrna and Betty are going to take you back to Wheatland. After I get off work this afternoon,Ruby, Stanley, and I will go to Wheatland, pick you up, and we'll all head for the mountains. I'll have to come back Sunday in order to go to work Monday, but Ruby and Stanley can stay."

Thus, it was arranged, and a DREAM-WEEK followed with all congregated under the home roof of the Barncastle.

Sam and Ursa Parker beamed with the pleasure of their family being together once more. "If only Leslie and Dorothy were here," their only lament.

"What a contrast!" exclaimed Wilbur to himself as he set foot in the familiar home surroundings, "What a contrast to what I so recently left...the war-torn, and devastated Marianas compared to the calm, quiet, serenity of Fletcher Park, Wyoming. "Home!" cried Wilbur's bruised inner self, "My God, I"m, HOME. No wonder I've been homesick. I was born in this wonderous, peaceful, serenity and it's a part of me!"

There were a lot of relatives and friends beneath the Barncastle roof that week, Myrna and Herman Johnson and their 3 children, Betty Pence and her girl friend, Waverly Parker, Alvin Menefee, Buster Burnett, Alta and Ina Lee hall... to name a few.

Perhaps, the din and confusion of company coming and going as they celebrated Wilbur's furlough was all for the best, in that it had the effect of pushing the war in the background. For a few happy days, war faded virtually into non-existence.

However, at night, as Stanley lay in the small home-made bed Sam and Ursa made for him, Ruby, before going to her own bed beside his, in vain searched her mind for comfort. "Please, God, let the war end while he's here. Don't let him ever have to go back!" Even before her words came forth she imagined she heard demoniacal laughter from the underworld. How many thousands prayed for their brothers and sons only to see them annihilated?

Seeking a ray of hope, she went to the window to open it so she could feel the refreshing rush of the clean, crisp, Fall air, laden with a scent of pine. Beyond in the moonlight she could see Cottonwood Creek gleaming as it trickled in and out the willows along its banks. As she listened to the night sounds a great sadness welled within her. Why did man want to erase beauty

from his environment? Why can't we live in
peace by our dear home stream? Dad and Mother
have worked so hard to maintain this remote,
mountain home. They've been real pioneers for
the State of Wyoming. Why does a country who
knows nothing about us want to wipe us out?
  "The world is filled with aggression,"
the voice of a friend echoed through her mind,
"And you can't get away from it no matter how
remote a place you may seek. Besides no one
can live on mountain scenery."
  More eloquent still came the profound words
of her dearly, beloved father, Samuel M. Parker,
"Maybe I'm trying to defend myself for not being a wealthy man in this wealthy country of
ours; but, you know, Sister, the good Lord didn't
create money. He merely gave us all the beautiful
natural things of this earth that money can't
buy...the hills, the streams, the mighty mountains, and the greatest wealth in the world
which is Love."
  As she mused, the soft breathing of an
innocent child came from behind her. Maybe she
was wrong in teaching Stanley the same principles her folks taught her...all about the beauty
of the earth, and treating your fellows as you
wanted to be treated...be considerate and kind
to man and animals alike. Now she was left
wondering if all these "good",thoughtful, teach-
ings would eventually injure his soul? In the
past few days she sensed the damage war had done
to her brother. He had steel bars about him. He
refused to talk about any part of his war experiences, saying everything was top secret.
She sensed a hardness in him that had never
been there before. As sure as though he'd been
physically injured he carried inward scars, she
was certain of this. There was a part of him
that had known death or at least, great injury,
and suddenly she was furious...furious and help-

less before the mass force that crowded all service men into brutality, immorality, and murderers.

"Maybe I wouldn't feel so moral, myself," she thought, "were there bombs bursting and tearing up our dear homeland. It's just that my folks are such gentle people and so vulnerable. They wouldn't hurt anyone. Still, maybe they were wrong in teaching us the same gentle ways, as I'll be wrong in training Stanley to believe in the same mold."

It was a most difficult lesson she pounded into herself to believe the animosity that filled the world. She may be cramming it down her throat, but she'd never figure it out. She ended tonight's lesson by turning from the window and giving thanks to God for the present moment. Afterall, she'd known this hour with her precious family beneath one, protective, roof. "Tonight," she thought, "We are all safe and I can hold this moment for a life-time, no matter what may happen to-morrow." She closed the window on the whispering, stirring, pines, and the gleaming, gurgling, stream, to the comforting, even, breathing of her son.

In another room of the Barncastle, Wilbur lay wakeful and wondering if his mind may be splitting asunder. "I can't go back to that slaughter," he despaired, "I can't go back to that man-made hell. I'll stay in caves and brush on Laramie Peak until they come dig me out. At least, I'd be but one man they'd be killing."

And then from the depths of the Barncastle, perhaps, from his father's shop, came the strains of a violin. Sam was playing softly so as to not disturb anyone's sleep. To Wilbur's ears came the poignant notes of "Whispering Hope": "Oh, how welcome they voice...." and, "Hope for the sunshine tomorrow...."

"If there *is* a tomorrow," thought Wilbur, trying to close out the vision of the black and smoking terrain...the human bodies strewn in disarray, bloody, mangled, crushed, stinking, and plastered on the face of the charred earth.

His father knew not what he was playing. No words or music could save a people for they'd not listen. They clammered for peace and hope only to make war. He was beginning to believe the only peace was obliteration. Nevertheless, should there be men left after this war, there would have to be a shred of *hope* that there could be a life of some sort worth the living. Perhaps, this, too, was the *hope* that kept him going.

Yes, this particular war would surely end some day, and by God, he was going to remain alive to come home and help his parents. He didn't know from whence the feeling came, but he'd never for an instance doubted, even when dead men lay about him, that he'd not come through the war alive.

Yes, by the grace of God, he *would* come home again; but *never* would he leave again. No future wars would ever claim him. Never again would he volunteer or be forced into "patriotic" service for mass murder. Instead, he'd take to the seclusion of the mountains and bury himself. The Japs weren't too, damned, dumb when they killed themselves rather than submit further to the horrors of another battle.

The viloin music lingered on..."...making my heart in it's sorrow rejoice." The world was not only in sorrow, it was in catastrophic terror that could mean extinction.

His comfort came in his family's innocent belief that there was hope for peace, at least peace in Fletcher Park, Wyoming. Their bright, loving, faces were almost a shock to see after witnessing the scenes and people he'd so recently left. His mouth would never utter words to wipe that hope from their dear faces.

    A worried mother, Ursa Parker, prepared herself for bed. As she did so she wondered if she had enough eggs for breakfast in the morning. The hens never laid as good in the Fall. Well, she knew she had at least two. This would be sufficient to make buttermilk pancakes, and she could always make a pot of steamed Quaker Oats.
    With the eating issue settled she worried about the more serious problems that disrupted her thoughts...the big upset being Wilbur's involvement in the war, and the war's final outcome. Wilbur seemed to be the only one of the four children interested in the home place. She and Sam often talked about this. When and IF Wilbur came back from war they would turn the place over to him, for there were signs of Sam's health beginning to fail.
    It looked, too, as if their oldest son, Leslie and his wife, would make their permanent home in California, this making Wilbur as heir, next in line. The girls, Ruby and Doris, hardly figured in the land problem for their futures lay with their husbands. A frown wrinkled Ursa's pretty face as she pushed back a stray lock of brown hair. Sometimes it seemed her daughters worried her more than her sons. Even though grown, was her family always to be a worry and a heartache? She shouldn't be worried about Ruby now that she was married to a good man, but Ursa knew her daughter too well...something was bothering Ruby. She was unhappy. Ursa just couldn't guess at the cause, and she was always so thin, and ill, too, much of the time. Maybe being ill caused her unhappiness, or maybe the unhappiness was causing her to be ill. Ursa shook her worried head and started thinking about her youngest.

Doris, still at home, was no less of a worry. She also, was unhappy and so restless. Ursa was beset with the fear her youngest daughter may marry anyone who may ask just to get away. All the men who came to see her were 20 to 30 years older than Doris. "Where have I failed?" moaned Ursa to herself, "How come I've reared such an unhappy family?" On the other hand had she been so happy herself? Maybe some of her anxieties had rubbed off on her children. There had been so little time for freedom and laughter. Since she and Sam were married in 1911, it had been a constant struggle to make a living...to keep food on the table, and the family clothed. Money-wise, things had been so much easier with the Government allotment Wilbur arranged for her since his entrance into the Service. However, she could do without most anything if the war were only over, and he was home safe and sound.

Would Sam stay well until the time Wilbur came to help them? Yes, there was so much anxiety about her family's future...Wilbur in the war, Sam and his health, Ruby's sadness, and who was Doris to marry?

She jerked from her nebulous cares...Where was Sam now? The hour was getting late, and he was probably in his fiddle shop dreaming over a fiddle scroll, or a fiddle back. She opened her bedroom door to stick her head out to be greeted by the musical strains of "Whispering Hope". Ursa smiled. Sam was always smiling and hopeful when she found no reason to be so cheerful. His optimism carried her through so many trials. "Stop worrying and go to sleep", he'd tell her now.

In her own, quiet, room of the Barncastle, Doris snuggled down beneath the home-made quilt. The nights were getting colder. Fall was definitely here. Soon snow would lay over the mountains and down the valley of the Cottonwood. Yes, she was facing another winter of isolation. She pulled her mother's hand-made quilt about her neck, and lay staring into the dusky room as she took up her inner war. It seemed each night she fought her own private conflict. It was no less frustrating than her brother's war in the Central Pacific, or so she imagined, in that she seemed to have no say about where it led or what it did to her.

"I'll be eighteen next month," she lay thinking, "And I'm still helpless to do anything about my life. My God, I want to *live*! I don't want to hole up like an animal all my days!"

Any sort of a life looked better, more eventful, more fulfilling than her own remote, mountain living. "I'd rather be like Wilbur, a man on the battle front, even if I got killed, than to stay here, stagnate, and burying myself alive. Ruby got away somehow into the swim of things. Still she really doesn't seem any too happy. Nonetheless, her life is better than mine. At least, she's not rotting in the mountains.

"Cripes, if I get married here, it'll have to be to some 50-year old geezer." She managed a giggle as she recalled the man she'd nicknamed Tee-Hee-Ha-Ho. He must be the world's one and only giggling cowboy. Whenever he spoke with her, he invariably broke forth into a long string of giggles...tee, hee, ha, ha, ha, ho, ho! Lord, her folks were actually afraid she may be interested in him! Then she recalled the words Ruby once said to her, "It's tough all right, Sis, living alone in the mountains. For comfort, tell yourself, it could be worse you could be married."

It had been great fun these past days with Wilbur home, and with all the company coming and going. "Hang on, Sis." Wilbur promised during one of their talks, "When the war is over and I come home, I'll take you places...anywhere you want to go."

How long would she have to wait? What if Wilbur didn't come back? "Oh, my God," she sobbed as she turned her face into the pillow, "What if my brother doesn't come back and I'm forced to marry some old geezer whose only conversation is tee-hee, ha, ho?" The ludicrous sight of this mental image caused a giggle to rise up through the tears. As she drifted of to sleep she was lulled by a violin playing,"Whispering Hope."

Wilbur left his home in the mountains, Sept. 25, 1944, to return to the holocaust, entitled, *World War II*. "*When #III* comes up I won't be there." Wilbur made up his mind to this.

Ruby returned to Guernsey to pack up all household belongings. As Wilbur arrived in Spokane, Washington, Bill, Ruby, and Stanley pulled into Granger, Wyoming, with the aid of their cousins, Herman and Myrna Johnson. Bill was to settle in on a new job in the pump station there working for the Standoline Pipeline. Soon the pipeline was to start covering the oil line by the way of airplane... riding pipeline would soon be a practice of the past.

While Wilbur was on furlough, and while his ship, the U.S.S.COLORADO was being restored so it could re-enter battle, heavy fighting was going on in all parts of the world. In the Central Pacific, as Wilbur was enjoying his furlough-freedom at Fletcher Park, there was heavy fighting in the Palau Islands. At Peleliu the American Marines suffered gigantic loses. The resistance of the seasoned Japanese defenders pushed the Americans back in their attack on Mount Umurbrogol. On September 22, 1944, as Wilbur and Ruby were guiding some cousins to a secluded fern cave in the Rocky Mountains, U.S.A. General Geiger in Peleliu decided to replace the exhausted Marine Regiment on Mount Umurbrogol with the 31st Infrantry Regiment. However, the Japanese dug solidly in their "termite nests", and continued to hold their attackers at bay. By September 26, the Americans at last began to gain a little footage, but not without a woeful price. A special unit of flamethrowers and tanks succeeded in blocking the Japanese termite holes with stones and by pouring flames into the slots of their strong holds.

In an eastern part of Palau Islands the Americans rightfully dubbed one Japanese position, "Bloody Hill."

Ruby was still unpacking in her new, prairie, home (Granger, Wyoming, is in the southwestern corner of Wyoming.) when Wilbur's first letters were received after his furlough:

Sept. 29, 1944
Dear Sister,
    Just another short line to let you know I arrived O.K.
    A sailor from the Yorktown, myself, and a couple of girls going to the University of Spokane got to playing cards on the train, and we had more darn fun until they had to change trains at Pendleton.
    Arrived in Seattle about 3 o'clock Wed. afternoon of the 27th. Got a room at a hotel, then while fooling around the Army-Navy Y, I got an invitation to a birthday party, and though I'd intended to go skating, I decided to go to the party instead. Had a swell lunch after which we all danced. The people were Swede and had a lot of dances that I didn't know, but had a lot of

anyhow. Met a lot of people most of whose names I don't remember.

Got my eyes closed Thurs. morning and caught the ferry back to Bremerton where I had breakfast before coming back to the shop.

Things have changed a bit...still in a mess, but out of dry dock. Think will leave Monday or Tuesday. Maybe for San Francisco...I hope! But I don't know yet.

After getting back at noon I rated liberty again at 3:00. Can you beat that?!! Makes me mad to think they could as well have given me another day on my leave. Hadn't figured to go out, but Sterling wanted me to meet his wife, so I went as I figured it might be my last chance to meet her. She is real nice. We went out and ate a chicken dinner and really had a good time but of course it put me in kind of late again, and now I have all my writing to catch up on.

It seems sort of maddening here now, but was wonderful to see you all again. Bye now, Wilbur

In his next letter, he'd returned to his ship and to the inevitable Navy Censor. The dot in his letter revealed he was in Los Angeles, and she wondered if the U.S.S. COLORADO were moving out, and so on to the war.

W.A.PARKER EM 3/c
U.S.S.COLORADO, Box 11
c/o Fleet P.O., S.F., Calif.
October 10, 1944

Dear Sister:

Just a short note in answer to that nice long letter you wrote.

Haven't had any liberty since I wrote last so there is really very little to say. This place sure feels hum-drum and awful after all the fun I had on leave. Had hoped to get liberty here but I guess we won't.

Worked all day Sunday, and yesterday out in the wind way up atop the foremast. One needs a tail and claws up there. I think I'd rather work on a flag pole or a church steeple, at least they wouldn't roll so much! But enjoyed the fresh air anyhow, though I did get a bit cold. Now you know how I celebrated my 29th birthday.

Last night I nearly roasted. One of the fellows got cold and stuffed his trousers in the vent. I could have murdered him with pleasure this morning when I saw him pull them out.

Mother wrote. She has been canning some more.

You didn't run across those papers for my car by any chance, did you? I hate to see it sit out and no one get any use out of it...don't suppose anyone could use it without the papers though.

Have a bunch of new men in the division and had to move out of one of my lockers. Ye Gods! How do they expect a person to get three changes of uniform, P coat, shoes, and all personal belongings in a box 2' x 2' x 1'? Anyhow, I can't and hated to throw them away so Stanley may get some material for a suit...more work for you.

Dorothy wrote a short line. Guess she and Les never have gotten their vacation.

That's about all, I guess...thanks for the clever little poem. Will try to write again soon.
      Love, Wilbur

As the rejuvenated and modernized U.S.S. COLORADO steamed out of harbor with Wilbur among hundreds of other sailors aboard, fighting in the Palau Islands was entering the "mop-up" stage...rubble and blood were mingled into one...rubble and blood and stench, the American's "victory". Nevertheless, even by October 18, 1944, some of the Japanese fighters resisted until it meant Kamikaze for them as they clung to their secluded pockets on Mount Umurbrogol on Peleliu.

Wilbur knew it went without saying they were headed for islands somewhere in the Central Pacific. The name of the island hardly mattered. Hell was the same in one place as it was in another. His ship was carrying thousands of tons of fire and brimstone with it. Most of the islands looked like an Eden until Satan ships anchored off-shore delivered their thousand-lb messages of Hell. (Note: Quadruple 40 mm Bofors AA guns were fitted on board all U.S. battleships from 1942 onward, displacing the ineffective 1.1 inch.)
October 29, Wilbur was in Honolulu. Ruby always "read" the dot before she read his letter. So the U.S.S.COLORADO had gone clear to Honolulu since she last heard from him October 10.

Dear Sister,
Don't mind my stationery. I received your last letter exactly a week...no, ten days ago so I guess it's about time that I wrote again. Hasn't much happened except last Sat. (week ago) I got to see Les and Dot. It sure was good to see them again, and was somewhat surprised to see them looking so well. We didn't do much but sit and talk the evening away, and they fixed a nice dinner at home. I thought we should eat out so Dot wouldn't have to go to all that work the way she felt after just getting home from the hospital, but she insisted. We got to bed for a nap about 1:30 or 2, I guess,they got up at four, got a bite to eat, and they brought me back in the early morning.
I got to go out skating one evening too, and enjoyed myself as I always do. The ice was better than ordinary and the rink wasn't at all crowded. I traded my skates off for a new pr. that fit me better. Now I don't suppose I'll have another chance to use them...ha.
After all the warning I put out, I still got an Xmas package from Les and Dot the other day.

It really was a nice package though.
   We had Admiral's inspection the next day after I visited D. and L., and I was so sleepy I could hardly keep my eyes open. We are going to have Captain's inspection again this week, but the water was so rough that they put it off.
   Got our booster shots just the other day, and my poor arms were so sore I could scarcely move them. I sure feel for some of the new fellows who have to be sea sick along with it. See quite a few leaning over and feeding the fish these last few days.
   Thanks for the picture. I liked it a lot.
   I'll probably have a letter from you when the mail comes in again, and I'll try to write more then. It's nearly 12 and reveille comes at 5----
--Goodnight----Wilbur

October 20, 1944, through December 5, 1944, brought about the biggest battle in history, and the last battle of the Pacific...the battle of Leyte Island in the Phillipines.
   General Douglas MacArthur disembarked from a landing craft on the Phillipines, October 20,1944. His saying, "I shall return" came true on that day.
   However, the U.S.S.COLORADO was still far from this battle scene as of November 6, 1944, according to the "dot". When Wilbur wrote his letter, his ship was still in the Hawaiian Islands. Ruby wondered much what the ship and its crew were doing there so long, and of course, there was no way Wilbur could tell.

W.A.Parker
U.S.S.COLORADO, Box 11
c/o Fleet P.O.,S.F. Calif.
Mon. Nov. 6, 1944

Dear Sister,
   Have received three letters from you since I

last wrote, though it's been only a week. Anyhow, I guess it's about time that I answered them. I'm afraid that I won't be able to write as well on nothing to say as you do. Gosh! I don't see how you can write such a swell letter. Sometimes I can hardly think up enough to make out a page or two.

Hasn't a great lot happened, and though, I've had two more libertys, I didn't do much but shop, mostly for Xmas cards. They don't seem to have as good a selection as last year. It's early yet, of course,but I was afraid to try to wait longer and maybe not be able to get them at all. Expect I'll have to send them out soon if I can so to clear my locker up a bit. It gets so stuffed with junk I can hardly get my clothes in sometimes. The darn thing isn't even big enough for the clothes to start with! Yes! I do have to wash pretty often...usually every night or every other at least. It makes it a lot easier not to let it pile up as well as helping to keep my locker clean, and a little room in it because I don't have to have so many changes that way.

Getting back to the original subject, I did have a swell banana split in town the other day....with good, tree-ripened bananas, too. Didn't go into town the other time but just fooled around the base. The several canteens have quite as good a selection of things as the store down town and a lot cheaper...that avoids a lot of the crowd and the struggle getting on the bus, too. Wanted to go swimming but I couldn't find my suit. I guess I'll have to buy another.

Keep up the good work on the studies. My heart is with you. Have wanted to get time to study myself, but seems I very seldom get to it.

No! of course, I don't care if you make Stanley *or* yourself a suit from those old Navy uniforms. They were just taking up my locker space, and I thought you could use them. You mentioned

something about making Stanley a suit when I was home; that's the reason I thought maybe you'd want them for him.
    Too bad you lost your $2.00 bill. I'll save you another. Betty said she had the same luck (about) with hers, only she rushed back and retrieved it...ha....
    The last Mother wrote she hadn't found the car title yet. Now where do you suppose that crazy thing went? I would sort of like to get rid of the car. It seems like a shame to let it set out and fall apart, and no one get any use out of it, especially when autos are as hard to get as now.
    Sorry Bill didn't have any luck hunting. Wish I could have been around to have helped.
    Over a deep dark ocean
        Far as the eye can reach.
    A sweet glad sky bends over the ocean
        Tell me, I beseech!
There on that golden horizon
        Where the water meets the sky;
Is it to some sad illusion?
        Or will we; you and I
Breathe again the sweet young freedom
        (Lost through all these years.)
Hand in arm in younder kingdom
        Come smiling through our tears?

            Always, Wilbur

    By November 15, 1944, the U.S.S.COLRADO was in the Phillipines and ready to do battle at Leyte, although she didn't really position herself and enter the direct combat until November 19, and then she belched destruction for 15 days.
    The Americans met extremely heavy fire from the Japanese that November day, and were forced into giving a little ground on Kilay Ridge.
    Wilbur ,knowing well what he faced, gave way

to the feeling his chance to get letters to his folks may be *now* or *never*.

As he prepared to write (maybe) his "last" letter, he recalled the *last* letter his great-grandfather, Edward Lapham, wrote to his great-grandmother, Jeanette (Lettie) Mosher Lapham during the Civil War.

Somewhere stuck away in Grandma Love Lapham Parker's trunk, she stowed this treasured letter. Wilbur recalled the tale Grandma Parker often told her granchildren. "When he left for war, Dad told my mother, 'If our baby is a girl and I don't come back, call her *LOVE*', and that is why my name is Love."

"Good, Lord," exclaimed Wilbur to himself, "that letter was written 80 years ago!"

That long ago day in 1864, people were fighting on U. S. ground certain they were going to bludgeon their enemy neighbors into a certain way of thinking. They were also certain this war of killing and dominance would be an end to all future wars. How many wars had there been since 1864? Hadn't history yet proven that war never ends dissension? Could man never profit from his own findings?

Nashville
November 12, 1864

Dear Lettie   A man just gave me this sheet and I will write at once. We are well and getting used to most everything---have seen some Rebels but they were all prisoners. I get kind of homesick sometimes, but you must not think less of me on that account as you are one cause of it. But it is so different from anything I was ever used to. If I could just see you once a week I could stand it much easier, but you have a full share no doubt. We hope to get to the regiment soon *and get some news from home, and if it is good* news I shall not be homesick for sometime. I will tell you something of our trip to Chattanooga. A captain and Lieutenant were ordered to take us from Camp Butter to Chattanooga. They had to wait so long for transportation that the officers of our regiment passed us on the road, and then we were given in charge of another Officer and sent clear back here again and now from here we go to Pulaskie sometime. It maybe in one hour and maybe a month, but I have learned to <u>wait</u>, <u>wait</u>, <u>wait</u>, Why, I can shoulder my knapsack, fall into line and wait half a day as easy as not. I have waited two days for rations, but there were plenty of peddlers, and I still have money, and we get along of course. The Office in charge of us now is worth a dozen such as we first had--- clever and accommodating, and more like a father than an officer; hope he may always remain so.

   O Nettie, you don't know how bad I do want to see you and the children. I suppose I have no business to write such stuff to you but it <u>will slip out</u>.

   Roy went to the theatre last night along with some of the rest of our boys. They say it paid well to go. Some of them were guarded and some went alone. The Captain let about thirty go out today, and I sent by one for something. I have not been in a store since I left Peoria, but the Settlers keep a good many things, and change their prices. We done our own cooking at Chatanooga and done it the best it has been done. I will tell just what utensils we have to cook with---two quart tin cups and two pint cups. We also made a frying pan of an old canteen. We made good coffee, cooked rice first rate--- had sugar and hard tack, and pork and beans. So you see that we are great cooks. This was all done out doors, and most of the time raining like fury. We were encamped on an old battlefield, and there were cannon balls, musket balls, gun barrels, and everything but wood. The Commissary would not furnish any. So we would go down at night, and while some were jawing with the guard the others would steal all that was necessary. It all belonged to Uncle Sam, and we were bound to have it

We passed along last Tuesday night between Lookout Mountain and the Tennesee River where the streams fell at least one hundred feet, and some of them struck the side of the cars we were setting on.

It is rather cold writing here as you can see by my penmanship, but there is not room by the fire, and when I am writing to you I don't think of it. You will write lots about home, won't you when you get well, and I hope you are before this time. You need not be afraid of writing anything that will not interest me, and I think I have set you an example. That is no _____ _____ _____ subject but it is our own business, and some day when I get home we can afford to laugh at all such letters as this.

Hoping this may find you and the little ones in good health and spirits, I remain
    Your loving husband   Edward Lapham

P.S. I sent the direction for my letters to Father and have not room here to write it plainly.

Two and one-half months after Edward Lapham wrote his "last" letter, his father-in-law, J.W. Mosher, received the letter that left Mrs. Edward Mosher Lapham a widow.

Huntsville, Alabama
January 25, 1865

Mr. J. W. Mosher
Sir
    Your letter of the 16th instant is at hand,

"The U.S. CHRISTIAN COMMISSION sends this sheet as a messenger between the soldier and his home. Let it hasten to those who wait for tidings."

Nashville November 12th 1864

Dear Nettie a man just gave me this sheet and I will write at once We are well and getting used to most everything have seen some Rebels but they were all prisoners I get kind of homesick sometimes but you must not think less of me on that account as you are the cause of it but it is so different from anything I was ever used to. If I could just see you once a week I could stand it much easier but you have a full share no doubt We hope to get to the regiment soon and get some news from home and if it is good news I shall not be homesick for some time I will tell you something of our trip to Chattanooga Capt Captain and Lieutenant were ordered to take us from

We were encamped on an old battle field and there were Cannon balls musket balls gun barrels and everything but wood the Commissary would not furnish any so we would go down at night and while some were jawing with the guard the Others would steal all that was necessary it all belonged to Uncle Sum and we were bound to have it we passed glory last tuesday night between Lookout mountain and the Tennessee river where the streams fell at least one hundred feet and some of them stuck the side of the cars we were setting in.

It is rather cold writing here as you can see by my penmanship but there is not room near the fire and when I am writing to you I dont think of it. you will write lots about home wont you when you get well and I hope you are before this time you need not be afraid of writing any thing that will not interest me and I think I have set you an example that is not easily beat for a little subject but it is our own business and some day when I get home we can afford to laugh at all such letters as this hoping this may find you and the little ones in good health and spirits I remain

    Your loving husband Edward Lapham

P.S. I sent the directions on my letters to Father and have not room here to write it plainly and its contents duly noted. I hasten to reply that you may as early as possible be in possession of the information sought. I will write what I know of the fate of Edward Lapham. We were together as we both belonged to the Pioneer Corps. During the day of the Second day's fight an Nashville, the Pioneers were called upon to build works for the Second line or first reserve. After this work was partially completed the Pioneers of the 36th were ordered to the front of first line of attack to throw up works to protect the line-This was done under fire. I remember seeing Ed while we were separated---I remaining there---he was going farther up the line-- as we were then ordered to go to spading. After we had thrown up sufficient works to protect our regiment, the Pioneers retired a short distance to the rear, getting behind trees and logs. It was at this time that I saw Ed was wounded. I did not see him shot, and did not know that he was until I went to the rear where I saw him lying behind a large log mortally wounded by rifle ball in the top and back of the head. I supposed he was wounded while working on the works, and carried where I found him, by someone.

    I did not at first sight recognize Ed, as his features were considerably distorted---face pallid, eyes closed, and the lids bloodshot. He had frothed considerable at the mouth. I thought he was dead. But just before the rebel lines gave way and we were ordered forward I saw him draw up his leg---I suppose this was his death struggle. This is all I know of him. I left him upon the battlefield where he was found by those whose business it was to care for the wounded and bury the dead.

    In conclusion I must say that during the short time that we were together I had learned to respect his many manly qualities---true courage,

and heroism. I never saw him flinch---and regret that fate has decreed a separation so soon. In him the country has lost a true soldier, and I am one would not be ashamed to call friend. I sympathize with his bereft wife and relatives. But they have this to console them and be proud of, he died doing his duty upon the field of battle for his country.
    Hoping that this may be received in due time,
              I remain
           Yours truly

              Warfield B. Todd
              Co. "A" 36th 2W Val Infty

    Grandma Parker had a portrait of her father, Edward Lapham, hanging on her living room wall. His bearded face rose before Wilbur as he wrote to his sister. He didn't believe it, but there was always the possibility this could be his "last" letter to anyone. Grandpa Lapham when he wrote November 12, 1864, didn't believe it to be his last either. Ed was looking forward to the day he and Lettie would be laughing over "such letters as this".
    "In war, death walks right by your side, ever-ready to bring you to its dimension. No one is immune," and Wilbur picked up his pen.

W.A. Parker EM 3/C
U.S.S.COLORADO, Box 11
c/o Fleet P.O. S.F. California
Nov. 15, 1944

Dear Sister,
    There isn't much to add to my last letter, and they will probably go out together, but I may not have a chance to write again for a while, so don't think anything of it if you don't hear.
    Have been trying to get your Xmas package off but sure am having a duce of a time. I hope it

Courage and heroism — I never saw him flinch — And despite that fact that he had derived a reputation so grim — in him the country has lost — a true soldier. And I am sure I would not — he (Adams) would be ever proud — I sympathise with his sorely-widowed relatives, but — they have this to console them and dis- tressed friends besides — in distinction — his name will live for him — Showing that this may be deemed in due time a minor

Yours Truly
Mansfield B. Lovell
Co "F" 20th Regt Illinois Vols

Adjutant General's Office,
Washington, D. C.,
September 23, 1867.

Sir:

I have the honor to acknowledge the receipt from your Office of application for Pension No. 149407, and to return it herewith, with such information as is furnished by the files of this Office.

It appears from the Rolls on file in this Office, that Edward Lapham was drafted on the 27 day of Sept., 1864, at Peoria Ill. in Co. the, 36 Regiment of Illinois Volunteers, to serve One years, or during the war, and mustered into service as a Private on the 27 day of September 1864, at Peoria Ills., in Co. the, 36 Regiment of Illinois Volunteers, to serve one year, or during the war. On the Muster out Roll of Co. D of that Regiment, Dated October 8" 1865, he is reported " Killed in Battle of Nashville Decr. 16" 1864."

The name Edward Lapham does not appear.

I am, Sir, very respectfully,
Your obedient servant,

Chas. S. Peck
Assistant Adjutant General.

The Commissioner of Pensions
Washington, D. C.

Memoranda
S. M.   Name of applicant
882   Address

won't be late. Doesn't amount to much but maybe will help make it seem like Christmas.

    We've been more than busy trying to get the work caught up. I feel played out already tonight, and have my washing yet to do. Oh, well! I've been feeling good anyhow, so shouldn't complain.

    The mail hasn't come for a good while. I sure will be glad to see it again.

    Will write again when I can., By now, Wilbur

(Note: November 27, 1944, the U.S.S. COLORADO was damaged by a suicide plane while in Leyte Gulf.)

U.S.S. COLORADO
November 23, 1944

Captain W. S. MACAULAY, USN
Commanding

Comdr. J.F. HENKEL, USN
Executive Officer

Comdr. H. P. KNOWLES, Jr. (SC) USN
Supply Officer

Lieutenant C. E. WEBB, (SC) USN
Officer in Charge
Commissary Section

J.E. WOOD, APC, USN	D. M. PATZ, USNR
Commissary Officer	Chief Commissary Steward

Thanksgiving Menu

1944

U.S.S. Colorado

November 23, 1944

THANKSGIVING MENU

TOMATO ASPIC

RIPE OLIVES   CELERY EN BRANCH   SWEET PICKLES

ROAST YOUNG TOM TURKEY

OYSTER DRESSING   GIBLET GRAVY   CRANBERRY SAUCE

PEAS PARISIENNE   WHIPPED POTATOES   ASPARAGUS TIPS

MINCEMEAT PIE   PARKERHOUSE ROLLS   BUTTER

NEAPOLITAN ICE CREAM

ROMAN PUNCH   CIGARETTES

Although the Japanese seriously damaged two U.S. destroyers off Leyte, December 5, they were unable to break American air and Navy blockade around the island.

December 3, the U.S.S. COLORDO remained ready, but her cover fire was no longer needed. Her weary, war-scarred crew needed news from home. After day and night detonation everyone was in a state of physical and moral collapse. So she eased back waiting for the mail carrier before going to her next point of destruction ...that of Mindoro.

W.A. Parker E M 3/C
U.S.S. COLORADO, Box 11
c/o Fleet P.O. S.F. Calif.
Dec. 5th, 1944

Dearest Sister,
   At last the mail is in again, and I have two letters from you, though I don't think it's all sorted yet...at least, I hope not as haven't one from home yet. Well, it sure was a long time coming this time...the last I heard was in October.
   After all this time I'm afraid this is going to be a flop for news. Things could go on like this for years, and there would still be nothing to write, but "am well" and "the water looks fine." Heck, I'd like to get ashore again somewhere and stretch my legs. The place I sleep in is about 2 feet wide, and it's got a post (stanchion) in it. I have to bend around and I think I'm growing crooked, (Ha), but it's cool there at least, and I prefer it to a bunk in the compartment. I've got so used to sleeping on the deck I can't stand a bunk anyhow. I find it a lot easier to come awake there, too. All I have to do is just stretch a little and I'm against the switch board. Boy! When I make a short circuit between there and the bulk head I'm out and on my g.q. station before the bugler can finish the call! The thing is

learning to stretch at the right time! All this
reminds me of the electrician who, working in
Central Station, tripped the warning howler. He
was on his g.q. station before he awoke to the
fact he'd set the signal off himself.
    Have found a little time for study but not
much. I got stuck on some of my problems and had
to get my algebra out and brush up before I can
go on. I have the darndest time remembering Algebra
anyhow...guess that's because I never went
far enough with it. Wish we could get together
on it maybe we'd get along faster, or would we,
maybe, gab about something else?
    Have your letters of the 7th and 13th now...
think I'll leave a little room here in case I
get another with questions later. Thought Stanley's
picture real good. They are not scratchy
and uncertain like most kids draw. Didn't you
help him?
    Mother sent me some pictures of us in the hats.
(I think the ones you mentioned). I believe she
said they were the ones you sent her. I've forgotten,
it's been so long.
    It sure would be nice to be skating with
Doris all right. You know after I got my new
skates, I never got to use them but once.
    The last few days I've been puttering around
the shop, building a new work bench. Guess they
have decided I'm better at that than anything
else. They sure seem to find a lot of odd jobs
of that sort for me to do. I like it though, and
it's nice working here in the shop where it's
air conditioned.
Guess I better quit for now and write Mother, and
whatever others I can get written, As Ever Yours,
                      Wilbur

Later:
    It does not look like we are going to have
that other mail call that I thought we would so
I'll just add a little bit to what I wrote the

other day while I still have the chance.

Of course, there is really nothing new to add but at least, it'll show I write when I can, won't it?

The boys are busy at a big game of Hearts tonight. We sort of take spells at playing cards.

I spent half my time today standing in line. Was hungry for some ice cream, but they run out before I got to the counter, so I bought some candy bars to console myself. (Ha)

They are having a show on the quarter deck this evening but think I'll stick around the shop and finish my letters, and maybe, do a little studying.   Love, Wilbur

PART II

ABOARD the U.S.S. COLORADO

with

WILBUR A. PARKER

Drawings by BONNIE PARKER ENGLE

Wilbur Allen Parker   EM 3/C
United States Navy
1944

For though to die is but to live
   And life is steadily turning...
All will lose what they most loved...
   The dearest to their heart.
That which they give alone remains.

Those that share will too partake
   When life has shut the door.
The Reaper wins the keeper stake;
   All this and nothing more.

And he so pious in his lot
   His sins will too define
His head is favored not.
   Is dead, still alive, not devine?

       ---Wilbur Allen Parker

No. ___

WILBUR A. PARKER F½
U.S.S. COLORADO
% FLEET POST OFFICE BOX
SAN FRANCISCO, CALIFORNIA

RUBY GOODWIN
(Sender's Name)
BOX 16
(Sender's Address)
WENDOVER, WYO.
AUGUST 30, 1943
(Date)

DEAREST BROTHER,
I'M TOO LAZY TO GET OUT MY TYPEWRITER TONIGHT; BUT NO MORE THAN THERE IS TO SAY I THINK EVEN A STINGY V-MAIL CAN CARRY ALL THE NEWS. DAY BEFORE YESTERDAY WAS A RED-LETTER DAY AS I RECEIVED YOUR LETTER OF AUGUST 17th. I JUST HAVE TO READ IT OVER AND OVER AND HUG THE JOY OF KNOWING YOU ARE O.K.
WE ARE STILL SITTING HERE AT CAMP 100, SAFE AND SLOW, IF A BIT DULL. I GO AHEAD WITH MY WASHING AN IRONING AND COOKING AS IF THE WORLD WAS AT PEACE, AND MY BROTHER CLOSE TO ME. STANLEY THOT YOU SHOULD COME AND HELP US EAT THE APPLE PIE I BAKED TODAY. HE STILL WORRIES ABOUT THOSE GUNS ON YOUR SHIP. I'D WORRY MORE IF THEY WEREN'T THERE, HA, HA.
DID I TELL YOU I HAD TO RIDE WITH MARGARET LOCKE WHEN I CAME DOWN WITH THE MAIL? SHE IS GOING TO CAN, SHE SAYS, EVEN IF EVERYTHING DOES SPOIL. OH, DEAR ME, WHAT A RIDE!
I'M LOOKING FORWARD TO THE DAY WHEN YOU BRING THOSE SEASHELLS HOME. I DOUBT IF WE GET TO MOVE NOW, ALTHOUGH WE HAVEN'T HEARD DEFINITELY YET. I HATE THESE NOTES; BUT I ALWAYS THINK THEY'LL REACH YOU QUICKER.
OLD PAL, YOU ARE EVER NEAR
IN EVERY JOY, IN EVERY FEAR
R.L.G.

ALWAYS — RUBY

V---MAIL

MINDORO

Not until the U.S.S. CLOLRADO was through her battle role on Mindoro did Wilbur get a chance to write again. The U.S.S. COLORADO's part in this operation lasted but 7 days...December 12 through December 18, 1944.
    During the night the U.S. 7th Fleet made sail from Leyte for Mindoro. There ensued the usual barrage from the naval guns as the US 24th Division landed on the island. Poor little Mindoro had but a total of 3,794 sq. miles to bomb.
    "By the time we get through with her," one of Wilbur's crew remarked, "she'll be lucky to have 3,000 sq. miles left."
    Lucky for this islet there was virtually no opposition from the Japanese, for they had stripped their Mindoro garrisons to carry on their opposition at Leyte.

W.A. PARKER EM 3/C
U.S.S. COLORADO, BOX 11
c/o Fleet P.O., S.F. Calif.
December 20, 1944

Dear Sister,
    Had mail call today but very little mail, and none from you. Probably, there is little use in writing now, but I just got to thinking about what you said in your last letter about not being able to get a spare tire. Now, I don't see why you mightn't just as well have Uncle Alvin send you one of those on my car. Looks as though they will just rot anyhow. They're probably not much good now, but might tide you over until you can get a better one. I do wish I could get rid of that old car. I hate to see it sitting there doing no one any good.
    Nothing much has happened here since last I wrote. Checked a book out of the library to read but layed it down beside me while eating chow

and someone stole it before I finished reading it. Had a show out on the quarter deck last night but I didn't go.
   That's about all for tonight. Will try to write more soon.   Love, Wilbur

Dec. 24, 1944
Dear Ruby,
   Have your letter of the eleventh and you say you have a new tire, so maybe there is little use in sending that other note, but I'll let it go anyhow.
   I guess I may have another note from you yet before it is all sorted, as there is still quite a few bags unsorted mail at the Post Office. That is all I asked for Xmas...just the mail, so I feel pretty good.
   We will probably be having a big dinner tomorrow, so I guess I'll lay off the beans today and go on a fast until tomorrow. (Ha)
   Yesterday I got ashore for a few hours, the first time since in October, so seemed sort of good though there is really nothing to do or see. Stood in line about an hour for a bottle of beer then went swimming. The water was wonderful...just right not too cold, but cool and refreshing. Stanley would have gotten a kick out of seeing Uncle Wilbur ducking under for sea shells. I found a few pretty good ones to keep for souvenirs. With Love Always, Wilbur

   1944 Christmas neared and passed.
   "The Leyte-Samar Campaign can now be regarded as closed, except for minor mopping-up operations", General MacArthur was quoted as saying, and,"General Yamashita has suffered perhaps the greatest defeat in the military annals of the Japanese Army."
   (On Leyte: The enemy lost 125,000 men, all but 500 prisoners killed. American casualties were

about 2,750 killed and 8,500 wounded and missing. During the period of the invasion, the Japanese lost close to 3,000 planes, far more than they could replace....From History of W.W. II by Francis T. Miller)

THE U.S.S. COLORADO DAILY 1943

Wilbur knew the rules of the Government... keeping a diary of vital war-facts while in active service was a big *no-no*. Why? There was danger the Big Wigs said that these notes may reveal the strategy of the fleet were they to fall into enemy hands. How could a diary possibly reveal more than the details in the U.S.S. COLORADO NEWS? Maybe he could just call his diary *THE U.S.S. COLORADO DAILY*.

Wilbur had kept a log of his daily routine ever since he was 16 just about the time he left home to herd sheep for Bob Sturgeon out near Garrett, Wyoming, in the year of 1939. He found it much easier to write letters if he could jog his memory by referring to his journal. In the Navy he didn't forsake this useful habit. Sometimes he kept his little $4\frac{1}{2}$" x 2 3/4" note book in his pocket and wrote in it while on watch.

In the past he found most everyday events had to be colored up to make interesting reading, while now during the seige of World War II in the Central Pacific he couldn't find words that would color an event highly enough to portray it well.

Most of the time the facts a diary states are dull and commonplace, not at all captivating unless you know the writer and are interested in what he's doing. However, from the Service's point of view it may disclose pertinent facts of a strategic area. Perhaps, when it was banned the stark realities of all war maneuvers that aren't entirely commendable may be what the Navy feared most in a diary.

Thus Wilbur thought, "What the Heck," and went right ahead ignoring the rules whatever the reason.

1943

October 22: Received package from Ruby - Shaving outfit, etc. before we left. Recieved letter from Mother.

Oct. 23: Went to Dr. with heat rash.

Oct. 24: Sunday - posted pictures in my album.

Oct. 25: They started to initiate the polly-wogs. Painted at the afterboard where they had welded.

Oct. 27: Stood watch at chgs-room on 8-12 and at after board 12-4.

Oct. 28: Put in first day as Turret striker - Helped Ball in morning and got a little shuteye this afternoon.

Oct. 29: Helped Ball in the turret in morning - crossed the International Date Line at noon so this afternoon is Saturday 30th.

NOVEMBER 1943

Nov. 1-5: Work in turrett. They had some sort of a fuss at the afterboard, and I'm not responsible for the cleanup anymore. Am I glad! G.Q. and watch - Watch and G. Q.

NAVY DEPARTMENT, BUREAU OF NAVIGATION

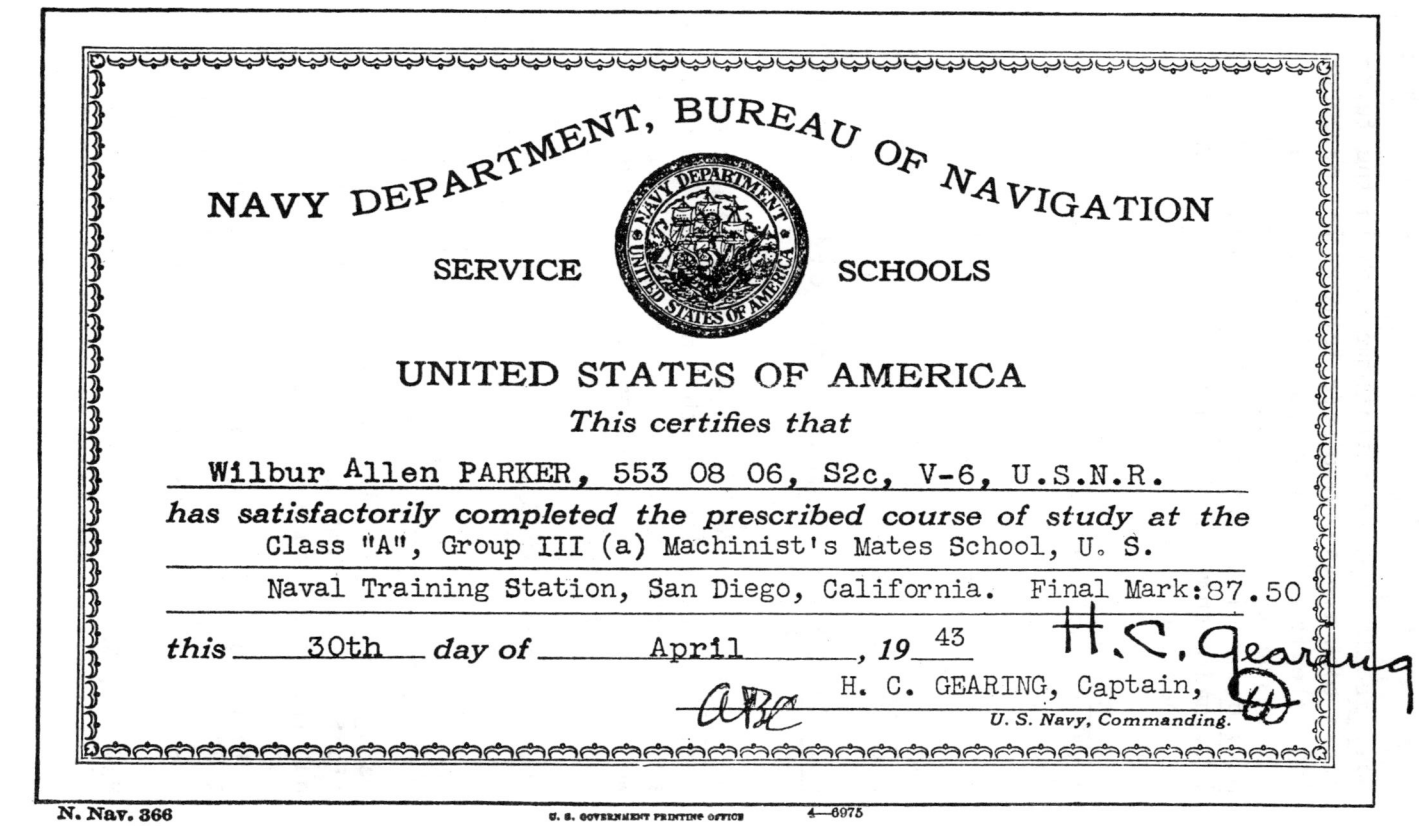

SERVICE SCHOOLS

UNITED STATES OF AMERICA

This certifies that

Wilbur Allen PARKER, 553 08 06, S2c, V-6, U.S.N.R.

has satisfactorily completed the prescribed course of study at the Class "A", Group III (a) Machinist's Mates School, U. S. Naval Training Station, San Diego, California. Final Mark: 87.50

this 30th day of April, 19 43

H. C. GEARING, Captain,
U.S. Navy, Commanding.

Nov. 5: No liberty - did some work in the turrett - took a nap, and wrote letters in the evening.

Nov. 6: Pulled into H-----H----- about 1900. They had a show, but didn't stay ashore for it as I had the 12-4.

Nov. 7: G. Q. at Y. until 8:00 - didn't do anything all day but write a letter in answer to one I rec. from Chloe.

Nov. 11: Saw the show - "Devil and Miss Jones."

Nov. 12: Watch 8-12 - Wrote - Cleaned up the turrett for inspection.

Nov. 13: Sat. & personal inspection - K.H. pulled out at 12:30.

Nov. 14: Sun. - Worked on knives for Beham and Lemon all day - Crossed the Int. Date Line so... again? Slept some in morning - did a little work on the switch boxes on circuit breakers - turret bow in afternoon.

Nov. 15: Mon. Stood watch, and worked on a knife for Hatche.

Thursday, Nov. 18: We went in G. Q. when enemy aircraft was reported. The word is that there were 4 squads, 18 fire squads, and one of our fighters shot down...had another alarm later, but they never came in close.

Friday, Nov. 19: Went on watch on Searchlights at 8-12. Saw search lights operating off shore about 9.30, but we had no G.Q. during the night.

Nov. 20, Sat: Reveille later than usual about 5

or 5:30 Went into g.q. and almost immediately closed in and started firing on Helene Island. Two subs. closed in on us, one on each side, at close range. We fired and presumed to have got both...the one at least certainly sunk.

A torpedo was supposed to have been sent under our stern. Another Sub. was reported close in and was fired on, but was soon distinguished as empty 40 mm shell containers.

About noon some of us went to the top side and watched the aerial bombardment off the Island. Our big guns seemed to have silenced the shore batteries, and we came out of g.q. about long enough for an early supper but on landing our Marines we encountered stiff resistance and had to retrieve. So we went into g.q. again, and our big gun went again into action about the time it grew light the morning of the 21st.

We had an air alarm on the eve of the 20th, and rushed to g.q., but it turned out to be our own planes from the carrier.

Sunday, Nov. 21, 1943: Kept the lights on all night with no excitement. Saw a few bursts of A.A. fire presumably toward the shore after reveille, then we went to G. Q. after which the lights were all to be fixed as all four 36 in. lenses had been broken.

It sure seems even our morning fire didn't quite silence all the job batteries as several destroyers fired for sometime while we were fixing the lights this morn, and bombers have been over the island all day in simulated attacks.

We went in close to the shore of Cora Island and went in G.Q. about time for supper this eve while I was on watch. We were supposed to bombard while the Marines made a landing there, but we rec'd the report that they were about 3/4ths across with little opposition, so we didn't fire and came on out of G. Q. About noon it was reported that the Japs had tried to cross from Helen I. to Cora, but were evidently repulsed rather successfully.

Monday, Nov. 22: Slept in Turret 4. (Very hot). They set condition Zebra directly after reveille and before G.Q. Jap dive bombers came in over Tarawa Island and bombed our Marines there. I managed with some trouble to get to my g.q. station.

Worked back in Turret Four on some resisters for the shell hoist motors. They finished putting the lenses in the other 36 in. lights.

Had quite a bit of excitement after I went on watch at 6:05. One of our planes tried to drop us a message but it fell short of the port bow. Then we got a sub alert and saw a sub surfaced out several miles, and two cans after it. One was said to have rammed it after which one of the U.S.S. COLORADO plows dropped two bombs and we saw it turn its nose high in the air and sink. (There were supposed to be some prisoners taken).

There seems to be some resistance on the Island, and I stayed up on the lights for some time, and watched the tracers arching across the sky from the two cans firing to the Island.

Nov. 23: Slept out on the rim of search light tower...got out at reveille---went on watch at 8-12. Lemon put me on the 24 in. search lights at noon. Sort of wanted to stay in the turret. Nothing much happened today. We pulled out quite a way from the Island and the transports got under way. There is (they say) still resistance on the Island.

Nov. 24 - Wed: Had thought we'd pulled away from the Island to take the transports out, but see The Gilbert Group still in sight this evening, and the Hospital ships lying close in. They say all resistance was overcome.

Nov. 25, Thurs: Hadn't thought of this being Thanksgiving until someone mentioned it. We had a good dinner. Worked on search light shutters this morn and slept all afternoon. (No excitement) We're still in the Gilbert Group.

Nov. 26, Fri: Worked on search lights all day. Watch 6-8. Some ornery devil stole my bed blanket. Had an alert out g.q....saw gun fire before I left the lights, and it was reported our fighters shot down one plane, but the word is we got 2 or maybe 3.

Nov. 27, Sat: Found my blanket but not my sweater or bed bag. 8-12 Watch. Found a blanket in one of the boats to sleep on.

Nov. 28, Sun: The Island still in sight this morning (Tarawa).

Nov. 29, Mon: It was announced over the loud speaker that we were to return to Pearl Harbor as soon as we refueled...guess we started about 7 last night.

Nov. 30: Exams are soon to come out, and I'm hardly ready. We are to have a study period at Power shop every other day.

DECEMBER 1943

December 1,2,3,4, Wed., Thurs., Fri., and Sat. Studied all spare time and worked on lights - Stood on Watch - Slept top side.

Dec. 5, Sun: Study. On watch 8-12, and nearly all day as it was Sunday.

<u>Dec. 6th:</u> Had the Monday exams today. Hope I made it. Had Martin stand my watch.

<u>Dec. 7th:</u> We weighed anchor about 8 o'clock, and liberty commenced at noon. Was in the liberty station section, but didn't go as had a bad ground in the Port light and wanted to get my mail anyhow. It didn't come out till late though. Wrote letters till midnight.

<u>Dec. 8:</u> (Wed) Tore the light switch and mechanism all apart today. Hope to get done in time for liberty tomorrow. Recieved lots of mail and a box of fudge from home.

<u>Dec. 9,</u> Thurs: Went on liberty in HONOLULU - Bowled with Carnes.

<u>Dec. 10:</u> Tore the S.H. motor down.

<u>Dec. 11:</u> Liberty by myself.

<u>Dec. 12,13,14,15,16:</u> Studying for the finals, and sure H- - - - of a lot of work, sure kept me moving.

<u>Dec. 17</u>: Weighed anchor. Have been too busy answering my mail and studying to keep this book up.

<u>Dec. 18:</u> Took the test...finals...have had a bit more time it seems, but have watch now, of course.

<u>Dec. 21:</u> Pulled in at the dock at Hunters Portal about 9-15. Stood watch until about 11 and had to get ready for liberty after that. Went to the Pepsi Cola and wrote some letters, then phoned Chloe. She wasn't home. They gave me a ticket there for the Follies at the Winterland

Ice Gardens so I went. Got to bed at the Harbor Club and stayed till morn.

Dec. 22: Got in about 7:30 - read my mail and tore the St. light switch apart - sewed my E/3 crow on tonight, and took off the stripe. (Aim to write a line).

Dec. 23: Went skating at the Cliff house.

Dec. 25: Was invited over to Aulds for Xmas dinner, and had a very nice one, came home about midnight.

Dec. 26:

Dec. 27: Went with Rickson and Powell, and we went out to Lemon's wedding. Met some swell people. I took Janet home after going to the Ship's Dome in San Fran.

Dec. 28:

Dec. 29: Left San Francisco for Long Beach.

Dec. 30: Put in for a special about 4 o'clock, but was too late to get it.

Dec. 31: Got off about 10 o'clock but had to get back at 1.2 midnight; but got to see the kids, Clara, and Parrs.

ORDERS FOR THE DAY, WEDNESDAY, 8 DECEMBER, 1943:
(RESTRICTED)

INFORMATION:
1. Duty Head of Department - Comdr. HENKEL.
2. FIRST Section is duty section.
3. Working division - Division "F" & "L".

GENERAL:
1. Moored alongside PENNSYLVANIA. Berth Fox 3.
2. Condition of Readiness III. Material Condition of Readiness YOKE, maintained day and night except when General Quarters is sounded, five minutes after which Condition ZEBRA will be set.

ROUTINE EXCEPT:

---- - Uniform of the day will be dungarees, blue dyed white hats.

---- - Call cooks and bakers of the watch.

0550 - MAAs call leading division POs.

0600 - REVEILLE.

0610 - Leading division POs report to MAAs that men sleeping in their spaces are turned out.

0645 - Breakfast.

---- - Gunnery division be prepared to transfer empty 16" powder tanks to lighter.

0800 - Muster on stations if ammunition containers are being unloaded, if not quarters for muster.

0830 - Sick Call

0900 - Liberty commences for PORT WATCH to expire on board ship at 1830 for non-rated men, 1900 for rated, and 1930 for CPOs.

1930 - Movies.

NOTICES:

1. Requests for special liberty will be submitted to the Executive Officer's Office prior to 1800 the day previous to that which liberty is requested. Men not staying at address given on pass are directed to report to Shore Patrol Headquarters, Old Naval Station, to have same changed.

2. The following from the Commander-in-Chief, Pacific Fleet is quoted:

    "CINCPAC IS VERY PROUD OF THE SHIPS RETURNING FROM THE GILBERTS AND OF THE OFFICERS AND MEN OF ALL SERVICES WHOSE GALLANTRY, SELF-SACRIFICE AND DEVOTION TO DUTY MADE POSSIBLE OUR SUCCESS IN THE CAPTURE OF TARAWA AND MAKIN X WELL DONE"

    W.A. BOWERS,
    Commander, U.S. Navy,
    Executive Officer

THE U.S.S. COLORADO DAILY 1944

JANUARY

Jan. 1: Went out about 6 in morn and had bombardment practice.

Jan. 2: G. Q. at 4 till noon.

Jan.3: G. Q. from 3.30 till 12.15 - Watch in afternoon. Should be back in Long Beach about 5 or 6 - liberty for the other watch.

Jan. 4: Couldn't get a special but went over to Les' anyhow, and we went night clubbing, met Smokers and really made a night of it. Stayed up and worked all day.

Jan. 6: Went out to where Dorothy works and looked the place over. Went out and looked George's (Parr) shop over. Had dinner out with Mrs. Parr, Clara and the kids (Les and Dorothy Parker).

Jan. 7: Managed a little sleep today, and did a little letter writing this evening.

Jan. 8 Took Ball with me and went out to Les and Dot's. Sure had a duce of a time getting him a girl friend. Eunice went but sort of hated to ask her she is so young. Had a lot of fun, but between Ball and the booze it sort of spoiled it for me, and no doubt the girls, too, especially Eunice.

Jan. 9: Sunday, so I didn't even try to get any work done, but catch up a bit on my much-needed sleep.

Jan. 10: My clothes need washing and I thought

I'd stay in, but decided to go as Weise said he could get his folk's car. He got it allright,but made it pretty late. I called Clara M. but they had about given me up. She sure is a sweet kid. I don't see why I couldn't be a bit younger or met a girl like her when I was. Stayed at Sterling's until morning and slept cold.

Jan. 11: Made it to the shop O.K. but sure caught a duce of a cold; but managed to stay up and work a bit.

Jan.12: Felt so tough I didn't even try to go on liberty. It expired at 10 or 12 anyhow, and my clothes were dirty. (Was in bed all day).

Jan. 13: Pulled out about daylight. Felt pretty low so didn't do much again today. Had 6 to 8 watch.

Jan. 14: Had a notion to turn in at sick bay but decided to try to fight it out, and had the 8 to 12 watch, and an hr. extra as they set the time back. Wrote a letter to Clara Mae, and started one to Mother.

Jan. 15: Are having G.Q. night and morning, too, this time out. Cleaned at aft Bd. this morning and drew sheet metal watch this afternoon.

Jan. 16: Sunday - worked on knife handle.

Jan. 17: Worked on stainless steel coffee tray.

Jan. 18: Had to give up my small locker.

Jan. 19: Pulled into Maui, Hawaii.

Jan. 20,21,22: The gun Captain on No. 2 Mt. is making us stand on the Mt. and we're having some argument over it.

<u>Jan. 23</u>: 8-12 Watch - warm - took it easy.

<u>Jan. 24</u>: Fixed shutter on 12 in. light - adjusted stbd 24 - worked on 36 in. for Stroud. Stood watch on the Mt. again, though the other watchmen stand inside, and think we will, too.

<u>Jan. 25,26,27,28,29</u>: These days have been spent on my knife some. Read a good deal and did the necessary work in preparation for the coming battle.

<u>Jan. 30</u>: No chance to work with everyone else C. out.

<u>Jan. 31</u>: They handed out sandwichs for breakfast, and we went to G.Q. At last the hour has arrived, and soon our guns began to boom as we strike the Marshall Island. We have most of the out-lying Island before night falls.

FEBRUARY 1944

<u>Feb. 1</u>: Before the close of this day nearly the whole of the Island Group is ours, and the lack of resistance almost complete is surprising.

<u>Feb. 2</u>: The Islands were in sight early this morn, but we pulled farther out and stayed until in the evening when much to everyone's surprise we pulled into the lagoon and weighed anchor. Fighting was still in progress, and we watched the Marines advance and mop up on two of the small islands close by.

<u>Feb. 3</u>: No G.Q. - last night on this move. No excitement. Stood watch 8-12 and fixed 12 in.

search light lens and held field day in the afternoon.

Feb. 4: Worked cleaning lights and stood watch 12 - 4.

Feb. 5: Group Inspection - read - Wrote to Clara Mae.

Feb. 6:

Feb. 7: Left Kwajalein about _____ _____ and got into _____ about dark. Stood watch in morn and 8-12 night.

Feb. 8: Took ground reading on lights, and tested battery. Worked on knife while on watch. Faree changed my G.Q Station to Turret 2.

Feb. 9: Helped Joe in the turret after checking lights, then worked on my knife, nearly finished it as worked a bit on watch, too.

Feb. 10: Was due at Camouflage but never got in, a tanker had trouble.

Feb. 11: 8-12 watch on Searchlights. Had an air raid over Camouflage Island.

Feb. 12: 12-4 watch - Had a round with Beckener, and went to sky control - had Captain's personal inspection in morning, and had to borrow Downe's trousers.

Feb. 13: Sunday - It was a wonderful day because the mail came in, and I had 6 letters from Clara Mae and several from Ruby, Mother, and others - scarcely did a thing all day.

Feb. 14, Mon: Helped Joe charge his firing circuit batteries, and wrote to Clara Mae, also cards to Mother, Les, and Parrs later.

Feb. 15: Tues. 8-12 Watch - ground a bit on a knife for McGinnis. Took my scabbard to the cobbler shop and had it sewed. Worked on lights late.

Feb. 16, Wed: 12-4 watch -checked lights and helped Herring in morning. Got some candy and locks at canteen.

Feb. 17: Ate a couple of rolls this morning and went into G.Q. for bombardment.
Can't hear much of what is going on here in the turret. Don't think much dope came over the speaker anyhow. Went out at chow time, and once before, and it appears to me there is very little, if any, opposition ashore.
Pretty hot in the turret, but couldn't find any other place to sleep.

Feb. 18: Fr. - Went to G.Q. - cleaned searchlight lens. 4.30 and we are in G.Q. and underway...preparing to bombard I think...got rid of all our 16" bombardment shells.

Feb. 20: Sun. - We stood by and fired the 5 in. all night, but weren't in g.q. They need the search lights a good deal, and burned one of the heads, so had to fix that, then went on watch at noon - dyed bits in evening.

Feb. 21: Mon. - fixed shutter in morning. They nosed in and fired the 5 in. all afternoon so couldn't do much. Wrote letters in evening as hear they may go out.

Feb. 22: Tues - took up a battery and worked on the windshield wipers all day. They finally secured the Island.

<u>Feb. 23</u>: Wed. - Clara Mae's birthday, and not a thing to send her. Watch 8-12. Fixed a shutter and worked some on windshield wipers. We got underway about 8 this morning for Majuro Lagoon.

Feb. 24: 12-4 watch - whittled - worked on windshield wipers.

<u>Feb. 25</u>: Worked all day on windshield wipers, and got them installed, but the switch is on the bum now. Anchored about noon in Majuro Lagoon. Got a letter from Clara Mae dated Jan. 14.

<u>Feb. 26:</u> Sat. - worked on windshield wipers- wrote to Clara Mae - changed tool boxes.

Feb. 27, Sunday 1944: A list of the Battle Ships with us here at Majuro Lagoon:

PENNSYLVANIA	38
NEW MEXICO	40
MISSISSIPPI	41
IDAHO	42
TENNESSEE	43
COLORADO	45
NORTH CAROLINA	55
WASHINGTON	56
SOUTH DAKOTA	57
MASSACHUSETTS	59
ALABAMA	60
IOWA	61
NEW JERSEY	62

Ground on a knife out of a file this afternoon as everyone was asleep at the board. Got three old letters and a Valentine from home.

<u>Feb. 28:</u>--- Pulled out of the Majuro Lagoon for Pearl Harbor.

Feb. 29: Quite a change in E Division. I have Sneider on the lights now. Fixed a switch and shutter.

March 1, Wed: Got called to Sky Control for relieving the watch late. Beckner got changed to a different section which certainly doesn't hurt my feelings. Had Sub alert all afternoon, and didn't get a thing done but got a hair cut and a gee dunk.

March 2, Thurs: 8-12 watch - fixed light panel shelf in thermostat room (started ring).

March 3, Fri: Checked lights, and helped drill shaft for one. Worked on ring - stood 12-4 watch. Hatcher is raffling my knife.

March 4: Hatcher brought back my knife as he couldn't raffle it off.

March 5: Sunday - Pulled into Pearl Harbor about 8.30 - didn't have the right station to get liberty...got quite a bit of mail.

March 6: Pulled out for the States about 9:30 so no liberty- got quite a bit of mail and now a knife. Wrote to Clara Mae.

March 7: Tues. -Tailored Joe's jumper - cut out a scabbord for Beckner, but was left-handed.

March 8: Wed. 4-6 watch - ground on Mc Cennion's knife, and finished my own (grinding) - sewed on 2 crows for Jack.

March 9: Worked on knife and tested sub lights and battery.

March 10: Stood 8-12 watch, and worked on knife

in afternoon.

March 11, Sat: Held field day and stood 12-4 watch on gun 8.

March 12: Pulled into Bremerton in morning - could see land since about 1 o'clock in morning- unloaded ammunition. No watch.

March 13: Moved over to the dock - found out we get a 16-day leave, and we'll go the 3rd (about) as am in second leave party. I got leave and went into Bremerton and bought some things. Got a watch for Clara mae like I had wanted so much - didn't get it at Naval store though, but don't think I got gyped as it was worked down from $165 to $135, which only came to $152.50 with sales tax.

March 14: I was pretty tired last night when I got in, and Oh! what a night of hammering and carving those Yard Birds did in the Turret!

March 15: Liberty again tonight. Bill and I went over and did a bit more shopping then went to a show, and came in early (9:30) so got a good rest.

March 16: Didn't have much to do, and the yard men got us up at 8:00 so press and tailored, and washed my clothes. Wrote some letters on watch.

March 17, Fri: Called Clara Mae, and saw two shows then went ice skating.

March 18: Slept till noon then went on watch. Wrote to Clara M. and Ruby.

March 19: Other than stand watch and write, I've scarcely did a thing all day.

March 20, Mon: Went over to Seattle and went skating after shopping around Bremerton. Took Clara Mae's watch over to have it engraved, and have her little necklace fixed. Met Zaic and some others at the rink, but the rink closed just as we were beginning to have fun, so we went to a show and stayed out all night as they were turning the COLORADO around when we got back.

March 21: Rated tonight, but stayed in - wrote to Clara.

March 22: Wed. - watch - moved battery down - made a scabbord for the knife that I won. Wrote to Clara.

March 23: Moved to dry dock - got ready for liberty early but didn't get to go off until after six. Went to Seattle and the ice rink, but they had had a fire and no skating. Went to a show, "The Gang's All Here", and "Happy Land". Slept at the hotel.

March 24: Worked today on some switch and fuse boxes for the turrets. Pressed clothes and wrote to Clara M.

March 25: Went to the store and got Clara Mae's watch, and my traveling book. Went to Seattle and bought skates. Went skating. Stayed at A M Y and like to froze.

March 26: Got up late, and went to ice rink. Met two gals, and we ate and went to a show, then I saw Marie home.

March 27: Turned to "on" switch boxes for turrets.

March 28: Did the same thing today.

March 29: Got off at 1:30 to get in the bank, but did no good. Went to Seattle and got a ticket at United Air Line's office on 9th - bought some Easter cards, and went to ice rink.

March 30, Thurs: Got up at 9:30 - worked a bit in Rheostat room - ironed and packed a bit, wrote letters, and stood watch.

(March 31 and April 1, 1944 - No entry for these dates).

April 2, Sun: We got off at 10 o'clock, caught the ferry to Seattle, rushed to the _____ building, and was nearly first in line, so seemed to have a good chance of catching a plane at 7:30 in the morning, so canceled my reservation with TWA. Reynolds and I got a hotel room, then went and ate, and had a little fun. I left him at the U.S.O. and went in and bathed and soaked my leg which had begun to look and feel pretty bad.

April 3, Mon: Got up at 4 o'clock, shaved and ate then got out to the air field and was nearly late. I was the last man that they signed to go.
    We stayed in Oakland from about 12:30 to 1:30 and ate there, then we stopped again in Bakersfield, then in Los Angeles at North American, and I caught a ride on out to the kids arriving about 6 o'clock, I guess, as I fiddled around trying to figure transportation to Cheyenne for some time.

April 4: Took Les' car and went over to Parr's. Clara Mae and I came back to the kids' in the evening, but they were going out so we saw Harley and Louise, then went to a show.

April 5: Clara Mae and I went to the show again.

Have been keeping hot packs on my leg.

April 6, Thurs: Clara Mae and I came over to the kids then we went out and ate, then went to Zamboango. I took Clara Mae home and stayed over there.

(No entries for April 7 and April 8)

April 9: We got up early and went out to the air field, but there were a good many waiting, and I got cold feet and didn't go home (to Fletcher Park, Wyoming), and we all went out on a picnic to Griffith Park.

April 10: Les didn't go to work, so we spent the day talking. Mrs. Parr called up in the evening about her mother, and we all went over, and did not get back until 12:00.

April 11: Got up about 10:30 - got a bite to eat, washed dishes, then my clothes. Bathed and pressed two suits, and swept the house. By this time the kids were home.

April 12: Went over to Parrs after cleaning up, and going to the ration board and getting some gas. Fooled around down town a while, and bought Clara M. some stamps, and we went to Shanon's to eat, then out to the ocean for a drive.

April 13: Walked part way to school with Clara M. Fooled around down town, worked on the car late, then Clara and I went over to Les & Dot's.

April 14: Les took yesterday off for his physical. We all drove out for a Spanish dinner. Clara Mae and I stayed up late and talked...the kids went to bed. I brushed Clara's hair, and it was nearly 3:00 before we could give each other up.

No. E 12 1232

Wilbur A. Parker F 1-c
U.S.S. Colorado
% Fleet Post Office, Box 11
San Francisco, California

Ruby Goodwin
Box 16
Wendover, Wyoming
August 9th, 1943

Dearest Brother;

Well, I will write another few lines this evening, this long evening spent in wondering where you are and how you are. Stanley is asleep, cuddling "Fluffy Pup". He thinks he can't sleep without the puppy Uncle Wilbur gave him, and he has taken good care of it too. And so the days eventually come to a close, and they are full days too, the fuller the better they suit me. I am ever thankful that I am strong enough again to do most anything I take a notion to do. It is truly a blessing.....Bill doesn't even have to help me wash nowadays, ha, ha. That is what I did today besides sewing and other little things. I'm making another dress. How much of a dress can one make for twenty-eight cents? I would like to show you, and it really isn't so very skimpy either.

I received another letter from Mary Delle Lightsey the other day. She is about through her summer school and will be home for a while before she starts teaching again. She says she got a school in Riverton this year, and is afraid she is going to miss Fletcher Park. The last time we were in Wheatland we went out to see Myrna a while. She said she had written to you at your old address, so I will have to send her the one you have now. Myrna looks well even though they have been looking working hard. The baby is so cute and looks like a girl instead of a boy. After leaving their place we went to see a show we had been wanting to see, "Random Harvest" starring Greer Garson and Ronald Colman. And it was surely worth seeing. And so that is about all of the latest, I guess. We went after another cow for Mr Herman yesterday, which was Sunday. We stopped to see Aunt Dode for a while and to look at your car. We were wondering if the papers necessary to get a license were in the car. I told Mother if she would send them to me I would get the license for her. Then when she comes down to have her glasses fitted I can drive the car back home for her as she talked like they would like to have it up there. Several little things have gone wrong with our car. I guess it is getting old and can't take it any more, and we have been so careful with it too. One can hardly get repairs now, and no mechanic to work on it if you could get parts.

I saved up the sugar to bake an apple pie the other day and was just wishing you were here to help eat it when some neighbors came to pay us a call and before they left there was no pie left, ha, ha. Can I send you packages now, do you know? I might bake you some cookies, but I think they say you mustn't send anything like that across seas. And can't you put the date on your letter? You haven't been, that is why I ask. I can't even get started on a letter with one of these V-mail things, but that won't keep me from coming back in another day or so. We have heard nothing of the other job we had hoped for, and I doubt if we will now. Well, we'll make more Bonds here than if we moved anyway, but was in hopes Bill would get a change before Fall to see if his health wouldn't improve. Write when you can, dear brother, as I'll be thinking of you and wishing you the best. Love,
Ruby

V---MAIL

Souvenir Photo

ZAMBOANGA
HOME OF THE TAILESS MONKEYS

3828 W. SLAUSON AVE.
LOS ANGELES, CALIF.

The World's Most Beautiful Polynesian Paradise

At the ZAMBOANGA CAFE, 3828 W. Slauson Ave., Los Angeles, California
Clara Parr, Wilbur Parker, Leslie Parker, Dorothy Parr Parker

April 15: We got up late, and then we started hating to think that I had to take the plane back. We just sort of held each other all day, and made poor Les get dinner, and do all the work. Then he drove past Dot's work, and out to the air field. It was awful to have to leave; but the time painfully came, and I took off. Gee, she is a sweet, brave girl. She didn't cry a bit, not at least so I could see.

I ate dinner somewhere out of L.A.. Stayed at San Fran, and Oakland and twice more. I slept out of Oakland - got to Seattle at 3:00. Stayed at the Olympic Hotel.

April 16: Up at 10 - cleaned up, checked my bags at the Y., ate a turkey dinner, and called a chiropractor. I saw him in the evening. He took an Xray, and gave me a treatment. Stayed at the Y.

April 17: Back aboard ship at 7:36, changed clothes, and worked on Search lights - slept in Turret 3.

April 18: Washed some, not much, and took a part over to the machine shop. Washed and got ready to go to the chiropracter again. I bought cards and went skating, back at 1 o'clock.

April 19: Got up at 10, helped Bill in afternoon in the turret. I cleaned the place up and pressed my suit after 4, washed, and I want to write to Clara M. as I got a letter today.

April 20: I got up about 9 and went to the machine shop to see about 56 sch. port. Then I worked in turret in afternoon after I washed one suit of blues. I didn't go on liberty as it started too late for me to see the chiropractor. Wrote to Clara Mae.

(No entries for April 21 and 22, 1944)

April 23: Cook and I went on liberty together. We saw a burlesque show, ate a bite, and came back to go to bed at the hotel in Bremerton.

April 24: I got up a bit late, and worked out in the rain all morning on the 36 in. searchlights.

April 25: Got liberty again, and though I didn't get off until late, I went over to see the chiropractor at his home. I had to be back at 12 and got to talking church at the Service Men's center, and missed the ferry!

April 26: (We went out for a trial run) Worked at aft. Bd. on a coat hanger all morning. Went to mast at 12:30 - got a warning. Adjusted 24 search lights in afternoon. Then worked on a lighting system for my locker.

April 27: My G. Q. station changed to the bridge. Worked on windshield wipers, and got set to put in a battery box. Cleaned out cabinet in Aft. Bd.

April 28: Took serial # of all s.p. phones on my G.Q station this morning. Worked on a shelf for the rheostat room in afternoon. Installed my locker light, but was grounded. Wrote to Clara M.

April 29: Held field day at the Aft. Bd. and was it dirty! Worked on bench shelf some in the afternoon, and finished my light.

April 30: Sunday - finished my knife , and started a scabbard also, finished the shelf. We left for Frisco about dark - took on about 500 passengers.

MAY 1944:

Monday 1: Checked the lights, and put in a shutter spring, took up rubber for a gasket for the battery box, finished my knife scabbard, and made a latch to hold my locker door open, and am now writing letters.

Tues. 2: Went on liberty in Frisco. We got in about 9:30, and I rated at 1 o'clock.

Wed.3:Went with Jack McDonald out to his wife's folks, bought Mother a box of candy - wrote letters after I got in.

Thurs.4: Was a bit sleepy, and I have the starting of a cold, so I didn't do a great lot, but write letters.

Fri. 5: Worked on searchlights. I didn't eat. Put a battery in on the Capt. Bridge.

Sat. 6: I didn't eat breakfast, but ate dinner and supper, and I feel worse tonight. Worked on 36 in. searchlights - sewed my cot.

Sun. 7: Worked on 36 in. searchlights all day, and didn't seem to accomplish a thing. Mr. Feree sort of gave us a talking to at the board this evening. By Cripes, I wish those guys would fix their own circuits! Mine works O.K. Wrote to Clara Mae.

Mon. 8: Worked on 36 lights until about 8 at night, and got 2 of them working.

Tues.9: Took grounds on 24 in. searchlights, and helped on 36 in. in the afternoon. Had G.Q. about dark after which I wrote to Clara Mae.

Wed. 10: Held field day at the Aft. Bd. today. We sure moved out a bunch of stuff. Pulled into Pearl H. about 6:30 in evening. Wrote to Clara Mae and Mother.

Thurs. 11: Expected liberty, but waited all forenoon, and it didn't come, so we continued field day. I got several more letters, and answered some of them.

Fri. 12: Vacuum cleaned the Fwd. Bd. and worked on 12 in. shutters. Jack and I went over on the MASSACHUSETTS.

Sat. 13: Jack and I went into Honolulu on liberty. I couldn't get what I wanted (silk hose) but I got Clara M. a big bath towel. I got in in time for chow, and stopped on the way home at the canteen. Washed my whites, wrote to Clara M., and went to bed.

Sun. 14: They put me on watch at the Fwd. Bd. I got out late as I didn't know it.

Mon. 15: Got under way They put me back on watch on 36 in. searchlights.

Mon 16: We went out on bombardment exercises, and ran aground about noon during G.Q. , and we never got off until about 2:30 next morning.

Wed. 17: Pulled out for Pearl and got in about 4 at Fort Island. We haven't any drinking water.

Thurs. 18: We moved about 8:30 to dry dock. I worked on the battery box and a 24' shutter motor. Have the 8-12 watch at Fwd. Bd.

Fri. 19: Bill Crane and I went out to Waikiki

"ALOHA" *Hawaiian Islands*

Sunset on Diamond Head

HAWAIIAN ISLANDS
Wilbur Parker

Aloha from Hawaii

KAUAI
NIIHAU
OAHU
MOLOKAI
MAUI
LANAI
KAHOOLAWE
HAWAII

LIHUE
HONOLULU
WAILUKU
HILO

DRISCOLL, HONOLULU

"The Loveliest Fleet of Islands that lies anchored in any ocean"
Mark Twain

War-worn Wilbur Parker

Beach and looked for a camera, but they were all rented, so we did a bit of shopping up town, and came back early.

Sat. 20: Worked on 24" searchlights, and stood 12-4 watch. (Wrote)

Sun. 21: I was pretty tired this morning, and I did not intend to go on liberty, but Jack and Hoey talked me into it, and we went out to Waikiki Beach. I wanted to get some pictures and negatives but couldn't. We played miniature golf until about 4, then came back in time for chow.

Mon. 22: Worked on signal Bridge Port light all morning, and most of the afternoon on the Rheostat. No mail. My cold I've had since leaving Frisco feels it may be leaving at last.

Tues. 23: Jack, Hoey, and I went over to Sub. Base. I bought Stanley a present, and a few other things.

Wed. 24: Took ground-reading on my lights. Started to the show, but came down and wrote.

Thurs. 25: Roberts and I went over to Sub. Base and Iea, played ball, swam, and I got my back and face burned.

Fri.26: Stood 8-12 watch - worked a bit on the knife I won.

Sat. 27: Crane and I went over to Iea. Got together with Cook and Ross and swam and played ball - bought some gum, finished burning my shoulders and nose.

Sun. 28: 12-4 watch (morning) and I didn't do

much but lazy around and write 6 letters.

<u>Mon. 29</u>: Went on a sight-seeing tour of the Island and had a lot of fun. The bus broke down and we were late getting in. McDonald had a transfer card waiting for him when he got in.

<u>Tues. 30</u>: Straightened up the E 3 locker in the storeroom - 4-6 watch.

<u>Wed. 31</u>: 4-8 watch (morning) and I didn't get relieved for chow. I read a book, slept nearly all afternoon on the signal bridge. We got underway about chow time (5:30) for Kwajalein.

JUNE 1944

<u>Thurs. 1:</u>   A blue stretch of water streaking from the Hawaiian to the Marshall Islands...Honolulu to Kwajalein...and somewhere on its heaving bosom, a ship bound South, "two days out!"

(Up early for G.Q.) Lights still seaward so no watch. Worked nearly all day on 12 in. light lenz and getting a battery hooked up, and windshield wipers fixed.

<u>Fri. 2</u>: Had a broken shutter, and we got an enormous supply of small batteries, which we carried from the store room.

<u>Sat. 3</u>:   Many ships in a great grey expanse of water as far as the eye can reach. Ships! bound together by the deep, grey, wall of approaching night...serene and apart as the stars are apart in this soft, warm, night with its tired old moon looking down from its nest on the grey cloud banks.
    I tried to fix the search lights, but couldn't find the right resister. I'm reading

"The Well of Loneliness" by Randolf Hall.

June 4: Did practically no work at all. Finished reading, "The Well of Loneliness". Saw a plane from a carrier land and sink in the water close by.

June 5:

June 6: Crossed the International date line so had no Monday. It's terribly hot. Had pay day and I drew $15.00.

 Perhaps the wan old moon has never seen a greater armada on the toiling breast of the tide that it has watched and governed; still it remains unobstructed. Surely it has grown tired of the insignificant strife, the repetition of restless men. Like the waters of the sea, men are as the moontide from generation to generation as they roll out in relentless armies. In waves...they roll out to pound and thunder the shores of an incomprehensible foe, beating themselves out one on the other till their blood runs dark as the filth thrown up from the ocean to become spent and silent.
 Ah, yes, they are civilized men of human corruption, men of peace and faith in God's salvation; boisterous men, men with lies on their tongues, and blood on their hands, all bent on the death of their brother.
 Yet faith! *May God forgive them*...these peaceful souls who long for their firesides and children...who find in the freedom for which they fight the bonds of their own self-destruction.
 Nay! Shall they buy freedom with slavery? Love with the sword? or peace with a heart full of hatred? Poor fools with their international law; their exchange of prisoners, and mocking

agreements. Could they not agree on a peace between them? No! Rather would they lose their souls than give a drop of blood in their foolish obsession, for over them all the men of greed gather the pennies of blood to abandon at the gateway of heaven.

June 7: Lost my flashlight at G.Q. this morning - got the resister back in for 24" searchlight.

June 8:   Still the moon gives no sign but shines down on the grim hatred of countless men as it has shown in its soft, radiant, loveliness for the world's lovers down through the ages, and on the 8th of the month along towards the evening may have marked the anchoring of many ships in Kwajalein Harbor, among these the good ship, the U.S.S. COLORADO, with her crew of 2,000. Here it was, nearly four months past (Feb. 17, 1944) that her guns rolled out, storming the beach heads in deafening thunder.

All lay quiet now, and along the beach many friendly lights shine, warm, and welcome as the windows of a properous young village. But the mighty fleet seems restless, and the second day following, she noses once again toward the open sea, worming her way ever West...West and North.

Among the men the destination is well known now. Maps of Siapan, the objective, hangs on Bulkhead and Shield for some to study, and the curious to observe this Fortress Island neatly surrounded by Jap outposts and fortifications, lying only some 1700 miles from Japan, and within distance of land-based planes. Surely here, the fleet shall meet strong opposition. Where is the fleet of the Rising Sun? Long has it lain in hiding; but the time will come! the time *must, for the great American Fleet shall*

soon be at the Gateway of the Capitol City!
     Step by ship the American Fleet has moved Northward from Guadacanal to Tarawa, and the Marshalls. And even now a great, gray, shadow of approaching doom circles Siapan, close to the heart of Japanese people.

June 9: Pulled into Kwajalein about 4 o'clock. Worked on the battery box on the Navigation bridge.

June 10: Got a hair cut. The mail came in, but no letter from Clara Mae. Slept on top side - Mast -

June 11: Pulled out about 8 this morn. Worked on angle for the bench.

June 12: They took down the life-lines today. Read and lounged around most all day.

June 13: Worked a bit on windshield wiper, and lights in the morning, but lounged around most all afternoon. (Word of the big W getting bombed).

June 14: The force ahead of us blasted Saipan today, and must still be at it for flashs can be seen from the mast. We are only 80 or so miles out. Quite a bit came over the radio today, but worked on lights this morn, and played cards on the Mast this afternoon, and didn't listen in.

June 15: 3 o'clock reveille - rolls and coffee, then up to G.Q. just before light. On the horizon was a Jap cargo ship set fire by one of our cruisers, and ahead the Island of Saipan.
     We only drew fire once or twice during the day. Secured for dinner and again for lunch

this evening. Having G.Q. on the bridge now.

June 16: Slept on the signal bridge - 3 o'clock reveille - rolls and coffee for breakfast. Ate battle rations on stations, and were in G.Q. all day. My lights O.K., but 36 is about shot. Evening slow at six, then we had an air alert. Several Jap planes came over but too high for our shells to hit, though the carriers farther out may have. Just before noon we had an accident, the machine gun in one of the planes went off accidentally and wounded four men.
     This afternoon we drew machine gun fire from the island across our stern.

June 17: Was in G.Q. all day - ate sandwichs for dinner. I was in the wash room after securing in the evening when some Jap planes came over, but they never got in close enough to get though we fired. Burnt the head on one of the 24s.

June 18: G.Q. before we ate this morning. Later we were served rolls and an orange on our station. We stood by all forenoon, ate sandwiches and fruit at the tables for dinner, and secured directly after, but I stayed up and read and slept. One of the lights burned out again, and the windshield wipers went out. I started fixing them about chow time, and scarcely got started to eating before G.Q. sounded. I took a bowl up and finished my pudding. Two planes came over our bow, but too high to hit though we did a deal of firing before and after. There was a glow of AA fire on and near the beach. Must have lasted nearly an hour.

June 19: G. Q. at 4 o'clock.
     Just about daylight some enemy planes came over. One ventured too close to the MARYLAND, TENNESEE G, and COLORADO, and we got him.

We received one 20 M.M. from TENNESSEE, and wounded one (some say four) men.
 We are said to have killed seven men on the MARYLAND.
 We had another raid tonight, and saw planes, but they never came close enough to bring down. They have burned the stbd. searchlight out twice now, and I worked on it all day when possible.

June 20: Slept on quarterdeck on my cot, and got out just in time for G.Q. Planes came in but not close enough to fire on.
 We saw one of our carrier fighters shoot a Jap plane down over the island just as he let his wheels down to land.
 Directly after dinner we went into G.Q. to fire on some caves on the Island of Saipan.
 Got my light back in order after working nearly all day. At G. Q. tonight some Bogies came within 10 miles, circled and went back out.

June 21: No excitement at G. Q. today. The arc image screen fell out of the stbd. light, and I fixed it, which, together with other adjustments kept me busy all morning. Made a door to drum clamp out of brass this afternoon. Finished reading my story "The Winning of Barbara Worth".

June 22: No excitement this morning at G. Q. Worked all morning fixing the hinges on the Port light, and spent the afternoon working on the Signalman's knife.

June 23: No excitement at G.Q. again this morning, but almost before we'd eaten we went back again for shore fire support, and stayed until noon.
 Word by radio that the U.S. Fleet (the other port, not us) were engaging the Jap fleet between here and the Philippines.
 We anchored about 2 o'clock here out in the

217

bay quite far at Saipan Harbor to refuel cans, and probably to remove empty ammunition cans, and so set zet before the second deck, and consequently did very little today. No G.Q. this evening.
    G.Q. sounded unexpectedly after dark. Seems a torpedo bomber sneaked in and dropped two torpedos, one of which caught the MARYLAND in the screws. We got under way incredibly and stayed in G.Q. to give fire support to troops in Saipan.

June 24: Nothing much today. We were in G.Q all morning, and again all afternoon for fire support.
    The dope is that the MARYLAND went back. The rest of the 5th Fleet encountered and sank 13 Jap ships including 4 carriers, one battleship, and shot down 300 planes.
    Worked on windshield wiper arms all morning. We have the Admiral aboard. G.Q. this afternoon. We fired a good deal, and went to the opposite side of Saipan from where we've been operating. G.Q. on A A and secondary tonight.

June 25: Worked on a knife for the signalman, one for a cook (George) and Lemon this forenoon. Played cards on the quarterdeck all afternoon.
    We left Saipan after dark last night for Eniwetok and we're supposed to arrive Wednesday so want to do some writing tonight.

June 26: Fixed elevating brake on the starboard searchlight and a shutter leave for the 12". Got a piece of bakelite for a knife handle. We had G.Q. this evening.

June 27: Worked on 12" shutter and finished a knife handle for George (the cook).

June 28: Tested and cleaned searchlights. We anchored at_____ about noon. Was wrestling

with Carnes and he sure put a kink in my neck. Hope it isn't out-of-place again.
 They are taking on ammunition tonight.

June 29: Had to rake up some material for new shutter springs today and was pretty busy all day. Still no letter from Clara Mae, and I've about begun to wonder if there will be any, for the mail must be nearly sorted.

June 30: Things were in pretty bad shape in Turret 3, and most of the boys worked all last night. 180° most all day in the Rheostat Room. Fixed a windshield wiper, and a shutter, and wrote three letters. Now I want to study a bit.

July 1: Saturday - Made some springs for 12" searchlights.

July 2: They took me off watch on the searchlights, which we haven't stood since leaving Pearl Harbor (about a month), and I'm at the afterboard. Got in a big bunch of new recruits today.
 Played Hearts nearly all day at the afterboard. Got a letter from Mother, but none yet from Clara Mae. Surely something must have happened!

July 3: Cleaned mechanisms on 24" lights. Played Hearts until about 10 at night in the Rheostat room.

July 4: 8-12 watch - studied - ate a heck of a big dinner, and took a nap in the Rheostat room after getting paid about 1:30. Had an air alert while in the wash room this evening and planes came within 15 or 20 minutes.

July 5: Set up steaming locker in Rheostat room.

Had mid watch. Got a letter from Dorothy.

July 6: Got and washed a new bed bag, then I got some stuff from the canteen and made shutter springs.

July 7: Field day! What a job! It hasn't been cleaned here at the Aft. Bd. for so long it sure was tough. Managed a nap on searchlight platform from about 2 to 4 in afternoon.

July 8: Personal inspection, but had the watch at Aft. Bd. Also caught the B-4 as they changed from battle-cruising to the port watch. Did a bit of studying.

July 9: Took a nap on the searchlight platform while they looked for me to give me a ballot card.

July 10: Haven't heard from Clara Mae, but decided to write a short line, and we're pulling out tomorrow.

July 11: Worked on windshield wiper while stood watch at Aft. Bd. (We're underway for Guam). They are painting the Aft. Bd.

July 12: Painted locker at Aft. Bd.

July 13: Studied after checking lights - Stood watch 4-8 and 6-8.

July 14: G. Q. early. We bombarded Guam with no opposition of big guns. We ate sandwiches on our stations. Some trouble with the 12" light bulbs.

July 15: G. Q. No breakfast, dinner or supper at the tables. Secured early - 12-4 watch.

I had a queer dream about a white horse. (after I awoke it seemed like the horse was Old Monte). I'd even forgotten there was a horse by that name, but it came to me instantly when I awakened. I was in the hills at home, and things were beautiful with the freshness of Spring, when suddenly there was an accident, a catastrophy, and the horse fell down, on down, and died. However, it seemed more than the horse that died, and there were bitter tears, and the saving of precious keepsakes belonging to someone dear was involved. Oh, well, what's in a dream? Sometimes they are so real, though, that they leave a queer feeling, and a sensation of unrest behind.

<u>July 16</u>: G. Q. and firing all day. We took off for Saipan after dark, and got here by daylight. Checked battery and played cards.

<u>July 17</u>: Worked all day and fixed shutter motor (24 lts.) and port windshield wiper.

<u>July 18</u>: 8-12 watch. Worked on windshield wiper in Rheo. room this afternoon. We're underway for Guam again.

<u>July 19</u>: Bombarded again. Ate sandwiches on stations at noon.

<u>July 20</u>: Bombarded, and they ran me out of my sleeping place on Turret 7, so I slept on a blanket with Joe.

<u>July 21</u>: Stretched my hammock in a new place on Turret 7, and nearly didn't get up for G.Q. We bombarded all day, and they landed the first troops. We had sandwiches and cakes on our stations. I practically slept all day - didn't get a shower yet - watch 6-8.

July 22: We left Guam and are back to bombard Tinian.

July 23: We've bombarded Tinia all day. They seem to have some gun implacements that are pretty hard to put out. We received special praise from some of the other ships for our good work in this respect.

July 24: Up at G.Q. and sort of stretched out after a nap in the usual place on the overhead st. bd. side of the signal bridge. We had been bombarding pretty heavily all morning, and the landing barges were going in in waves for a beach head, when we caught it.

It seems we hadn't got all of their guns out. In fact, there must have been quite a nest of them   , for we caught some 22 direct hits in about 4 minutes. The first I knew of it I saw water fly abeam, and I looked down to see where the first one had hit the focicle, and saw some blood and half a man here and there. I stayed with my perch for quite a while, but I couldn't tell where they were coming from, and I got a glass to look around. Then we started to turn and a shell hit to spray us with schrapnel. I felt its burning sting, and right then I began looking for the sheltered side. Several on the bridge were hit, and an arm, blood, and pieces of flesh strew the deck blown up from the 2 m m mount where the projecticle hit. After it was all over we had close to 40 dead, and about twice that number wounded.
    I was pretty busy with the electrical work as a fire started in the flag room, but later I found time to help carry the dead back to the officer's wash room where we piled them up like cord wood. I was might well-played out at the end of the day!

July 25: At anchor at Saipan. I worked on my lights, and sort of got them in shape, but one cable is cut somewhere. I tried to trace it down, but the circuit Nos. are all mixed and I got the wrong one.

July 26: 8-12 watch. I was going to fix that cable but there were others working there and no room for one more, so I let it go for an early start tomorrow.

July 27: Heck of a place to work, but I got the light working, though there is still a bit of work for Johnston this afternoon while I'm on watch. We got underway for Guam (I guess) to unload our ammunition through the guns preparation to leaving and to get fixed up.

July 28: We arrived at Guam last evening, and I went to G.Q. to stand by all day. We never fired a shot all day. One can drew fire from the beach, and I saw what appeared to be a mine go off among some ships close to the beach.

July 29: It was a little cooler today, and I had a good rest. We were standing by all day again, but we never fired. A big game is going on at the board, so I guess I'll take another shower and seek my hammock.

July 30: 8-12 watch. Studied, checked lights, washed, and fooled around this afternoon.
    We are supposed to have a storm sometime tonight, but it's 12, and I don't think it's bad yet. I stood by on the Secondary Unit and fired star shelis.

July 31: We're still at Guam standing by. Had 12-4 watch, wrote letters, but I couldn't mail them.

AUGUST 1944

August 1: I was sleepy, but I worked on the bridge all morning in the rain. Most everyone flunked out this afternoon, but Mr. Page lined me out for some more work on the bridge. (Ha) Lemon says I'm to change to I.C. tomorrow.

August 2: We were at G.Q. for shore bombardment all day. I didn't change to I.C. One of the 24" lenses broke.

August 3: We left Guam for Eniwetok early this morning. I had the 8-12 watch, so I didn't get the search lens in until this afternoon.

August 4: I changed to I.C. today. I showed Reynolds the set up on lights this morning, and I had the watch this afternoon.

August 5: I helped Schewell (I.C.) put some cables in machine shop to Case Mateo.

August 6: Herring and I layed out on the quarter deck and slept all morning, then I straightened my locker, and did a bit of work in O.D. shack this afternoon.

August 7: We struck out for Pearl Harbor at 5:30 this morning. I had the 8-12 watch, then I helped Hoey in casemates this afternoon...wrote to Mother, Ruby, and Aunt Alta.

August 8: Reimensnider and I worked on box in casemates. 12-4 watch.

August 9: Bias and I worked on sound power phones.

August 10: 4-6 watch and 6-8 watch, worked I.C. tracing a sound power cable.

August 10: We crossed the International date line so this is the 10th again! Oh, well. 8-12 watch, studied, and I did some sewing for Herring and Elmhirst.

August 11: 12-4 watch. I studied, but I won't be ready to go up this time.

August 12: We pulled into Pearl Harbor about 5 o'clock. I had the watch at the Aft Board, so I didn't have to change to whites, and go up.

August 13: NO liberty. Quite a bit of mail came aboard. I had two letters from Dorothy, but still none from Clara. My watch was changed from the Aft. Bd. to I.C., and I sleep at the Fwd Gyro now.

August 14: We left Pearl Harbor for Bremerton about 6 or 7 this morning. It was a lovely morning, and I stayed on deck until about time for quarters, and I enjoyed it.

August 15: I finished up a sheath for Lemon's knife, and one for mine, too. I've done a lot of running since I came to I.C. but I took it a bit easier today.

August 16: I stood watch at the Fwd Bd. this morning while Young went up for the exam. I worked on a knife for one of the cooks this afternoon.

August 17: I had quite a bit of trouble with the 2J V circuit in the Ice room. Worked on the Move bridge, too.

August 18: This morning I got up as soon as the lights went on and washed my top hammock. It was sure dirty. 8-12 watch. I sewed a jumper and crows for Drown.

August 19: I sewed a jumper for Stroud on the 12-4 watch last night. Then I got up early this morning again and washed my other hammock, got it dried, and ready to sleep in this evening.

August 20: I could see the lights from shore when I went off watch this morning. We entered the sound some two hours ahead of that. The morning was cold and hazy, much damper than when we left in_____ it seemed, and more foggy. I stretched out in the I.C. room, and I didn't get up until nearly noon chow; but it was still hazy out. We made one stop for some Yard Big Shots to come aboard.
At 4 this evening before I came down for Watch, the weather was swell. I would have liked to have stayed out, but didn't have blues on.

August 21: I rated liberty at 3 this afternoon, but I stayed in and wrote some letters. We aren't in dry dock yet, but they are doing welding, and other repairs.

August 22: I didn't rate today. I had the Fwd. Bd. watch 4-8, and I wrote some more letters.

August 23: I was going on liberty, but Lemon's wife was up. He was worried about going over and getting her straightened out, so I stayed in his place. I wrote a couple more letters and Lemon took them to P.O. for me.

August 24: I haven't done a thing all day. I did fix this pen at Fwd. Bd. and loafed. Watch 8-12. Stuck some snapshots in my album. Received letters from Dot, Ina, and Ruby all 20th and 21st of July.

August 25: I went over to Bremerton on liberty this evening and got little Stanley some color books, then I sent Clara some roses. I saw a show and came home about 11.

August 26: Worked on Main Control putting in a 2JV circuit. Stood watch 12-4.

August 27: We moved our ship, the good, old U.S.S. COLORADO to the big crane.

August 28: I went over to Seattle and went to the P.O. to get some stamps and mail Dot's letter and one to the Studio for some enlargements. Went out to the ice arena to find it closed, so I went skating at Ballard.

August 29: Rated again this evening, but I stayed and let La Point go in my place.

August 30: Stood the 8-12 watch, then I had to get up at 3:30 for we are moving to dry dock. I got a nap though before going on watch.

August 31: I went on liberty. I took my skates and bought a bag for them. I phoned Clara Mae, which cost $8 something; but I could hardly make out what she said, so I'm still more or less in the dark. At least, I know she got my last letter and the flowers. I went on over skating...got in about 2 and slept till eight.

SEPTEMBER 1944

Sept. 1: I scarcely did a thing today but loaf around the shop. We are eating ashore now. 4-8 watch.

Sept. 2: La Point and I went to the Ship's dance at Craven Center. We fooled around a while afterward and didn't get in until late.

Sept. 3: I got up late and went over to Seattle and fooled around until about 7 then went skating. I met Rickson, and he introduced me to his girl friend and her friend. I was surprised to find I already had met them. I got in pretty late, so I got a bunk and slept at the Y in Seattle for about an hour and a half, then bunked with a queer. What a night!

Sept.4: I sneaked off and took a nap in T 4 this morning as I didn't have a great lot to do.

Sept. 5: I got off without a watch today, which was plenty lucky. I spent a good deal of time answering Dorothy's letters thanking me for the pen and asking me down. It sure looks like things are off between Clara Mae and me. I hate it like H---- but I sure can't grow any younger!

Sept. 6: I'm standing by for Reynolds tonight. About all I did today was make a cake turner for Lemon.

Sept. 7: Got liberty in Reynolds place tonight. Terrill and I went skating. Zaic came out later, and we had a lot of fun.

Sept. 8, 9, 10: (No entry)

September 11: I've rated a leave.

Sept. 12: My leave started this morning. Reynolds and I were the first in to see about air transportation. He got a ride South, but I couldn't catch one East, and I nearly gave up going altogether. I spent all day looking for a job, but decided, after sleeping on it, that I didn't want one. Anyhow, I took the train for

Cheyenne, Wyoming, about 12:30, September 13.

Not much happened on the road. I played cards, and I slept what I could. We got into Cheyenne on the morning of the 15th at about 8 o'clock.

I was surprised to find I didn't have much trouble in hitch hiking to Wheatland where I visited with Grandma Menefee, Uncle Alvin, and Uncle Wayne's. Then I borrowed Wayne's car and Myrna and I drove over to Guernsey to Betty's, and she helped us to find Ruby's place. I stayed with Ruby and Bill the night of the 15th, then Myrna, Betty, and I drove back to Wheatland about noon. Betty and I went on a drive with Uncle Alvin in the truck. We went to a show afterwards.

Bill and Ruby came over about 6 and we went up to the hills to the folks.

Bill, Doris, Betty and I went out hunting, but with no luck. Bill and Betty left in the evening, Sunday 17th.

<u>Monday, Sept 18</u>: We got up late, then Ruby, Doris, and I went over by Tom's Mill and got the gun.

<u>Sept. 19</u>: Ina and Glen came over after their mail, so I got to see them. Doris and I went hunting across the Park afterwards.

<u>Sept. 20</u>: Ruby, Doris, and I went across the Park again. Aunt Alta came for a short visit Thurs. 21. Buster and Ina came in the evening after we returned from hunting and stayed all night. Buster and Ina went hunting upon Laramie Peak the next morning, and got a big one about noon. I nearly broke my back carrying it in.

<u>Sept. 23</u>: Saturday - Stanley and I went fishing

up the Cottonwood.

    Bill came in the evening, Sunday the 24th. Betty, Myrna, Herman, Uncle Alvin, etc. came in, and we all went down on the North Laramie River fishing. So much fun! And we danced at the Barncastle to Dad's fiddle after we got in. Company didn't leave until about midnight, so we got to bed about midnight.

Sept. 25: Monday - We got out a little earlier and we got ready to go. It was time to travel back to Bremerton.

    I fooled around in Wheatland with Ruby and Bill until about four, then I caught a ride to Cheyenne. I spent a couple hours in Cheyenne, then boarded the train for Seattle. I had a seat with an Army flyer. He and I got with some other people, and we played cards. They changed my seat the next morning while we were over having a game at a different car. There I sat with a couple of girls. We got acquainted and went to dinner together. At dinner another sailor joined us. We played cards, and had a good time until they had to get off and change trains at Pendleton at two o'clock. I sure didn't get much sleep. I changed trains at Portland, and played cards with Lemon until nearly 3 o'clock when the train got into Seattle Sept. 27.

    In Seattle I got a hotel room, ate a bite, (ate at the Y after bathing) and I was going skating, but from the Y I got off on a supposed Birthday party with other sailors. We had lunch at the girls' house (May) and then we all went dancing until about 1 o'clock, so I missed my sleep again.

Sept. 28: Thursday - Arose at 8 o'clock, and caught the 9:30 ferry back to Bremerton.

Pipiz and I had a ham and egg breakfast in Bremerton, and got back aboard ship ½ hour early (before noon). I unpacked my things and read my mail, then readied myself to go out with Weise as he wanted me to meet his wife. We went to where she and his mother stay. We then went out and ate. After eating we went on over to Art's.
   Red and Zane were there. They had a few drinks. The three of us, Red, Zane, and I took the bus back, and we finally managed to catch the ferry after so long a time. We stayed at the Y in Bremerton over night.

Sept. 29: Guess it's about time to settle down and get on schedule again.
       Well, I'm on watch at I.C. So much for catching up in the diary. Now it's letter writing next.

Sept. 30: Rated liberty, so Adams and I went over to Seattle ice skating. It was pretty crowded, but we had a bit of fun, anyhow.

OCTOBER 1944

Oct. 1: Worked on a ground on the 3 E P. Main Control. Liberty expired early for the other watch.

Oct. 2: We pulled out away from the dock this morning...got the 3EP clear finally.

Oct. 3, 4, 5, 6: These days we fooled around in Pudget Sound. We were in and out. Got our mail at Port Townsend, then we pulled out for Long Beach or San Pedro.

Oct. 7: Pay day. I didn't draw any, so worked.

231

Oct. 8: Sunday - Worked on fire alarm circuits with Adams, on wind indicator with Spencer, studied Math, mustered on quarterdeck...The *news* is NO liberty in Long Beach.

Oct. 9: Well, here it is again...my birthday, and the most exciting thing that happened was the mail call, and a letter from Mary Delle and Mother. I worked all afternoon on the foremast, wired the indicator, G.Q. this morning.

Oct. 10: Worked fire alarm circuit, bought 3 Parker fountain pens, wrote letters in the evening before G.Q. at 8:30. It is rumored that 38 of the COLORADO fellows took one of the whale boats last night and went over the hill to Long Beach. G.Q. practice 8-10:30.

Oct. 11: G.Q. on the battery a lot today, and zet set, so I didn't do much (slept a bit)... saw some whales while working on a phone bell up at sky control this evening.

Oct. 13: The planes went out and brought the mail in. I worked on the wind indicater.

Oct 14 & 15: G.Q. and drill is about all this week has been. Fired on Island.

Oct. 16: Put in a bell and SP. phone at Ice Machine.

Oct. 17: Battery problem in morning, fueled a can in afternoon, worked on bridge.

Wed. 18: Pulled into Long Beach. The other section rated and went ashore. I had to change lockers, hold field day, and what not. Anyway, I was on the run all day...wrote and received several letters.

Oct. 19: I pushed around trying to finish, and get ready for liberty and inspection at the same time...got ashore about 2:30 or 3. Zaic and I fooled around, drank beer, and went out ice skating at 6:30 until 11, drank beer there until 12, ate, and hitch hiked back to Long Beach, caught the 2 o'clock-in-the-morning boat back to the ship.

Oct. 20: Reveille at 5, so I had about 2 hrs. sleep, then I missed chow for another 2 hours. I had to get ready for Admiral Inspection at 8:30. Then I stood around until noon in dress blues. I got a nap between 12:30 and 2.

Oct. 21: I wanted to get off early, but couldn't. I slept behind the board a while, and just caught the first boat over. Hitchhiked to Hawthorne. Les and Dorothy picked me up while after groceries. We had dinner and talked until about 1:30. Then we slept until four. We ate breakfast, and they drove me back.

Oct. 22: Sunday - I got no sleep at all for I've spent most all day writing to Clara Mae. Here's a little bit of what I wrote: Yesterday I was over to see Dot and Les. How good it was to see them both looking so much better! Yes, even Dorothy after her operation! And the best thing, they seem to be happier together, too. I guess it takes a little scare, a little pain, and a little care now and then to show people how much they really have even IF it isn't the perfect bliss they dreamed of. Yes! our illusions soon fade. Believe me, Clara Mae, nothing will ever be perfect unless we believe it is. NO couple, Dot and Les, Buck and Ellen, or any other shall be happy unless they think they are. Do not look for a perfect happiness for there is none until you have built it.

Oct. 23: Monday - I took liberty at 1400 and took C. M.'s letter over. Zaic and I went skating out to Hynes again, and I traded my skates off on a new pair that were larger. They cost me $14 with some guards for the blades. We stayed at the A M Y overnight.

Oct. 24: We left Long Beach Harbor, and got underway about 1400 for Pearl Harbor. I was a little disappointed as I thought we might get to S. F. I guess, I'm more blue than disappointed. It seems I'm only wasting my life, and I'm already too old to be wasting anymore years!
   Clara Mae's picture came in today's mail. Gee, it's good! What I wouldn't give to be her age again, all the good times, the vitality, enthusiam, and all the hopes of youth ahead. "Well, God bless you, Clara, and keep you safe, and guide you straight on a harmonious path of life and Love. God has also decreed I can be no younger than I am today."

Oct. 25: Worked up at Radio 5 nearly all day running cable and putting in a sound power box. I made a mistake on these notes. I got C.M.'s picture today instead of yesterday. I put a glass over it, and stood it in my locker.
   We got our booster shots today, one in each arm.

Oct. 26: I felt like the duce all day, and worse toward evening...a fever, headache, and my arm is sore.

Oct. 27: I felt better today, held a little field day, and worked on a reel for a S.P. phone line for off the ship service.

Oct. 28: We were supposed to have Capt's inspection, but the water is so rough and coming over

the rail, so they postphoned it. Good! I
did some more work on the reel, and I felt first
rate this morning after all night in.

Oct. 29: I sort of loafed today, worked on
sound power circuit this morning but didn't
do any good.

Oct. 30: Monday - I worked on the same circuit
this morning. G.Q. this afternoon. We pulled
into Pearl Harbor about 5:30 or so.

Oct. 31: I thought I'd get liberty today, but
didn't so I wrote four letters. Some stores contain wool mits, and winter overshoes. It looks
like we may go North.

NOVEMBER 1944

Nov. 1: Wednesday - The other section rated
today, and got off at 11:30. I worked on SP
circuit JS all morning, and on a SP circuit
on the fo'c's'le this afternoon.

Nov. 2: Got liberty at 11:30. I rode right into Honolulu, and after buying an ice cream at the
Y I spent the rest of my time shopping; mostly
for Xmas cards.

Nov. 3: Stenciled some clothes, put up a cabinet for blue prints in the I.C. room.

Nov. 4: Terrill and I went over on the base in
our dungareens today---Sub Base Iea and fleet
landing canteen, bought a few Xmas presents.

Nov. 5: Today being Sunday, no one worked very
hard. I spent most of my time wrapping Xmas
things, and addressing cards.

Nov. 6: We pulled out from Pearl Harbor, and we're headed somewhere near Yap, I guess, and maybe later to the Phillipines. Worked putting in a new cable on the focicle this morn, and wound twine on our S.P. telephone line rest of this afternoon.

Nov. 7: I've been sleeping behind the I.C. board because it's cooler. I got up at 7:30 and we had personel inspection at 8. I bought $6 worth in stamps and 2 towels, a shirt, and comb, and a pocket knife. Worked up by ships canteen. Watch afternoon, and mid. Wrote to Myrna, and a letter to Standard Art Studios ordering enlargements.

Nov. 9: Worked on the Q circuit and morning Howler all day. Wrote a few letters.

Nov. 10: We crossed the International dateline, so there was no 11th or Friday.

Nov. 12: 8 to 12 watch. Worked on a bell and front (wood) for Dygart's radio. Worked on cable up by canteen. Got my hair all cut off. Wrote. Worked a bit in forenoon, but took it easy in afternoon.

Nov. 13: Worked on focicle and below at canteen.

Nov. 14: Helped Hoey up at C.I.C. this morn and worked on focicle and by canteen in afternoon. I'm still sleeping behind the I.C. board; but it's too hot to sleep good. We're just having G.Q. in morning...must be moving to the Phillipines.

Nov. 14: I had the 8-12 watch, so worked around the shop. I sent Mother & Dad's Xmas package off, and must get the rest of my cards off as tomorrow is the last day the office will be open!

Nov. 15: Worked in I.C. room on a box to plug the coffee maker in. 12-4 watch. Darn it's hot sleeping behind the board!

Nov. 17: We anchored at _____ sometime between 7 & 9 this morning. We had a mail call after the show this evening but I didn't get any.

Nov. 18: Reveille at 0400 and we were underway for Leyete at 5:30. I worked in the I.C. room...coffee maker, etc.

Nov. 19: 8-12 watch - fixed a knife sheath for Brown, basked in the sun at noon, and slept behind board afterward.

Nov. 20: We reached Leyte and sent boats off. (No mail). Worked around the I.C. room. 12-4 watch. Got a steaming locker in I.C.

Nov. 21: It was beautiful this morning at G.Q. These islands look as though they might almost be worth fighting for. Hoey and I worked on the 23 T S.

Nov. 22: Bias and I fixed the 23 J S this morning. I fooled around the shop figuring on a bench this afternoon.

Nov. 23: THANKSGIVING - 8-12 watch. Worked on bench - Nice dinner - G.Q right after dinner, and one Jap plane ventured in close enough to be fired on, but don't think it got hurt any, at least, it looked O.K.

We've been having several such raids each day, but it's the first time yet they've come in close enough to see. I sort of took it lazy like everyone else this afternoon.

Nov. 24: I went out on the quarterdeck at 7:45 with a line (telephone) for refueling, but didn't use it. 12-4 watch (G.Q. watch). Two planes came close in, and some of the ships fired. We didn't fire, but we saw a P 38 shoot one of them down. G. Q. again about 7-9. There seemed to be quite a lot of Jap planes scattered about. Some of the other ships fired several different times.

Nov. 25: Alanzo Stroud left this morning. I worked in his place up near CIC today. G.Q. and air alerts several times as usual.

Nov. 26: Most everyone flaked out today. Lemon, Spencer, and I worked this morning up at CIC. I made a shelf for my locker door up at the ship fitter's shop this afternoon.

Nov. 27: Nothing exciting at G.Q. this morning. 8-12 watch. Worked on bench in I.C. room till chow call blew and soon after G.Q. sounded. We hadn't much more than got manned when they announced we were under air attack. We could see them closing in. It was impossible to estimate how many there were, for there was a heavy layer of low-lying clouds, but with occasional holes, and a higher and lighter layer of clouds. The first we saw was two ships (dive bombers) coming down on the ST. LOUIS. The first they shot down, and it fell short of the target, the second was also apparently bad hit, but managed to hit its objective. The Jap's object seems to be purely suicidal, and they must have locked their controls, coming straight in from aft to crash on the deck.
    There is word that the MONTPIELIER got a hit, too. The fire wasn't out on the ST. LOUIS yet when we saw two planes coming in from Aft on us. The guns opened up. When the planes got in close I moved around to the forward part of the mast

as I could see the one was going to crash us, so I didn't see just as much as I could have. The plane dropped a bomb through the galley deck pay office, and strew rubbish all along the port side, then crashed into the water. I don't know just what happened to the other, but I guess, it crashed close off the port side, too.

Either the bomb or the plane took the barrel off about the middle of the 5 in 51 in the aft casemate (Port side). We brought the fire hose down from the bridge, and picked up several Jap souvenirs. We ate late noon chow, then I came down to the shop a while, went up and washed, and just made it to evening chow. I'd just gotten through when G.Q. sounded again. Nothing happened this time, though they got several close enemy contacts.

It is being reported that the Japs used our I.f.f. (signal code) this the reason they got in so close before they were spotted as Enemy Craft. Also, 2 P 38s and one _____ are reported down, probably by our own fire. 23 Jap planes were downed altogether. The task force got 11, 3 of which are reported credited to the COLORADO, and 12 were downed by aircraft.

Nov. 28: The Captain said over the speakers this noon that only 10 enemy planes shot down altogether, one by a P 38. There were around 20 attacking planes.

One dived on the MARYLAND, too, but sustained a direct hit in mid air, and missed its target.

Enemy planes were overhead again at 2 o'clock this morning, and we went to G.Q., but it was pretty dark. The clouds were pretty thick, and they never attacked.

After the regular 5:30 G.Q. this morning I never ate, but came on down. I slept behind the board, and didn't get up till chow call at noon. Worked on bench afternoon while I had the watch. Went to G.Q. once during that time, and again right during chow at evening. At midnight we had G.Q. again. One plane is said to have come in and scraped a destroyer missing with its bomb.

Nov. 29: 12-4 watch last night. Had G.Q. at 12 just about time to relieve the watch so I stood till reveille. We were up on the bridge early with our telephone lines. We were up there all day in the rain, and we got 6 destroyers refueled and some of them supplied. We're getting rid of our fuel as we're going to Manna (sp?) to get patched up again.

I'd just come down and relieved the 4-6 watch when G.Q. sounded. They cast the lines off quickly, and the destroyer was hauling out fast when I got up on my station. It wasn't long before the firing started abeam of us. The clouds were low and couldn't see the planes for some time. Then one came down out of the clouds off our port beam, diving on the cruiser _____ close by. A good many ships including our Port battery turned loose. Our 40s screamed and seemed to be right on while still high in the air the plane burst in flame and smoke to come plunging down to a watery grave a very good distance from its mark. It sent up a large pillar of smoke, burned furiously for several minutes then dissappeared. The COLORADO, the ST. LOUIS, and 4 destroyers headed out for Manna, and were just emerging from the low cloud bank to move opensky when 6 more Jap planes came in, close tailed by P 38s. They eased down but went back up as our guns opened fire.

Later, far back under the fog, we saw the fleet open up with great bursts of AA fire. There were huge spouts of water very close by the MARYLAND, and then a great flame and cloud of smoke. A bomb had struck her bow. We pulled steadily out behind. The firing ceased. The moon came out. Soon we secured for the night and all is quiet.

Nov. 30: G.Q. a little later this morning. We turned directly around early this morning and headed back for Leyete. The ST. LOUIS went on.
 The rumor is that the Japs were in the bay on the fleet again last night after we left, and the MARYLAND sustained another hit. She is going back in our place.
 Bunks were let down at 0900, and nearly everyone flaked out who wasn't at G.Q. on the A A battery. I put the shelf in my locker and made 3 more keys for my padlock.
 At evening chow we're back in Leyte Bay.

DECEMBER 1944

Dec. 1: 8-12 watch. I drew prints for lockers in the battery locker below, and one for a coupling for the fan we're installing. There was a submarine alert this evening, and they dropped a lot of depth charges. Torpedos were said to have been fired about chow time. At 11 o'clock Condition Zd is still set below the second deck.

Dec. 2: Zet set nearly all day. Hardly did a thing but paste pictures in my album. Have the 12-4 watch, so guess I'll turn in early.

Dec. 3: Not a very hard watch, but worked all day with Hoey on the 31 J S at combat while everyone else flaked out. Pulled out (for the Palau Islands I think).

Dec. 4: Worked on the bench cutting angle iron. Stood in canteen line. About 4 in the afternoon we anchored at Palau Island.

Dec. 5: 8-12 watch. Worked on bench. Wrote letters.

Dec. 6: Worked on bench. Wrote 2 letters. They had a swim call this evening, but I didn't go.

Dec. 7: Worked on bench in morning. Stood in canteen line about all the afternoon.

Dec. 8: Cut a top out for the bench.

Dec. 9: Worked on a small bench for the fan. Still at the Palau Islands.

Dec. 10: Sunday - 12-4 watch. Fooled around all day. Changed my bunk from behind the board to on the new bench I made. We left the Palau Islands, and we're headed back to Leyte Gulf. From there we go to the other conquest in the Phillipines.

Dec. 11: 4-6 watch - fixed 36s, fixed light for my locker.

Dec. 12: We refueled 3 cans today, fixed 36 v fireroom 6, and checked others. Washed one of my hammocks.
    We have 56 ships and 200 planes in this and one other group. We're pulling into Leyte Gulf tonight, and then on into the strait.

Dec. 13: We went through the strait, and on out into the Sulu Sea. Nothing happened at G.Q. this morning as expected. About 1300 we were called to G.Q. One of our planes crashed into the water coming in. I could see the smoke yet when I got on the bridge. Nothing more happened until right after I'd finished evening chow.
    Then G.Q. sounded again. I had hardly reached

my station before two planes were seen coming in on a destroyer. They launched torpedos. One went back out, then the other one crash dived and a cloud of smoke rolled up from the destroyer where the plane had hit and took off her stack.
    The last we saw her she was way behind still smoking. Fighter planes went aloft from our carriers. We didn't fire a shot, and the enemy planes came in several times before we secured. Most were shot down or driven off by our fighters, or by ships farther out. (Washed other hammock today).
    Kistner says, "Morinduque Island is our objective," but I say Mindoro is.

Dec. 14: We kept running to G.Q. all day, but it was usually all over by the time I got up on the bridge, and didn't see much. Bogies kept coming in but only in very small groups or alone, and were mostly intercepted and shot down by our fighters before they could get over the ship formation. One flew directly over us in the evening, but too high to reach with AA fire. Our worst losses were plane crashes in landing. Three cracked up this way today. One was close enough that I watched the men get into their rubber life raft. 12-4 watch - fixed SP phone on hoist 11, and in the afternoon made up a test phone.

Dec. 15: (written Dec. 17) Air attack was heavy today. In the morning quite a number of planes came in. It was pretty cloudy and most of them were too high to see but we and other ships sure laid down a barrage. Schrapnel flew, and hit close by making one feel like ducking behind something. One heavy Jap two-motored plane came in low, dead ahead and unobserved until close in. I was looking directly at it. We opened fire as he dived on the carrier _____ close off our stbd bow. I ran from the Port to the Stbd. side

243

and saw him crash in the water close by with a huge explosion, flame, and smoke to burn fiercely some time.

Dec. 16: For some reason or other we turned around and headed back toward Leyte. Was at G.Q. off and on, but no real excitement.

Dec. 17: G. Q. about noon as we started back through the Straits. Through the glass I could see cabin-sailing boats, and what looked to be people on the beach.

Dec. 18: Fixed 22 JS at combat. 12-4 watch - Got a little mail today. Betty sent her picture too. Wrote some letters this evening. Guess we headed right on out of Leyte Gulf and for the Palau Islands. No. G.Q. today.

Dec. 19: We pulled in at the Palau Islands. Worked putting up geer lockers at fwd. bd. Pay-day but I didn't draw any.

Dec. 20: We left the Palau Island for _____ about noon. I finished setting up the lockers below at the battery locker.

Dec. 21: Today we crossed the International date line - my mistake - we cross the Equator tomorrow but they started indrifting today and cut off all the polliwog's hair. I helped Dygert with a gadjet for his radio and cut a piece for the fan shelf at the foundry.

Friday Dec. 22: We crossed the Equator this evening about six o'clock at 145° 19 N 1" east. Helped Hoey on A. calls at O.D. shack this morn and had the 12-4.

Dec. 23: Saturday - Ground knives for Lemon and Baker at the power shop this morning and went on liberty over on Peleliu Island this afternoon - not much over there. I got 2 bottles of beer and went swimming. Found a few sea shells I'm going to save.

Dec. 24: Sun. - Sort of laid around today. Wrote letters and waited for the next mail call. Got out the Xmas box Les & Dot sent me and we ate the cake and candy. I don't know where they got the where-with but a lot of the fellows were sure getting pie-eyed.

Dec. 25: Mon. - Christmas Day though it didn't seem like it. There were working parties all divisions. I worked in C.I.C. a while this afternoon. Got a few letters but still none from Leslie or Clara Mae. Ellen said Parrs have moved back to Calif. though.

De. 26: Tues. - Worked with Munn this morning. Finished the souvenir necklace I was making out of part of that Jap plane. This afternon we

LEFT THE ADMIRALTY ISLANDS

Dec. 27: When I awaken this morning my bed has oil all over it from that motor on the overhead leaking, so had to wash my hammock this noon. Worked this morning putting a phone in at steering motors, and fixed the fan shelf this afternoon.

Dec. 28: Shewelle gave me another map yesterday as I lost mine after I last wrote from the Philippines. Worked on the drawer slide for the work bench today. I'm starting to grow a mustache. It is now seven days old.
    General MacArthur is quoted as saying, "The

Leyte-Samar Campaign can now be regarded as closed, except for minor mopping-up operations. General Yamashita has suffered perhaps the greatest defeat in the military annals of the Japanese Army."

(On Leyte: The enemy lost 125,000 men, all but 500 prisoners killed. American casualties were about 2,750 killed and 8,500 wounded and missing. During the period of the invasion, the Japanese lost close to 3,000 planes, far more than they could replace....from <u>History of World War II</u> by Francis I. Miller)

U.S.S.COLORADO, Box 11
c/o Fleet P.O. S.F. Calif.
Dec. 28, 1944

Dear Sister: This old year surely is close to an end, so I guess I'll write you just one more letter in this old year. There isn't anything to tell, of course, but I do want to let you know that on Christmas day I rec'd your letter with the picture. I'm sure it is the very nicest gift you could have sent and I like it a lot. It is so much better than the one you and Mother had taken together.

Bet Stanley thought Uncle Wilbur's present was kind of a fraud this year. It was all I could get at the time though. I just came very close to having to leave the poor kid out altogether.

We had a swell Xmas dinner but nearly the whole ship had to turn to and work as there was an unusually lot to do. Maybe that made us enjoy our dinner more.

Still haven't heard from Leslie and I don't suppose we will be getting any more mail for a while now. I do hope this goes out. Will write again when I can. Love, Wilbur

<u>Dec. 29:</u> Fri. - Held field day so didn't do

much else. While drilling a hole to anchor the fan I broke the handle on the drill motor.
    Pulled in at the PALAU ISLAND.

Dec. 30: Saturday - Had Captain's inspection this morning - wash room hours are in effect again. Mail came in yesterday, but I didn't get any.
    We are heading back for the Philippines to complete that campaign. We are to have in our force 6 B.B., 6 Cruisers, together with destroyers, mine sweepers, etc. (4 carriers). After about 3 days of bombardment another force consisting of about 200 ships, a large number of which will be transports are coming in to land the Army, and we are to stand by until they are firmly established ashore, then we are to return by the Northern Passage.

Dec. 31: Sunday - I got fouled up on my dates some place. Yesterday was Sat. and not Wed.
    I didn't do much today. Studied a bit this morning, played cards on the quarter deck all afternoon until time to wash. I was going to the show but some other guy claimed my seat and it was so crowded that I came on down.

    (Author's Note: By the end of 1944, the U.S.S. COLORADO had steamed a total of 143,983 miles for the war years of 1942, 1943, and 1944. There was a total of 56,798 miles for the year of 1944 alone.
    By 1945, the U. S. was at the heighth of its strength with 3,4000,000 in the Navy...2,400,000 in the Army Air Forces.)

NEW YEAR'S EVE 1944-1945

ABOARD the U.S.S. COLORADO

via

Wilbur Parker's Diary

It could hardly have been expected ten years ago when yet the ends of a small but wonderful world reached only as far as the low foothills; melted away at the edge of a few small towns where the friendly mountains gave way to the vast open stretch of the Great Plains, or even six years...while the world was yet new with hope, with the fire of love like a promise of better things yet to be reflected in the white snow of the distant mountains.

Oh, no! no suspicion, no dream was there then of this distant Island; this tropic sun and far reach of water, of ship and shell, of war with death and horror. But all things must change (as this night gives evidence) and all on the pages of the past are the fairer pictures.... youth, the golden summer; hope, the clinging vine; Love, the budding tree that perished; the snow-clad peak; home, and peace, all on the pages of the past; while over PALAU the heat waves dance.

In the gulf is a vast Armada; Life, not a living but an existence; a future of memories. Still as the vine clings 'round the old dead stump we go on; toiling, the old year out, the New Year in, as silently the hands of the old clock turn 'round ticking off the last minutes of the old year.

No loud Hurrah! is there. No banging of pans or clanging bells, only a rustle as the men move in darkness on their stations.

Here give pause for some reflection, give

thought to the adage, "All things change," and guide this new year accordingly in the light of a better self.

For though there is small evidence the world will change overnight, or the greed of the men in power will be quenched in pity for their slain brothers...still is there in every man (even as these) many possibilities for improvement.

Certainly life has not taught Kindness, Honesty, or Respect for ones fellow man as a virtue to be cultivated, and the SERVICE! perhaps I should say; The NAVY, has marked it intolerable to one valuing his own welfare. Yet are there other virtues, and in these shall we trust...to these ends shall we strive to find and build a shrine of self-respect that in the loneliness of the future shall stand unashamed, clinging as the withered vine to life's last page.

JANUARY 1945

Jan. 1: Monday - Studied a bit at the I.G. room this morning and worked nearly all the rest of the day getting the J L circuit at sky control in order. Wrote a little if you might call it that and played a few games of Hearts with Ross, Hoey, and Specer.

We had a very good dinner between Palau and the Philippines. Oh, yes! at 0930 the Dr. gave us a little talk on skin care, etc. in the tropics.

Jan. 2: Took the fan apart and greased the bearings this morning while on watch. Finished fixing my other test phone this afternoon and studied this evening. Had G.Q. on the A.A. battery several times and we must be nearing Leyte Gulf,

New Years Eve 1944-1945

It would hardly have been expected ten years ago when yet the ends of a small but wonderful world reached only as far as the low foot-hills; melted away at the edge of a few small towns where the friendly mountains gave way to the vast open stretch of the great plains. Or even six years while the world was yet new with hope, with the fire of love like a promise of better things yet to be reflected in the white snow of the distant mountains.

Oh no, no suspicion, no dream was there then of this distant Island, this tropic sun and far reach of water, of sky and shell, of war with death and horror. But all things must change (as this night gives evidence) and all on the pages of the past are the fairer pictures, Youth, the golden summer, Hope, the clinging vine, Love, the bending tree that perished; the snow clad peak; home and peace, all on the pages of the past; while over Palau the heat waves dance. In the gulf is a vast Armada; life, not a living but an existence; a future of memories. Still as the vine clings 'round the old dead stump we go on toiling, the old year out the new year in; as silently the hands of those old clocks turn 'round ticking off the last minutes of the old year.

No loud Harrah! is there, no banging of pans or clanging bells only a rustle as the men move in darkness on their stations.

ON THE U.S.S. COLORADO

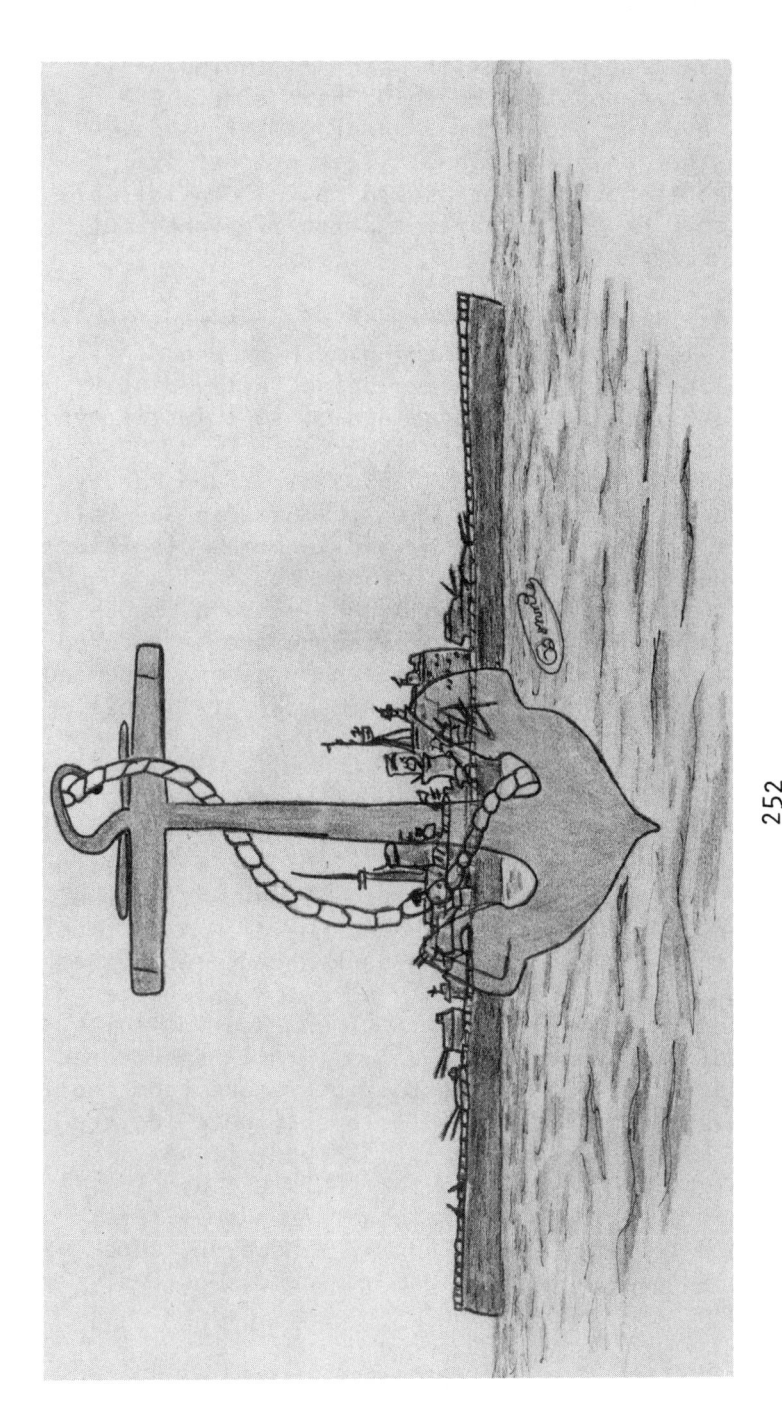

The NAVY has marked it intolerable to one valuing his own welfare!

Jan. 3: Wednesday - 12-4 watch - studied a bit as want if possible to go up next time. G.Q. this evening about dark. Heard an airplane motor hum as a Jap plane either crashed or dropped something far astern making considerable splash. G. Q. again right after midnight, but no excitement.

Jan. 4: Thursday - G.Q. right after I went on watch this morning. Nothing much happened. I'd no sooner got in bed after being relieved at 4 o'clock than G.Q. sounded again, so I just stayed up there until daylight.
   At evening chow G.Q. went again. Had hardly gotten upon the bridge when the Bamadie Bay (aircraft carrier) was hit by a dive bomber (suicide). It sneaked in on her before she could fire a shot. I have never seen such a cloud of smoke from a wounded ship before and before we secured, the crew had abandoned her, and she was torpedoed and sunk, though the fire and smoke still rose from the burning oil.

Jan. 5: Friday - Didn't try to do much today on account of G.Q. Studied a bit.
   Early this evening a number of Jap planes came in. At first all the firing was way aft in the other group of ships. Then as we drew away from the open sky toward a fog bank ahead, two planes dived   from ahead. They were low which prevented us from firing without endangering ships ahead. One dived for a can. I think she scored a near miss. There was too much smoke from shell fire and fog, and I was too busily watching the other and nearer plane as it dived. It came straight in and crashed the LOUIVILLE about center sky (though it was bad hit and afire) with a terrific explosion which, however, quickly cleared away. Report: one man dead, one badly injured and 15 others.

253

AMERICAN PLANE

Later a group of several planes came in aft again, and I saw these huge explosions and smoke as crash divers hit ship far astern in the other group. It was too far to see what actually did happen, but one aircraft carrier, a cruiser, and an Austrailian can were reported hit. I believe the damage to anyone was not very severe.

<u>Jan. 6</u>: Saturday - There is little use in trying to relate all the incidents of the day. Even if I could remember them all clearly enough for that purpose. It was indeed a long and trying day and it seems one's mental faculties are not at the highest at such times.

Had the 8-12 watch - got up at reveille to relieve the watch, and had just eaten and relieved the watch, gathered my clothes and rolled my bed when G.Q. sounded. I didn't get down again until after seven this evening.

It was a lovely morning, but with a rather high wind, and low-soaring cloud banks. I think I shall never forget the Island as I first saw it against the pink-edged thunder heads.

We lay fairly well out under open sky, but many of the other ships, especially aft, were under the clouds.

Our planes did a good job this morning, however, and not many Jap planes got through to the formation, and what did were shot down. I finally decided to nap and did so from about 9 till eleven, when we ate and planes started getting through again.

We didn't fire much this morning and did very little bombardment though we sent a few five-inch shells toward the Island. We opened up on one twin-motored bomber that crossed our bow. He dropped a bomb and just missed a destroyer ahead, but never was hit I believe, unless it was he turned back, for about that time a plane dived in from that direction through the smoke

and flack and was shot down quite a way ahead of the starboard beam.
About mid afternoon the ships all lined out and started into the Gulf (Lengayen). It was a beautiful sight...a great, long, string from horizon to horizon, grouped close, and steadily moving forward.
I read a story. We turned and went in toward land and back toward the way we had come. Fixed Salno from the 16-in. guns, which broke a search light lens, which I was trying to fix when the real trial came.
The Jap planes began to get through in rather alarming numbers. Three ships ahead, including the LOUISVILLE (again), the NEW MEXICO, (I think) and a can were hit almost simultaneously, a little later, men on life rafts and in jackets were seen in the water. We shot one down trying to crash us. The smoke was so heavy one couldn't see. The flack obscured the sky and schrapnel shell hit close off the stern, so I gave up even trying to see, and sought the sheltered side.
Finally things cleared up and we could see again. Firing continued further off, but no more got in close to us. I had some repair work to do on the phones and darkness slowly settled down. We secured and came to chow, which I don't know how the cooks managed to get together.
I forgot to mention the crash-diver that hit the CALIFORNIA this morning, and also, the plane that hedge-hopped off the Island, starboard straight for us soon after the formation lined up in a straight line to come in. We got him but he sure was in close before we did.
This is all a rather confusing picture of what really did happen, but as I say, a man isn't quite at his best at these times, and is inclined to look sharply ahead and put past moments aside with so little reflection that they are almost

"...the ships all lined out & started into the Gulf...what a beautiful sight!"

instantly forgotten.

Jan 7: Sunday - Things were a little more settled today though G.Q. started early and lasted all day until about 8:00 at night and a few planes got through. No damage was done, and I don't believe any planes were shot down by this unit of ships...the Japs dropped one flare before dawn. After that I slept till nearly eleven, after which we started bombarding. We went in first and bombarded the town (I guess it's the Capitol) there are several large buildings.
 Some fires were started but none to compare with those at Tarawa, Tinnian, etc.
 The bombardment lasted until about 1600 after which we started moving our way back out of the gulf. About dark the Japs came over (high) and dropped mines. We saw quite a few of these mines later on our way out. No planes were shot down, however, as they crossed high over the formation.

Jan. 8: Monday - Early a few planes tried to get through but were beat off.
 It was getting quite light and I was trying to take a nap when one finally succeeded. He was followed in by two of our fighters, which for some unknown reason were taken for Jap planes also. The Jap was first shot down, and one of our own soon followed. I saw it crash not too far out over the moates on the port side near the Island. The pilot got out so they say. Not much later another Jap plane got through, and tried to crash an Australian ship off our stbd. beam. He crossed with a great flame just the other side of her.
 We bombarded the rest of the day without being bothered.
 Refueled an Australian destroyer about noon and also one other. We took on some survivors from the destroyer. Their ship was torpedoed

and sunk today, though I didn't see it go down.

<u>Jan. 9</u>: Tuesday - After breakfast G.Q. sounded as scheduled, but things were pretty quiet and I decided to take a nap until we started bombarding. The guns woke me up and I got down off the overhead by the skylights about daylight. Two Jap planes came over soon after, and I don't see how they could dodge so many shells. One of them practically stalled overhead, and I thought he was going to dive on us, but he went on over and vanished over the Island. Soon we saw our fighters shoot one down in that direction. I slept again after that as the troop landed about 9:30 and we ceased firing.

Secured from G.Q. at 10 but I came down in time to eat late chow, and had not much more than finished when G.Q. went again...didn't get up then in time to see but two Jap suicide divers came in and hit the NEW MEXICO and the Australian. They soon secured after that, but I stayed up and finished my book, came down and washed my clothes. They played Hearts for a while before eating supper to relieve the watch.

Was playing cards again after relieving the watch when they passed the word to set zet soon after which they blew G.Q. It was a mess with half the hatch closed and everyone trying to get to their stations. To top it all off by the time I got to the Q deck they were bringing down the wounded.

I finally made it up on my station and started helping.

After a lot of looking and inquiring, I doped the story out thus:

A Jap plane passed over our bow...must have been pretty low and one of our own ships (probably the PENNSYLVANIA) caught as with her fire in battery. It caught us on the ft. bd. side (beam) of sky control. Though I helped carry down the

259

dead and wounded I got a very poor idea of how many there were. Perhaps, (It's said) 17 enlisted, and 5 officers dead...about as many wounded.

Jan. 10: Wednesday - Jap torpedo bombs came in last night. There are several rumors and though they did some damage, I don't know just what the extent of it was, probably not very great as we never went to G.Q. They did set zet set and I had a time getting up and back this morning to relieve the watch.
 At G.Q. this morning they laid a smoke screen over the transports which we gradually drifted into.
 Jap planes came over and we did a deal of firing, but did no good. The plane crashed over among the transports but missed.
 8-12 watch, then helped carry stretchers this afternoon.
 I was lying on the quarterdeck asleep this evening when a Jap plane sneaked in and we started firing about the time G.Q. sounded.
 What a commotion! Everyone trying to run over each other! I stayed on the quarter deck until the firing was nearly over then beat most of the others on my G.Q. station I think.
After a while the plane circled around again and we finally saw it crash-dive on a transport after much A.A. fire. A bomb was also dropped over that way.
 To top the evening off one of the searchlights shorted out and burned Mr. Berry's hand.

Jun. 11: Thursday - We started to pull out of Lengayen Gulf during that air raid last evening so are well under way now. The water was pretty rough last night. No excitement on G. Q. this morning so I slept and waited until G. Q. was over and then relieved the 8-12 watch. Worked on S P phones. Seems quite a few have gone bad

260

during all this G.Q.

Jan. 12: Friday - No excitement at G.Q. this morning. Worked on the 21 J S and J H all day. Ross worked on hand sets at the hoists.
   The water was rough all day.
   Had one Bogie contact and G. Q. about noon. About 1600 there was a Sub. nearby.

Jan. 13: Refueled the old tub today. The water sure was rough. Worked J. A. circuit. Got gedunks and played cards in afternoon.

Jan. 15: Monday - Nothing much of interest. We're back in Lingayen Gulf.

Jan. 16: We're still in the Gulf. Finally got the motor drill fixed. Have caught a darned cold from some place. G. Q. each morning but nothing happens.

Jan. 17: Did very little today. I should have studied but didn't feel like it. We're out at sea and the water is very rough.

Jan. 18: At G. Q. we're back in the gulf again. We must be for I see land and star shells in the sky. 8-12 watch. Worked on x 1 6 v in afternoon. Studied this evening after G.Q. which sounded unexpectedly about 6:45. I guess there was some aircraft fire after we secured.

Jan. 19 Worked on a drawer for the forward bench I.C. room this morning. Had to take care of my bed roll in the compartment as it had gotten damp. A sudden G. Q. at chow time, but soon secured. 12-4 watch.

Jan. 20: Saturday - It was pay day. Although I did not draw any I see I have $317. on the books.

I had all my hair cut off again.

Jan. 21: Laid around all day and played cards.

Jan. 22: Monday - 12-4 watch - Worked all morning on S.P. at main control. Afternoon bought shoes, etc. at small stores. Changed berths today, and came near to having an air raid this evening about 2100.

Jan. 24: Wednesday - I still have a cold, so I didn't do much today...fixed a S P phone in the morning and fooled around all afternoon.

Jan. 25: Had a couple of air alarms today... nuisance raids you might say, though planes were directly overhead this evening. Stood by for call fire and went in close in the afternoon, but only fired 2 16-in. salvres and came back out and anchored.

Jan. 26: Friday - We're still in Lengayen Gulf. The lights by the landing look like a young city.

Jan. 27: Not much to write about today. 8-12 watch, and worked nearly all the time till 4 at night in the Main Mast. Admiral's Inspection.

Jan. 28: Sunday - Aircraft is in the vicinity, and there was A.A. fire last night, but we didn't go into G.Q.
Not much doing today. They say the exams are coming up soon, but I'm going to have to hurry if I make it.

January 30: Tuesday - Same old thing. It's sort of tiresome.

Jan. 31: In LINGAYEN GULF - Still occassional air attacks and A.A. fire in which we seem to take little part. Fixed a guard for the board A.C. room.

U.S.S.COLORADO

February 1-5, 1945

We're still sitting in Lingayen Gulf.

There are occasional light air raids, but we seldom go to G.Q. and we haven't fired as we are banned from firing unless this ship is the target of an attack. There hasn't been much work lately and have done a lot of card playing when I should have been studying. We haven't had a mail call yet.

<u>Feb. 5</u>: We got under way this morning but were only out for drill, and we were back in the gulf before evening.
We received the report that our troops are going into Manila and things sure look good on the German front with the Russian Army only 50 miles from Berlin...makes a person dream of getting home, and I sure have been thinking a lot about it.

<u>Feb. 6</u>: Tuesday - Worked on w Z in F Div. all day.

<u>Feb. 7</u>: Wednesday - 8-12 watch - worked all morning on the 2Jv at Main Control and finished the 2 J Z this afternoon.

<u>Feb. 8</u>: 12-4 watch - Spent the day working on the X 3 J down in #204 store room.

<u>Feb. 9</u>: Had field day and had Captains's inspection of crew's spaces.

Feb. 10:Saturday - We left Lingayen Gulf this evening, and we finally got the mail also.
   I worked pretty hard today getting circuits back in shape.

Feb. 11: I was going to do some tall letter writing this evening, but I didn't even finish one letter. I really didn't do much all day but read a book.

Feb. 12: Didn't get much done today, either, but read my mail and answer a couple of letters.

W. A. Parker EM 3/C
U.S.S.COLORADO, Box 11
c/o Fleet P.O. S. F. Calif.
Feb. 11, 1945

Dear Sister,
   It's been a good while since I wrote. Before Xmas I guess, but at last the mail is in and I'm here to scratch off a few lines. There sure was a stack of mail and I imagine the men in the office will be glad when it's all sorted. I have six letters from you besides a pile of others...all of which I'll probably never get answered.
   The weather must be pretty disagreeable in Wyoming. I've roasted so long I feel I could stand a good freezing, but suppose I couldn't stand much with my blood about as thick as water.
   After all this time there should be something to write about but I'm afraid there isn't.
   Every day we see the same thing; mostly just the water stretching off to the horizon, and at night the dark with perhaps a few bright lights of efflorescence tumbling in the wake of the ship.
   I've been studying a bit, read a few books, and sometimes we get together in the evenings

for a few friendly games of Hearts or Pinochle and have quite a bit of fun. I know you never cared about playing cards, but I always get quite a kick out of it.

The war news looks pretty good now, doesn't it? I've begun to plan already, foolish, I know, for it will be a good while yet, and I probably won't get out for six months or a year after it's all over.

One thing I don't like the looks of is this bill why are working on to induct women. God knows it's Hell enough for a man to have to live like this, and though nurses may be needed, I'd rather die than see one of my sisters here! If women want to volunteer, of course, that's their business. A lot of them are more than equal to the task of looking out for themselves.

We have been talking about going to Alaska again. As soon as we are out and the war is over, of course. That makes four of us in the group now since we have a new member, Harry, big and blond. Quite a bunch. Joe is short and stout; Al is tall, slender, and pale. Then me, of course, halfway between something and nothing at all. I don't suppose anything will ever come of it. We probably won't even all be together when the time comes, but it's fun to talk and think about it anyhow. I don't believe I'd want to stay up there unless I could get the folks to come up too. It would be a nice trip though.

I had the nicest letter from Aunt Hazel. They seem to like it fine up there. I'm going to try to wheedle a little information out of her.

Glad you liked your Xmas gifts. I'm afraid poor Stanley sort of got ruped, but it was the best I could do at the time...the letters he wrote were O.K. Tell him that Uncle Wilbur liked them fine. They weren't so hard to make out

either...much easier than Jap...Ha! I should
talk, his letters really were quite plain, which
reminds me, did you hear the one of the old back-
woodsman that goes like this:
PA: Hey, Ma! come here and see, I've larned to write.
MA: Gosh, Pa! you sure can. What does it say?
PA: Don't know, Ma! ain't larned to read yit.

The censors don't like long letters so I guess I better quit and write again though I can't see what makes the difference between one long letter or two short ones.
Sure hope this finds you all feeling O.K. I've been feeling good enough myself and get lazier and more no good every day.
Will write again when I can, and hope the mail won't be so slow next time.
As always, with love, Your Old Pal, Wilbur

Feb. 13: Tuesday - Pulled in at Leyte Gulf this morning and out again this evening. Went down in A - 124 store room and over to Central Station and finished fixing the x 3 J circuit.

Feb. 14: Wednesday, 1945 - U.S.S.COLO. - They went up for tests but I wasn't ready so didn't go. Put up a box at Central Station for the X 3 2 phone.

Feb. 15: Talk is strong of going back to the States in April. Fixed a pipe and hangers for buckets.

Feb. 16: EULITHI - We arrived at Eulithi. We found there are to be eleven 2C rates, so hurried around to go up, but doubt will make it on such short notice.

Feb. 17: Saturday - They are sorting the mail mostly 3rd class - I got a V-Mail from Dorothy. Hoey and I went back to Main Control and took the progress exam.

Feb. 18: We're at Eulithi. Helped fix the J H circuit this morning and studied. Wrote one letter and took it easy the rest of the day.

Feb. 19: Hoey, Sickles, and I went down to Main Control and had Finkbone and Hogey give us a little dope for the exams.

Feb. 20: Did a little more work today but got some studying done, too.

Feb. 22: - Thursday - Eulithi - Put up bill board in the I.C. room.

Feb. 23: Spent the better part of the day at Central studying.

Feb. 24: Went up for the test this morning. Though it was an easy test I didn't finish completely, and doubt if I passed. Took the P.O. this afternoon.

Feb. 25: Stayed up until 4 playing cards last night so I felt a bit lousy today. Rated liberty today and went over... swam and had a pretty good time though I nearly played myself out.

Feb. 26: There wasn't much work to do today so I read a book (Klondike Mike).

Feb. 27: Still at Eulithi - Painted the shop today which was quite a job.

U.S.S.COLORADO, Box 11
c/o Fleet P.O. S.F., Calif.
Feb. 27, 1945

Dearest Sister,
    It doesn't seem so long since I last wrote, but I guess it has been a couple of weeks; besides I got a nice long letter from you in today's mail so I'll just have to scratch off a line even though there isn't anything to say.
    We spent most all day painting the deck in the shop together with some of the machinery and benches. It looks pretty snazzy now, but smells pretty bad, and still so damp that I'm afraid I'm going to have to hoist my bedding up the top side and run my chances with old Man Weather again tonight. Maybe If I get up there before the show lets out I can find sort of a sheltered place before someone beats me to it.
    Got liberty last Sunday and was on the beach nearly all day. There wasn't a great lot of fun. Took a lunch but the sandwiches were so bum we took the meat out and ate the bread alone. They had beer and a little coke over there and I managed to get a bottle of each.

We stayed on the beach the rest of the time after eating. It was the nicest, cleanest, beach you ever saw...not a speck of dirt in the sand; (sure would make good cement) and the water was just as clear and warm as it could be. It was so nice I clear forgot I hadn't had my trousers off out in the sun for a long while, and oh, Boy! did I get a nice burn. I can hardly sit down yet.
    There were no pretty sea shells to be found but I found the reddest piece of coral you ever saw...don't know if I can cram it in my locker or not, but it isn't very large so I'm going to try.

Cripes! don't worry about that old car title. I imagine a person would have to want a car pretty bad to buy that one now anyhow.
    Sure glad Bill is feeling better. Am run down so will close and try again another night.
    As Ever Your Old Pal, Wilbur

<u>Feb. 28</u>: Went over on liberty again today with Les and Hoey.

MARCH 1945

<u>March 1</u>: Fixed 3 J V and 2 J V at Main Control. They broke out _____ today. I got Stroud's and must now get them ready to send to him.

<u>March 2</u>: Friday - Held Field Day and had inspection of machinery spaces. Read quite a while out on the quarter deck this afternoon.

<u>March 3</u>: Fixed 2 J V No. 1 thrust. Went on liberty with Munn.

<u>March 4</u>: At Eulithi - Sunday, so took it sort of easy - played cards all afternoon. 4-12 watch. Wrapped one of those pictures for Betty this morning. Worked on and soldered this new Sheafer pen. 12-4 watch tonight.

<u>March 5</u>: There was no liberty party today.

<u>March 6</u>: Worked on a drawer cabinet for screws. In evening stood by for Harry Howell at fwd. Bd.

<u>March 7</u>: Tried to solder that drawer today but I didn't have much luck and finally had to take it apart and rivit it.

<u>March 8</u>: Had the duty today. Most of the strikers in the shop made 3rd Class, so I'm back to

carrying the trash again as I didn't make second.
Worked on the screw cabinet again today.

W. A. Parker EM 3/C
U.S.S.COLORADO, Box 11
c/o Fleet P.O., S.F. Calif.
March 10, 1945

Dearest Sister,
    Your letter of the 26th came today. That is making pretty good time, isn't it. It sure does seem good to get a letter that isn't months old. Bet I would have a hard time taking the cold there now. Gosh! you know it has been about five years since I have seen any real winter weather!
    I went over on liberty again the next day after I wrote you...I think it was...and sunburned myself again right over where I peeled off. Pretty dumb, eh? Guess I'll never learn. Am about over all the effects of it now though as we haven't had any liberty for several days.
    Guess I just can't stand being comfortable, for yesterday evening I scalded a big patch of skin right off the back of my hand with a pot of hot coffee.
    Hasn't much happened around here. Haven't been working very hard, but manage to keep busy. Am doing some more metal smithing...making a cabinet for nuts and bolts. Have been cutting down a little on the card playing and trying to do a little more studying as I want to go up for second as soon as I can.
    Went to the show last night, the first I've seen for I don't know when though they have shown one nearly every night for the last two or three weeks. It was in technicolor, and the name of it was "When Irish Eyes Are Smiling". I managed to get a seat and enjoyed it quite a bit.
    I don't know how you find so much to write

about. I'm run down already.
   The fellows just got back from the show, and some of them that sleep in the shop here have mid watch, and want to get to bed, so I guess I'll close as I'm run down anyhow, and move out of their way so they can put their cots down.
   Probably be back again in a week or so. Tell Stanley and Bill Hello and Goodnight.
   As ever Your Old Pal, Wilbur

March 11: The show was interrupted by an explosion, a carrier was hit.

March 12: I was going to the show, but they decided not to have it.

March 13: Cleared the J L 5 of a ground. Wrote letters in the evening.

March 14: Had liberty again today that is I went in Schneider's place. I got off early as it is a long way over and I got back about 3:30.

March 15: Finished the rivet cabinet. Played Pinochole till way late.

March 16: Fixed shower for Signal Bridge. G.Q. drill at 8:15. Rec'd letters from CM, George, Ruby, and Myrna.

March 17: Saturday - Got those photos of me ready to send to Ruby, Les, and Ina for their birthdays, also one each to Mother and Doris. Put a clasp on the screw cabinet to hold it shut.

March 18: Sunday - Straightened out my locker this morn. Wrote in the evening.

W.A. Parker EM 3/C
U.S.S. COLORADO, Box 11
c/o Fleet P.O. San Fran. Calif.
March 18, 1945

Dear Sister:
   This is Sunday and there hasn't been very much going on around the shop all day. Most of the fellows are up to the movies now, and it is about quiet enough for me to write a little I guess.
   I straightened out my locker this morning and threw away a lot of old letters. Boy! I sure have got a lot of good out of this writing folder you gave me. It's just right. I keep it so full though it looks like a trash pile inside most of the time. It's getting a little frayed on the corners from so much use, but it sure has stood up good.
   It isn't long until your birthday now, and I haven't even so much as a card to send you, but all the good wishes are here just the same. I'm sending a picture that I sent away and had enlarged. It flatters me too much to really be good. Haven't got a frame for it either, but maybe you can rig up something.
   Went ashore again last Wed. and it rained on us all the way over, and while we were eating lunch. One really doesn't mind though, it is so warm a little rain helps keep you cool. It turned off nice after lunch, and we went swimming again, but have a pretty good tan now so I didn't burn this time.
   One of the fellows is here and playing the phonegraph for me while I write. He says to tell you "Hello"! (Ha). I keep telling him you are the married sister.
   No, I never did get very far in Geometry, but I sure liked it. Wish I were there to finish it with you. Poor Bill, he <u>would</u> have troubles then.

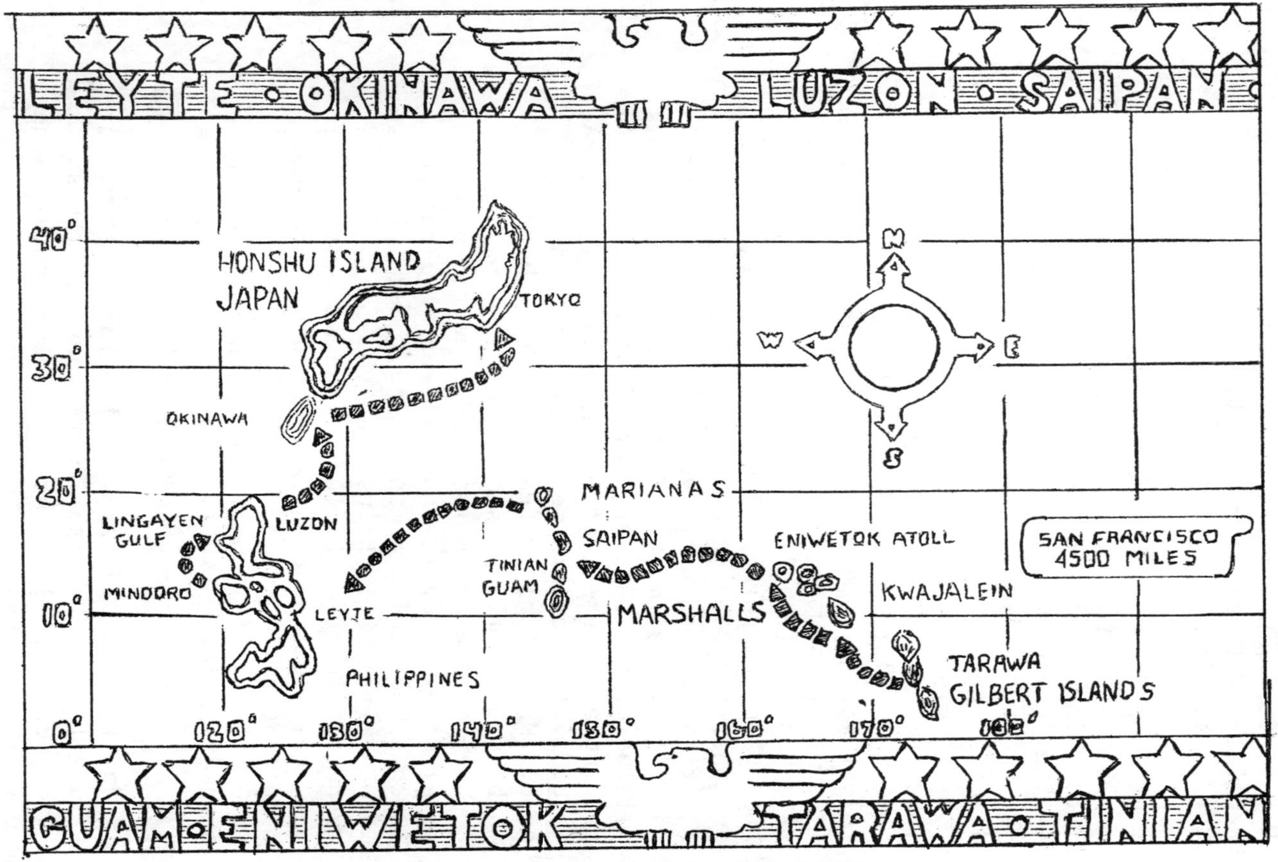

Route of the U.S.S. COLORADO

I don't seem to find much to say, so guess I may as well quit, and study a bit just in case I may want to go up for another rate some day.
    We played Pinochle all afternoon. So Happy Birthday, and Love, Wilbur.

March 20: I went on liberty in Edington's place. Had a flash red over there, but still got time for a good swim.

March 21: Wednesday - Dawn G. Q. - Water rough all day. Getting some cooler as we move North. I bought a warm jacket yesterday.

March 23: Friday - 8-12 watch. We refueled cans today. Helped Munn on #6 hoist bell.

March 24: Dawn G.Q. - It's getting quite a bit cooler as we move North. We got #6 bell fixed this morn. Slept nearly all afternoon.

March 25: We were supposed to bombard today, but didn't.

March 26: Monday - Didn't bombard again today though we went to G.Q several times and were in sight of the Islands nearly all day. Some transfers 3/C came in yesterday. Weis and Pipig, probably Zeine, are getting them.

March 27: Tuesday - Early reveille, chow, and then G.Q. I got up on the overhead but it was too cold to rest.
    As the sun came up and with the dawn some evening planes came in...the first from the port stern ran an awful barage of A.A. fire, came down low and flew along the water for a long while before he was finally brought down.
    During this burst of fire two shells exploded over the boat deck, A piece of schrapnel went

through the forward smoke stack, and other pieces injured 12 men...only four very serious I think.

    The next plane came down in a dive off our stbd. beam, straight for the NEVADA which was directly ahead. It was badly hit and burning furiously but crashed (apparently between Turret 3 and 4) with a huge burst of flame and smoke, which however soon burned out.

    Another plane was soon spotted in about this same direction. Rather far from us yet he came down in a dive and dropped a bomb which missed after which, like the first plane, he seemed bent on escaping...flew low along the water, running a terrific barrage of flack, was hit and burning but slowly and continued for a good while before finally crashing and roaring into flame on the water. This is the first Jap plane I have observed to burn without exploding or burning fiercely immediately.

    One ship also got hit is the word though I didn't actually see it.

<u>March 28</u>: Wednesday - Only one plane came in at G.Q. this morning which drew the usual fire but I doubt they got it. It was low and quite a way out on our Port beam.

    We bombarded lazily all day and fired few shells (sixteens only). The weather was warmer than it has been and caught a few disturbing naps.

    At 8 this evening we had a warning signal and some planes came in high off our st. bd. bow, working around to the stern, still far out and drawing some fire from a number of ships further out.

    There seems to be quite a number of effective guns still on the Island and usable aircraft (grounded) were spotted.

March 29: Thursday - Bombarded again today. We're still rather far out and undecided as though targets are not well known.

March 30: Here in OKINAWA we pulled into sort of a harbor between two rugged looking islands & took on ammunition.

March 31: Saturday - At G.Q. again all day... got into the beach a little closer and bombarded more earnestly. Also, afternoon saw our bombers dropping bombs and rockets on the Island. Once I saw machine guns return fire on a ship close by, the first return fire on our ship I've observed.
 I lay on the Signal bridge and read and slept nearly all day. The gunnery officer didn't seem to like my beard.

APRIL 1945

April Fool's Day & Easter Sunday: Up at 0455 and G.Q. shortly after. That lasted until 1700 at evening.
 Started bombarding early (almost sunrise) at which time some evening planes came in and I saw one shot down by other ships a good way out. None got close enough for us to open fire.
 Bombarded heavily all day. Afternoon saw our troop landing on Okinawa. Resistance ashore was said to be light at which one will not wonder who saw the hail of shell and rockets they landed behind.
 G.Q. again at sundown. We were sitting quite a way from the Island, and most of the other ships so didn't get to fire when evening aircraft came in. Must have been quite a few judging from the amount and duration of A.A. fire, a few of which came uncomfortably close to us. I could barely distinguish one plane as it came down in flames.

SHOREBIRD
TODAY IS—
1945
FOOL No. 1
BANG!
CLICK
BING
I DON'T WANNA GO HOME.
LOOK AT ALL THE DOUGH I'M SAVING!
APRIL FOOL'S DAY
AND EASTER!
GREETINGS FROM BUNNY SHOREBIRD
ME, TOO!
AND L-DAY!
SHOREBIRD
READY, AYE, READY!
READY FOR "L" DAY

The WEST VIRGINIAN was reported hit by a dive bomber.

April 2: Monday - Evening Aircraft overhead again at dawn. Most of the activity though was over the Island and the transports further in. We only fired at one time (5 in.) G.Q. and shelled with 16 in. all day.

April 3: G.Q. 2:30 this morning - A.A. fire in the distance - G.Q. again at 4 - Secured for breakfast, then back to G.Q. for the rest of the day. Fired main battery all day and did considerable good I guess, from the reports.

April 4: AT OKINAWA.........Dawn G.Q. - breakfast - G.Q. at 0800 for shore bombardment (but didn't fire) - chow - and call fire again at 1300 - fired some five inch.

April 6: Friday - G.Q. at 3 this morning. Our air force doing a good job but the Japs seem to have decided to throw everything they have at us, and a few planes got through G.Q. - lasted quite a while and I came to the compartment and slept and ate early chow - slept till 10 at I.C. then worked a bit.

G.Q. again at 3 this evening. A good day for planes to get through as it was cloudy and rainy and cold all day. Inspite of weather conditions, however, we came in close to the beach and anchored about 10 with a large number of the other ships, mostly transports and took off cans and on ammunition. G.Q. lasted from 3 until after dark. An awfully large number of planes seemed to be in the air, but at first I thought nothing was going to happen and came down for a while. They shot a plane down close by and I went back up and saw them shoot down another quite a way off. Three fighters and one bomber came in low directly astern. The arms back there sure did good work on them. They got uncomfortably close, but one after the other they plunged flaming into the water. A can was reported badly damaged (too far out to see).

    Another plane started bearing in from far out ...on our port side apparently straight for us. The cans opened fire and then our 5 in. It seemed as I looked that one of our 5 in. hit it directly but guess it wasn't hit very bad as it kept coming and finally crashed uncomfortably close. Everyone else left for the stbd. side.

    The smoke was rising from the water where another plane had been shot down. I moved to the stbd. side and almost immediately I saw a huge smoke and flame as a crash diver crashed a can. Then two more divers crashed this same can before the end of the day. It will probably sink. Two flames rose toward the sky from back in the bay where we were and the transports still lay at anchor. No doubt two more crash divers had found their targets.

    I don't remember just how many more planes I saw go down farther out, but A.A. fire continued, and I was just inside when they shot another down off our port side. Darkness finally closed, and I brought a pair of phones down to fix. They secured and I washed and came back to the shop.

April 7: A Jap plane came over before dawn and launched one torpedo, which exploded harmlessly close by. At dawn G.Q. - A.A. fire was light and far out. Evening - Jap surface craft including fast battle ships, cruisers, and destroyers, reported sunk by our air force.

    While fixing phones for hoist 5 G.Q. sounded. I ran up there just as we opened up. A Jap dive (crash) bomber crashed the MARYLAND.

ON THE U.S.S. COLORADO

April 1, 1945

"The plane came down in flames."

April 8: Sunday - The Jap fleet never showed up so guess they probably turned back. Stayed in the compartment for G.Q. this morning. Nothing much seemed to happen. We are in at anchor in the lagoon between the two rough looking islands where we anchored the first time.
   Everyone seems to be getting a cold (me too). I got sort of disgusted with the cold running into my mustache, so I cut it off and the beard, too. Too bad! with it almost $1\frac{1}{2}$ inches long! The mail came in and I rec'd a letter from Chloe, the last one probably from the sounds of it!

April 9: At G.Q. this evening a plane came in low and turned its lights on. There was some firing and they finally got one enemy craft quite a way out, and probably the same one. I had a letter from Ruby.

April 10: Didn't get up above today for G.Q. which we had all morning and fired some...our target a radar screen. Read a book..(Yukon Trail)

April 11: Not much excitement at morning G.Q., and no evening G.Q. except A.A. battery. Fixed 2 circuits and layed around the rest of the day.

April 12: Thursday - I was asleep after noon chow when they sounded G.Q. so I came up to the compartment and stretched out again as Mr. Berry said there was no use of my going up on the bridge. They started firing like H- - - ! about 2 or 2:30 and I woke up. There were 12 or 13 planes shot down very close...only one of them managed to crash its target (a can). G.Q. lasted nearly all afternoon. I went upon the bridge for a while and stayed. It was so nice and sunshiny.
   We are in G.Q. again now for call fire. It started about 10:30 during a Heart game and must

be 12 now. I stayed on the bridge for a while as it was so nice up there and looks as though they may use the lights. Looks like a Fourth of July carnival and celebration over on the beach, and even most of the ships seem to be lit up here in the bay.
We just got under way a while ago.

April 13: We received word of the President's death today at noon.

April 14: Saturday - Slept nearly all morning. Was out on the focicle about noon for a little air when they announced the rumor that the war in Germany is over. Soon after, the mail-boat pulled along side with 12 bags of mail. What a day! Some light air attacks.

April 15: G.Q. this morning...air attacks heavier then, and also again this evening. We have been in G.Q. a good deal all day. Fired some 11 in. and are firing star shells again this evening. Bogies still reported close by... about 8 o'clock, I guess, and still G.Q. I have my mail all read and six letters answered.

U.S.S. COLORADO, Box 11
c/o Fleet P.O., S.F. Calif.
April 15, 1945

Dear Sister,
  With mail call over and a bunch of letters to answer, I guess I better get busy. I really hadn't expected the mail to get in, but I'm sure glad that it did. Guess your letter of the 26th is the latest one I have. Glad you got the picture. I sent Leslie one, too, but haven't heard from them. Mother didn't have but one letter for me either so I expect they have been snowed in. Ina wrote a couple letters with her usual crazy chatter, and had a letter from Aunt

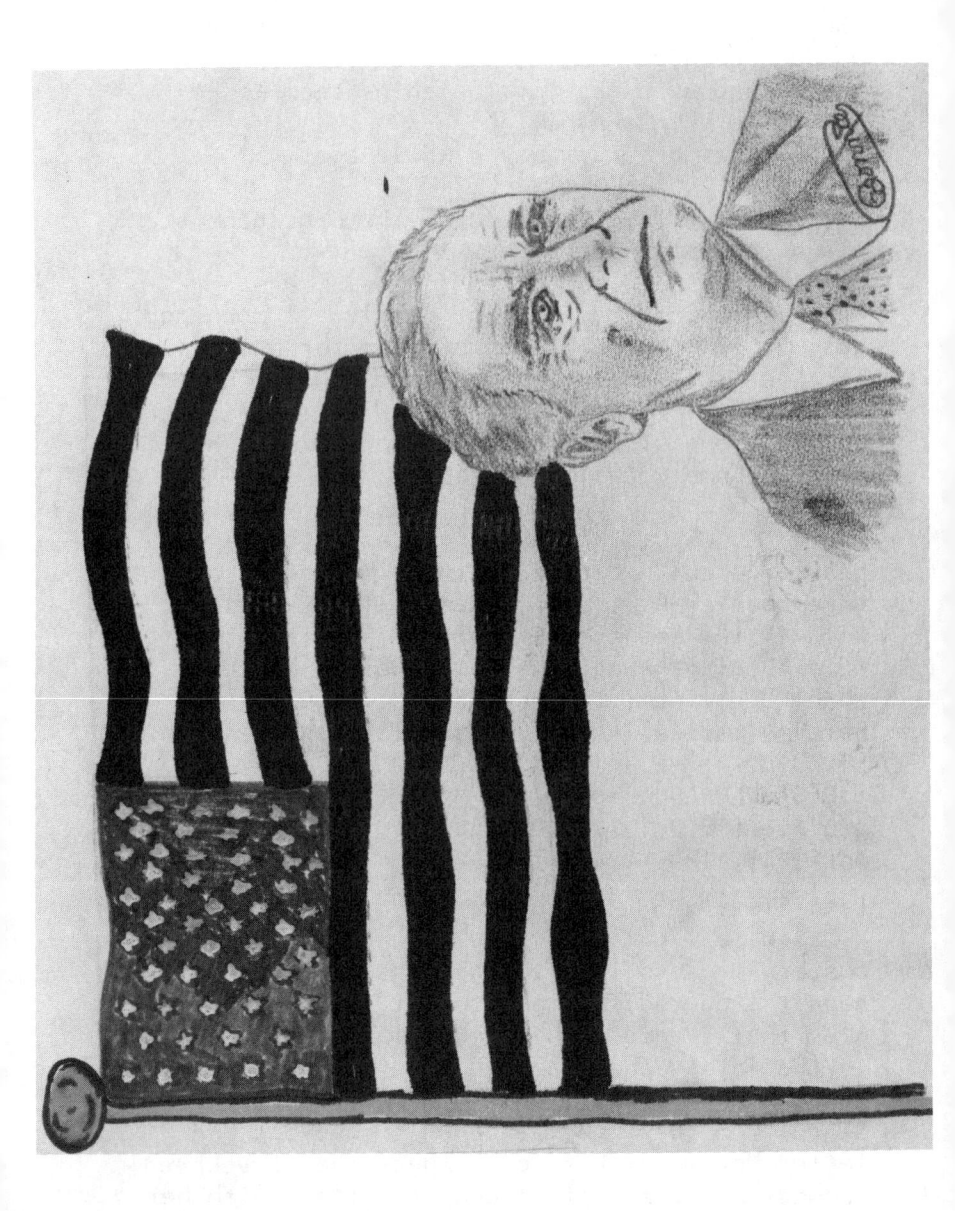

Friday, April 13, 1945

President Franklin Roosevelt's death

Hazel telling me about Jr.'s being forced down somewhere over France, and probably a prisoner of war. I know she feels pretty bad, and I must answer as soon as I can.

Things have been monotonously the same from day to day here, so there is very little to say. I have read a few books. We still have a few Heart and Pinochle games, but I'm about discouraged trying to study...yes, electricity...it's interesting but darn, it takes concentration, and it's hard to rush from it to something else every minute or so and back again. A person needs quiet and a table maybe, with a pad to jot down notes. I sure admire your persistence and sure am glad you are coming so well with your course. Yes, I wish we could take it together, but I suppose, even if I were home I'd find some excuse of "too busy" even if it were to hunt or fish. (Ha)

Well, I've hardly been out to see daylight for weeks, and consequently have lost all my sun tan. I have a cold too which really annoys me. I can't seem to get rid of it. I had a growth of beard about an inch long that I cut off last week. Maybe that's what brought this cold on! (Ha). You should have seen me!

We had turkey and ice cream for dinner today, and not bad at all, which reminds me, it is nearly chow time again, but for some reason, I don't feel very hungry.

Think I must close and try to get some of these other letters answered now.

Tell Stanley and Bill, "Hello". As ever,W.A.P.

April 16,17,18: Rather large scale enemy air raids especially on the 16th. Have been G.Q. quite a bit and have been bombarding the Island either with 5 or 16 in. or both almost continuously day and night. I haven't read a great deal nor have I lost too much sleep.

April 19: Thursday - We were in G.Q. and firing steadily all morning as troops were making a landing. Had a bit of trouble and worked on the K 3 J Bridge and quarter deck all morning. In G.Q. a good while this afternoon, too.

April 20: Anchored to take on powder today. Had a fire in #2 Handling Room...killed one man and injured 2 or 3 others when a can of powder dropped and exploded. Had a heck of a long G.Q. this evening.

April 21: Was mighty busy all day. Put in new phone hangers (61 on bridge and 21 on quarter deck). Most all strikers on Working Party.

April 22: We're still at anchor between these two rugged, sharp, islands, and still taking on powder. Mail came in and I was pretty lucky. I slept a little and did a little work. Wrote.
 There was an air raid this evening. They got in at 2700 yards once. First over the Island but never came on over, and the COLORADO never fired a shot. A thick smoke screen was layed, but for the most part we were sticking out as we're on the windward side.

April 23: Stood by for Munn most all morning as he was tired, and I wrote letters...took a nap in afternoon...went to G.Q. for shore bombardment which didn't last long. The mail came aboard again. Evening played Pinochle, after which I went out on the quarter deck and watched the bombardment off the beach. They are going at it pretty heavy . They were still at it this morning when I went out.

U.S.S.COLORADO, Box 11
c/o Fleet P.O. S.F. Calif.
April 23, 1945

Dearest Sister,
    Hasn't been more than a few days since I last wrote, but I had a couple of swell letters in the mail yesterday...yours of April 2nd and 9th, so I guess I can afford to scratch a line just to let you know I'm still here. (Ha)
    There isn't a thing new to tell about. Wish I could get ashore and look around just to have something to write about.
    I'm glad you had a nice birthday. Guess there is nothing better than to feel and look well. Gosh! I always forget Bill's birthday, though it shouldn't be hard to remember coming so close to yours. Stanley has one in about a month doesn't he? I hope by that time I'll be able to do something about it, but doubt that, too.
    Yes, I left the shells I found before with Leslie. Most of them had layed out in the sun too long to be very nice. I have a few more now besides some other things, so I'll save you a souvenir. I lost the winder (stem) off my watch here a while back. I've been thinking about trying to make a new one but it's pretty fine work. I don't know if I can or not. Haven't much ambition anymore, anyhow.
    I feel sorry for Ina, too. I've had my doubts about anything coming of her engagement for quite a while, but don't doubt but what Buster will be the one to be sorry in the end. It seems to me he won't be able to remain a kid all his life no matter how hard he tries. Maybe I haven't much room to talk, I'm just an old bachelor myself, and sometimes I feel mighty old but at least, I don't go around making promises I don't intend to keep. Guess that sort of sounds like I'm running him down. He is probably about as good a friend as I have, but that sort

SHOREBIRD — "I MUST GO BACK TO THE OLD COUNTRY"—
I'M LOSING MY "SCHOOL BOY" WAIST LINE....
MY MOTHER WON'T KNOW ME!
SEE WHAT I MEAN?
MY NERVES ARE SHOT—
THE HAIR I HAVE LEFT, IS TURNING GRAY, —AND FALLING OUT.
I'VE GOT THE 'OLD COUNTRY' BLUES
BUT—BUT—(SNOB)— — — NO BODY, NO ONE AT ALL, SEEMS TO CARE!
AND I AM SLOWLY GOIN' CRAZY!
BSG

of thing makes me tired.

    Isn't much to do today, but guess I better quit now, look around, and do what little there is. Chow will be ready by the time I'm through. We had chicken yesterday, but it was Sunday, and today we'll be back to beans.

    I'm all run down now, but hope that old mail man keeps coming in, and if he does, I'll be back again. As Ever, Yours With Love, Wilbur

April 24: Tuesday - 8-12 watch...worked rather hard on several different phones this afternoon, and 23 J S on Bridge went out after dark.

April 25: Worked on 23 J S and other circuits (C.I.G.) all day, and still didn't finish the work in the book. Fired main battery nearly all day but no all-hand G.Q.

April 26: Pretty well finished the work all but the broken selector switch C.I.C. - Secondary fire all day and nearly all last night. I got my hair cut.

April 27: Worked nearly all day on selector switch C.I.C. but fixed a number of other circuits too. They sure are giving that old Okinawa Island Hell! We fired secondary a good deal all day and night. Got a letter from Ruby and one from Mother.

April 28: They took the repair watch off at I.C. so I'm standing first section alone now. This firing sure has jarred the old ship up! We were anchoring after evening chow when G.Q. went, and we stayed there until midnight. One evening plane crashed and possibly sank a Hospital ship close by. Fixed phone in Ex. Officer's cabin.

April 29: Sunday - I slept until 9:30 after securing from G.Q. and eating chow. I fixed a couple of circuits, ate chow, relieved the watch at noon, and wrote a letter. Went to bed early as had 12-4 watch. They took the repair watch off at the I.C. room.

    Had an alert and G.Q. about 230 in the morning. Went upon the bridge. They were trying to lay a smoke screen beneath low rolling clouds and in a lively breeze! Red flashes and the boom of heavy guns were constant as the shelling of Okinawa continues unabated. G.Q. lasted about an hour with no conflict.

April 30: After securing from morning G.Q. and eating chow I lay down on the bench and slept until about 1030. Fixed phone transistor in afternoon, and a crystal for Lester's watch. Mail call was late. One letter from Ruby.

MAY 1945

May 1: Tuesday - Fixed selector switchs C.I.C.

May 2: 8-13 watch. Started a picture frame. Played cards with Lemon and Ryan in the evening. One of our 5 in. guns gave out today. I don't see how the Island can hold out much longer!

May 3: Over the radio comes the word of Hitler's death...AND surrender of troops in Italy!
    12-4 watch. Air raid in evening again. Two of our ships were hit the other side of the island. Also fired a few shots at planes this morning.

May 4: I tried to get a nap this morning but was rousted out to fix 22 23 2S at combat after which I fixed 42V and had G.Q. until

ON THE U.S.S. COLORADO

Wednesday, May 3, 1945 - Hitler's Death

chow call. I napped nearly all afternoon until time to go on watch 1-6.

May 5: Back at anchor and taking on ammunition. I didn't do much today. Studied a bit.

May 6: SUNDAY- 8-12 watch. Worked on X2J but didn't finish.

May 7: 12-4 watch. Fixed X2J and 21 hoist. We fired 16 in. (main battery) and are still at it now at midnight. CRIPES! this continual firing is getting tiresome! As I came on watch they passed the word: GERMANY HAS SURRENDERED UNCONDITIONALLY!

May 8: 12-4 watch again tonight as they changed me from I.C. shop to I.C. repair watch. Mashed my finger on the hatch (I.C.) this evening and it throbbed till I couldn't sleep. Sure are firing steady tonight.

May 9,10,11,12: Every day is about the same. The bombardment continues day and night with occasional days lying at anchor to take on stores of ammunition. We don't go to G.Q to fire anymore, but have dawn G.Q. and occasionally an air raid that drives us to ct - like today - for a few hours this morning.

U.S.S.COLORADO, Box 11
c/o Fleet P.O., S.F. Calif.
May 11, 1945

Dear Sister,
   Got another nice letter from you today, so I guess I better try to scratch off a line. Your letter came through in good time...only eleven days.
   I had a letter from Betty, too, and one from

Mother yesterday, one from Dorothy. Probably Dorothy and Mother wrote about the same things to you as they did to me. I've been wondering how Leslie will come out with his 1A, and if the turn in Europe will change the draft quota. Betty has moved to Linn, Missouri. She said Orlie was married the seventeenth.
    Of course, there isn't a thing to write from here. I just feel like throwing up my hands, laying down my pen, and never trying to write again. Cripes! I could just send out an empty envelope now and then and it would be just as good. Feel especially bad tonight, I guess, because my good pen played out and won't hold ink anymore...caught my writing finger in the hatch and mashed the nail, etc, etc, grouch! Pretty soon I'll have you feeling low, too.
    Well, as I said, nothing new here. Up at 4:30 every morning, stand four hours day watch, and four at night, three meals a day (if you can call it that) and sleep where and when I can, do a little work, and if there is time, play a game of cards, or read a book.
    Tell Stanley, Uncle Wilbur likes his drawing, and says "Hello". As ever Yours, With Love,W.A.P.

<u>May 13,14</u>: The ARKANSAS was hit pretty bad on the 14th.
    I sat out on the focicle after eating a gedunk and watched the bombardment of the town of OKinawa. We fire +. 3. and a lot of other ships were firing, planes were scaping and bombing. L.C.I's were scraping the beach with 40 M.M. and firing rockets; besides, what the Army may have been doing. It sounded as though they may have some pretty heavy artillery fire, too.

<u>May 15</u>: Don't know how that place holds out! We're still pounding them day and night. I studied a bit. Made a dog tag chain. 8-12 watch.

May 16: Started a picture frame out of lucite. 8-12 watch. G.Q. about 10:30 or 11. A big twin engine bomber nearly hit us. Arthur's on the B6 searchlights said it nearly scraped the mast. After G.Q. worked on X 3 J annunciator and bell between bridge and main control.

May 17: Thursday

May 18: About noon we went to G.Q. A can got grounded on a reef and Jap shore batteries opened up on her damaging her severely. This afternoon after securing from G.Q. I could see her far out by the point of the island a spiral of smoke rising from her to the sky.
 We fired more or less all day. Have fired over 1600 rounds from the main battery on this operation.

May 19: 8-12 watch. Worked on picture frame. Didn't fire quite so much today. It seems as though the Island may be about secured.

May 20: After G.Q. I slept on the bench till ten, ate chow, went on watch, and worked on phones all afternoon till late. G.Q. after evening chow until 9. Got a couple hours sleep and up to fix a phone on bridge. Watch 12-4. It's 1300 now, and we're firing steadily (star shells). They are meeting heavy counter attack on the beach to-night.

May 21: Monday - We unloaded our ammunition in preparation to go back to Leyte (PERHAPS). Still at the Island tonight though, and there were evening planes overhead this evening.

May 22, 1945: WE PULLED OUT FROM OKINAWA

May 23: The Captain gave a few words of "well done" for the last 60-day operation.
8-12 watch. There was sun bathing today.

May 24: Cleaned overhead in the shop and A C O Board this morning.
We got another shot. 12-4 watch.

May 25: We pulled into Leyte Gulf about noon. I rec'd 3 letters. Played Pinochle in the evening instead of studying as I should.

May 26: Rated liberty but didn't go as had phones to fix in aft engine room and wanted to study. Stayed up until after one o'clock studying.
Poor Carlson got on the 240, back on the quarter deck while working and got electricuted.

May 27: Sunday - Studied a good deal as no work was necessary. Got 2 letters.

May 28: Worked on box in old C.I.C. Studied at night. Power went off in the Engine Room and that sort of fouled me up, as it didn't come on for a long time.

May 29: I went over to the repair ship with Mr. Jones. We got back about noon and I studied a bit.

May 30: I went ashore today. It rained to start with, but I had a little fun anyhow, and saw more than I expected to. It is really quite nice and green, good grass, and water with a lot of coconut trees. The Natives are numerous and friendly but wise and hard to barter with. I picked some coconuts and ate a few, but didn't buy any souvenirs.

May 31: There was an Army show aboard tonight

but I didn't go. I studied a bit and chased circuits until midnight when I took a bath.

JUNE 1945

June 1: Friday - I chased grounds J L circuit all day. Wrote letters until midnight.

U.S.S. COLORADO, Box 11
c/o Fleet P.O., S.F. Calif.
June 1, 1945

Dear Sister,
    I have your letter of the 21st, which came this afternoon, also, a couple of others that I should have answered before this, but really, I've been terribly busy. The mail has been getting in every day, but I haven't written for over a week, so I'm going to have to hurry if I get all my letters answered as I've gotten two or three letters nearly every day. I expect if I stay up until my usual late hour I'll finish though. I haven't been going to bed before 2 in the morning, but revielle isn't until six now, so that gives me a longer nap than I'm used to. The watch I have is a 24 hr. watch every four days, but it is a sleeping-in watch so I get by mighty good.
    I had liberty to go ashore day before yesterday. Like all the other libertys here it really doesn't mean much only a chance to get one's feet on solid ground again, which always seems good after a few months at sea. We had more room to move around than a lot of the places we've been on liberty, and we took a short tramp back in the woods. It rained terribly hard just before we went ashore, so the trees and bushes were wet and the ground muddy and sloppy but we didn't mind. I climbed a tall tree, got all wet

and dirty, and skinned my arms and shins sliding down...ha...just like a kid.

I have a letter from Aunt Hazel, which I was very glad to get. She says she has word from the War Dept. that Jr. has been liberated from a German prison camp and is definitely safe. I can bet that sure is a relief to her and Uncle Floyd!

The censorship regulations have been lifted a bit for the present so I can say that I've been in the Philippines and Okinawa Campaigns. I expect any further word on the subject would be censored though, and I shan't attempt it.

Stanley's birthday and Mother's Day both passed and caught me with nothing to send nor nothing I could do about it. I know Stanley is just the age to look forward to the mail and be disappointed by no remembrance. Tell him Uncle Wilbur is saving up for a big present next year. Gosh! you know I haven't drawn a cent since I got back from leave and I'm getting quite a bit on the books now. I don't expect to have another leave, but here's hoping the war won't last very much longer!

As Ever, My Love, Wilbur

June 2: Worked on J L.

June 3: Sunday - I rated liberty, but I didn't go. I guess it's pretty poor from what some of the other fellows say. They're taking the liberty party to a different place now and they say it's more like a convict's holiday than a liberty. I slept nearly all morning. Played Pinochle at Central in the afternoon and I want to study a bit this evening.

June 4: Strung cable on main mast. (It was pay day, but I didn't draw any).

June 5: Had 8-12 watch as the battery electrician in Labeto's place as he is on working party. I studied a bit in the afternoon, but I was too sleepy all day to do any good.

June 6: Just got up in time to start writing out the test this morning. Although it has been a trying day, I have hopes I may have passed this time.

June 7: Chased grounds again today and tried to get a welder, which I finally did and got the JL Box on the mast up.

June 9: Went over to the repair ship , the Pamenthaen (sp?), and got the meter and other parts. Tied up the J L on the mast after I got back. Went to the show for a change.

June 10: Sunday - Finished reading "Spirit of the Border" by Zane Grey, and wrote a few letters.

U.S.S. COLORADO, Box 11
c/o Fleet P.O., San Fran. California
June 10, 1945

Dearest Sister,
   It hasn't been long since I last wrote, and there is little more to say. I suspect I may not get around to writing again for a while, so will dash off a line.
   Being Sunday things have been sort of quiet. We still have plenty of work to do, but have sort of slacked off since the exams. Examinations for advancement in rating were held the sixth. It seemed fairly easy though it took an awful lot of writing, and I have hopes I made it alright. Hope so! Those tests sure are a headache.
   We went over to the repair ship yesterday for some spare parts, etc., and stayed for noon chow. The change in eats seemed good, though I guess,

it wasn't much different than we get here. We had a real good steak dinner today with pie and ice cream, usually we get pretty good chow on Sunday. After chow (noon) I went out on the focicle and read for a while (I'm reading "Spirit of the Border" by Zane Grey). It's about those old Indian hunters...gets pretty interesting, but decided I'd better quit and scratch you a line. Wrote to Mother this morning.
    There was a U.S.O. show including five girls aboard the other day, but I didn't try to crowd my way in. I know it must have been a mad house. Even the picture shows are always so crowded it's hard to get comfortable enough to enjoy them. I went to one last night for the first time in months. My dogs got darned tired (especially the one underneath), but I did manage to enjoy it somewhat. The name of it was "Mark Twain".
    We had inspection yesterday while I was gone, which was a lucky break for me. There has been a liberty party every day, but I haven't gone again. From what the other fellows say, it is pretty poor liberty, and they practically keep them in a pen. Can't see why they have to be that way; for liberty here is poor enough at the best, but I suppose the fellows do bring it onto themselves to a great extent.
    The shop is just about crowded enough to make it impossible to write right now, so as I'm about run down anyhow...if I can get the tablet out from under this one guy, I'll sign off and fold this up.
    I'll be back again, As Ever Yours, Wilbur

<u>June 11</u>: Monday - Installed one S P bracket. We went out on a run and had G.Q. this morning and A.A. practise. Lemon said I passed the test with good marks.

June 12: Fixed warning howler Off.'s country. We came back into port at Ligayen Gulf last night and remained all day.

June 13: Worked rather hard today fixing J X J on bridge, and running cable.

June 14: I bought cigars at the canteen to give out on my 2/C rating.

June 15: Held field day and had shop inspection today. Worked on the A calls.

June 16: I got Eddie to cut my hair last night as there was supposed to be inspection today. However, there was no inspection, and I wouldn't have had to go anyhow as had the duty.

June 17: Sunday - Washed my bed and cot.

June 18: Fixed 5 J Y at C.I.C.

June 20: Slept all morning. Got paid ($100) in the afternoon. I stood by for Harry while he went to the show.

June 21: Thursday - Worked on J S all day.

June 22: Field inspection below deck.

June 23: Captain's personal inspection today. Went over on liberty. Took so long going and coming that didn't have long to stay. Walked around a bit, drank one beer, and purchased some Jap money. Were only 5 of us from E went.

June 25: There was an explosion from gas fumes back in the aft part of the ship which caused the death of one man (a shipfitter).

June 26: Tuesday - Read a bit. Put an angle iron on the shop work bench. Wrote to Ruby.

U.S.S. COLORADO, Box 11
c/o F. P.O. S.F. Calif.
June 26, 1945

Dearest Sister:
   Received your letter today so must scratch you a line.
   I guess you will be home by now, so that is where I'm sending this. Really, I'm afraid there isn't going to be much to say that I haven't already written to Mother, and I know you will probably exchange reading letters so there seems little use in repeating myself.
   Bill will feel a little lost for a while perhaps, and so will you, but I just know you will be a lot happier, and therefore better off. There just isn't anything in a job. When I look back I see I've worked out a long time myself, and when and if I get out of here, I hope to find something better. Alaska, maybe. I've thought of it a lot and it seems like as good a bet as any. Just dreaming again, maybe, but a person has to look forward to something. By that time I hope you and Bill will be well established, but if not, it sure would be fun to take off together. Golly, it doesn't seem like you two have been married eight years. What a long while it's been since we two walked together on old Castle Ridge! I'll never forget that path, the long talk we had, and the sinking feeling in my heart then, and when Bill came to drive you back to Wyoming. Funny thing how our emotions change with time. Don't guess I feel much anymore or at all...don't get all sad or glad, and excited inside like I used to...just sort of drift along on an even keel, knowing the sun will come up tomorrow the same as it did

today, and that there will always be someone to enjoy it. However, I still think it's sort of pleasant looking back on little things like that, and one can even manage a smile knowing he's getting old...damned old! Why I aught to be married and have a couple of kids. (though right now I'm plenty glad I'm not). That's a funny thing too, how some people just sort of fall into things, and others drift around them. Even in his own mind a person can't place themselves in another's shoes and make them fit.

Looks like I'm in sort of a gabby frame of mind. I had to fill some space up with something but that must be enough, or maybe more than enough.

I've been thinking now you are back close to home, maybe you could get some good out of that old car of mine, so I'm going to give it to you. I don't want to be an Indian giver, but I don't believe the folks will ever do anything with it, and for that matter, I guess I never really gave it to them. At any rate, it's quite qpparent it will never do me any good, nor the folks either, so if you can get the least bit of good out of it in any way I wish you would. Maybe Bill will want a saw engine or can use the tires, or even sell it for a small amount. If I can find out where to write I'll see if I can get another title. Sacramento is the place, but I'm not so sure of the Bureau.

I had less money on the books last pay day than I did a month ago. Now isn't that something when I haven't drawn a cent!!!? Seems they got tangled up someway, and took the allotment money out all in one sum...sure made a hole! I still don't quite figure how it came to so much. By Golly, it's nearly as bad as working on a job. There are so many deductions, it takes a mathematical genius to figure it out!

Think I'll close now as there has been nothing new or exciting happened to tell about.
Sure hope this finds you having one swell visit. Your Loving Brother, Wilbur

June 27: Wednesday - Finished the bench

June 28: Worked on 21 J.S. sky control to combat.

June 29: Field Day. Fixed a phone center shift alley.

June 30: There was to be inspection but it was postphoned. I wanted to go on movie trip but had shore patrol.

JULY 1945

July 1: Sunday - Did very little today, but played Pinochle until midnight, and fixed the X S.J. on the quarterdeck afterward.

July 2: Monday 1945 - I got some books from the library...small ones....

    Small books though they were, Wilbur never got them read. Time for diary-writing abruptly ceased as he was caught up in a violent course of events that was to splatter Japan into bloody, effacing, submission.
    Okinawa was truly the beginning of the end for Japan. It was the longest of all the campaigns for the U.S.S. COLORADO...a total of 63 days she'd battered Okinawa.
    Even after their loss of Okinawa the Japanese resumed their Kamikaze and Baka attacks. Most of the Navy casualities were due to these attacks, and the little ships, Wilbur refers to in his diary as "cans" suffered the most.

By the way of kamikazes (suicide) planes the Japanese were literally begging for the insane horror of annihilation. The kamikazes were the reason for the charred ruins of Okinawa, and they were the main fear of the seamen, for the ships and men of the Navy were the primary targets of the kamikazes and the Japanese suicide squadrons. Okinawa was eventually termed the toughest and most costly battle of W.W.II. The Americans paid a great price for its victory with some 12,500 killed and missing, and 36,600 wounded.

(The U.S.S. COLORADO alone had fired two thousand tons of main battery ammunition upon the Island of Okinawa).

With Okinawa secured at last by the Allies, June 21, 1945, it became the "jumping-off" point for the invasion of the Japanese home islands.

Okinawa seemed to prove there could be no other way of winning...one country or the other would have be practically wiped off the map to be conquered. It seemed to become a question of who could be obliterated first, or who could deal the most horror? The mass kamikaze attacks of Japan's Imperial Navy seemed to be the answer. It had the top answer for horror. However, the Americans had been working for sometime on *their* answer.

It was July 16, 1945, that the first atom bomb was successfully tested at Alamogordo, New Mexico. Three weeks later, (August 6) the United States by dropping the atom bomb, virtually wiped out the Japanese city of Hiroshima.

Wilbur had never been so glued to any book he'd ever read as he was to THE COLORADO NEWS one August morning in 1945. "Go get your own paper," he snapped as eager hands of other sailors reached forth in an effort to grab the paper from him.

-THE COLORADO NEWS-   8 August 1945

WASHINGTON:

The most terrible destructive force ever harnessed by man, atomic energy, is now being turned on the island of Japan by United States bombers. The Japanese face a threat of utter destruction and their capitulation may be greatly speeded up.

Existence of the great new weapon was announced personally by President Truman in a statement issued through the White House at 11 A.M. (E.W.T.). He said the first atomic bomb invented and perfected in the United States, had been dropped on the Japanese Army Base of Hiroshima, sixteen hours before. That one bomb alone carried a wallop more violent than 2000 B-29 Superforts normally could hand an enemy city, using old-type TNT bombs. Secretary of War Stimson followed through with a report that the blast stirred a cloud of smoke and dust so impenetrable as to make immediate accurate observation of results impossible. The power of the bomb, Stimson said, is much as to "stagger the imagination" and he asserted it would "prove a tremendous aid in shortening the Japanese war." Stimson's emphasis on this point renewed speculation all over again as to whether Japan may be completely crushed by air attacks without invasion. Mr. Truman noted that the Japanese rejected the "Big

Three" surrender ultimatum from Potsdam, and that this had been intendant to spare the Japanese people from utter destruction. The announcement heralded an Anglo-American victory at a cost of two billion dollars, in one of the grimmest battles of the war, the battle of laboratories to unlock the secrets of the atom and yoke its energies to military use. The Germans were striving desperately to win this highly secret contest in the closing months of the European struggle.

GUAM:

The United States unleashed, Monday, the most terrible weapon in the history of war, an atomic bomb, carrying the destructive power of 2000 Superforts, that crushed the annihilating force on a Japanese Army Base, Washington announced.
Official sources there remained silent but Secretary of War, Stimson, declared in Washington that the big base and port of Hiroshima, on Japan's inland sea was engulfed in "an impenetrable cloud of dust and smoke." Transmitters of nearby Saipan and on Hawaii and in San Francisco bombarded the Japanese homeland with broadcasts declaring that this was the annihilation promised at Potsdam for scorning the surrender ultimatum. The messages of doom crackled across the air waves even while the smoke of spreading ruin rose over four more Japanese cities, struck early Monday by 580 Superforts, unloading 3850 tons of fire bombs. The Japanese said a small force of Superforts raided Hiroshima at 0820 Monday morning, Tokyo time, but made no mention of damage. One Superfort failed to return as the wave on wave of sky giants roared through heavy flak, putting the torch on the industrial cities of of Nishnomiya, Sebashi, Immibari and Saga, all forewarned they were marked for annihilation.

As the raiders thundered back toward home they reported all four cities wrapped in flames that sometimes were visible 150 miles at sea.

WASHINGTON:

President Truman has clearly indicated that the scientists who made the atomic bomb have done two things. First: They have created a monster which could wipe out civilization. Second: Some protection against the monster must be found before its secret is given to the world. The terrible implications of the destructive force of the bomb are contained in these sentences from the President's statement "normally everything about the work with atomic energy would be made public, but under present circumstances, it is not intended to divulge the technical processes of production of all military applications pending further examination of possible methods of protecting us and the rest of the world from the danger of sudden destruction."

NEW YORK:

If the Germans started first with atomic bombs their leading was probably only a few days. The atomic explosives possibilities sprung unexpectedly from calculations by a German-Jewish woman mathematician, Lize Meitner. Within two weeks the whole scientific world knew of her theory and had verified it. Hitler might have had a few weeks start. His first act was to set a large number of physicists to work on the ideas of Lize Meitner.

PACIFIC:

General MacArthur announced that American bombers sank or damaged 23 Jap ships in patrol down

the Asiatic Coast, from Shanghai to Saigon, and into Makassar strait. General MacArthur reported that his ground forces are steadily closing in on the Jap Philippine Headquarters at Baguio on Luzon. Despite a stubborn daytime defense and persistent night counter-attacks.
Fleet Admiral Chester W. Nimitz reported the destruction of at least 2280 Japanese planes since March 18, start of the Okinawa operation, which included U.S. Carrier Aircraft blows at Southern Japan to April 18. About 1600 of these enemy planes were smashed in the air or on the ground by Vice Admiral Marc A. Mitscher's fast Carrier task force, with the other 600 knocked down by anti-aircraft gunners, other escort Carrier planes, and air craft based on Okinawa. British Carrier planes accounted for 80 enemy aircraft. There was no change in the lines on the Southern Okinawa front, while to the North Marine Units were meetingsmall pockets of Japanese resistance. Nimitz said that mopping operations continued on Iwo Jima.

LONDON:

A London and Northeastern railway sleeping car has been converted into an armored coach for Gerneral Eisenhower and is now on the continent for his use. The car contains a conference room and a combined dressing and sleeping compartment. The roof sides and ends are armor-plated and the windows of bulletproof glass have steel shutters.

Adolf Hitler, calling for a death stand, announced that the Third Army had opened its final all out offensive against Berlin as the thunder of 1000 Russian guns shook the Nazi Capitol, and Russiantroops won high ground only 23 miles away. Berlin reports indicated that four Russian Armies with perhaps two million men were on the move. The long-expected offensive burst upon the Germans, the German high Command announced, and drove forward along a blazing 120 miles front within 85 miles of a lineup with American Armies that might end the war.

NEW YORK:

General Eisenhower was quoted in a W.O.R. shortwave broadcast as saying, "There will be no V day until Germany is completely occupied including all pockets of resistance and the German Army is completely destroyed". The broadcast was by Howard Bardes, New York Herald Tribune correspondent,who also represents W.O.R.

LONDON:

Chubby"Potato Pete" whose face has peered at Britons from millions of posters was fired Monday by Ministrey of Food. He did so well the job of persuading people to eat potatoes that once plentiful spuds are now scarce.

LOS ANGELES:

Charlie Chaplin was adjudged to be the father of Joan Berry's child Tuesday by a jury of the Superior Court. The Jury of eleven women and one man brought in the verdict after deliberating thebitter contested case for two hours and 55 minutes. Last January the first case ended in a mistrial when the Jury was unable to decide whether the Comedian was the Father of the baby, now 12 months old, Carol Ann.

LOUSIVILLE, KY:

This is gratitude! A crisis hit a cafe when two waiters attempting to serve 150 diners suddenly walked out. Two regular patrons donned aprons and finished the job with the remark, "We all gotta eat." They received 65 cents in tips.

PHILADELPHIA:

Misty, chilly weather caused the opening game of the Major League baseball season between the New York Yankees and Washington Senators to be called off. The game had been dedicated to the memory of the late President Roosevelt and the postponement was made with considerable reluctance. Speaker Sam Rayburn was selected to pitch the first ball marking the first time in baseball history that the honor has gone to a member of Congress. It usually is reserved for the President or Vice President. The dedicatory cremonies to Mr. Roosevelt will be carried out Friday when the Senators face the Yankees here after a three day series in Philadelphia.

NEW YORK:

Irving Berlin came home from a three months tour in the Pacific war areas with a new song, "A servicemen's lament to be home again, don a blue serge suit, have breakfast in bed, and date a girl wearing a dress, not a uniform".

Page #3
Aircraft of the Fourth Marine Aircraft Wing sank two boats and damaged two buildings in the Palaus on 6 August. On the preceding day aircraft of the Wing struck enemy targets in the Palaus at Yap and in the Marshalls.

CALCUTTA:

Allied patrols have thrust across the old Sittang River channel at a point sixty miles northeast of Rangoon in lower Burma while other forces battled to wipe out Japanese remnants still trapped west of the river, the Southeast Asia Command announced Monday.

LONDON:

The United Nations Relief and Rehabilitation Administration close to scraping the bottom of its financial barrel will open its Third Council Session Tuesday hopeful of getting new funds to carry to through the winter at least.

ATHENS, GEORGIA:

Chester Fletcher of Alabama City, Alabama, although minus one arm, is making a strong bid for a guard slot on Georgia's football team this year. Fletcher who tips the scale at 170 already is rated good enough to get into action as a substitute and with some experience might break in as a starter, coaches say.

HOLLYWOOD:

The Times Ways reports Oona O'Neil Chaplin, 20 year old wife of Charlie Chaplin, is expecting another baby have been confirmed by close friends of the couple. The Chaplins were unavailable for comment.

HOLLYWOOD:

Frank Sinatra, belying his reputation for emaciation, highlights the Hollywood happenings of the week by making a spectacular dive into the Harbor at nearby San Pedro to save the life of a 3 year old boy. Frank's feat occured when the boy, Duke Jones, fell thirteen feet from a railing onto a yacht dock then rolled unconscious into the water. The Crooner who had spent the day as crewman for a sailing boat in a match race rushed across the dock leaped into the water and pulled the youngster to safety.

LOS ANGELES:

Major Richard Ira Bong, 24, America's Ace fighter pilot in the South Pacific before returning to this Country to become a Test Pilot, was killed today in the crash of a jet plane. He had shot down 40 Japanese planes.

VENICE, CALIFORNIA:

A power cable blew out and plunged the Venice Ocean Pier into darkness, but 6,000 dancers kept right on for three hours. They had to. Checkroom attendants couldn't identify their belongings.

SAN DIEGO, CALIFORNIA:

Apprentice Seaman George Lee, 22, San Francisco Chinese-American, correctly identified 300 slides of Allied and Enemy aircraft flashed on a screen at split second intervals. First 275 planes were flashed at intervals of 1.5 seconds the next 25 at 1.25. Lee set a record. "It is easy", he said, "My boyhood hobby was model plane building."

CHUNGKING:

Chinese Troops have broken into the South China port of Yeungkong and cleared a fifty mile stretch of the Chinese "invasion coast" West of Hongkong, General Issimo Chiang Kai Shek's headquarters said Monday. Savage, block by block street fighting is raging in the strategic coastal highway town, 121 miles southwest of Canton, a communique said.

COLUMBUS, OHIO:

If the new Atomic bomb announced Monday by President Truman gets its energy from large scale breakdown of atoms it could possibly mean the opening of a source of power "Almost revolutionary", Professor Cecil Boord of the Ohio State University Chemistry Department said Monday.

WASHINGTON:

Senator Hiram Johnson of California, Militant opponent of the League of Nations and the San Francisco Charter for a United Nations Organization, died Monday at 79 years. The Veteran Republican Senator succumbed at a Naval Hospital where he had been confined for two and one-half weeks. His death was attributed to thrombosis of a cerebral artery.

PARIS:

The Conference of Representatives of France, Soviet Russian, Britain and the United States on re-estableshment of International Control over Tangier, scheduled to open Monday, has been delayed until later this week at the request of the British Government.

SAN FRANCISCO:

Uranium, essential to atomic bombs, does not exist in pure form in Nature, but is a lustrous white element derived from pitchblend, the source of radium, or from carnotite, a mineral found in sandstone.
The United States has deposits of both pitchblend and carnotite, so has Austria and Portugal.

In the spring of 1940 scientists extracted a minute quantity of substance which they named U-235, a close relative of Uranium. One pound of U-235 was said to equal energy of five million pounds of coal, or 400 gallons of gasoline, or 15,000 tons of TNT, and in a one-ten thousandth of a second explosion would create one million times the pressure of TNT or nitroglycerine.

Science then thought, however, that one pound of U-235 in exploding would produce a crater of much less than 300 feet in diameter, and only 75 feet in radius.

If it could be regulated and controlled over a period, ten pounds of U-235 could run an ocean liner or submarine for an indefinite time, for it would be equal in power output to 25,000 tons of coal.

Uranium salts have been used in photography and in coloring porcelain yellow, orange, brown, and dark green.

Uranium U-235 differs from regular Uranium only in atomic weight. It was the only form of Uranium before the war which could be split into nearly two equal parts under impact of neutron rays. Like Radium it is radioactive, but it is less powerful. It was Uranium which in the laboratory of the French scientist, Becquerl, forged photography place and led Madame Curie and her husband to discover radium.

SAN FRANCISCO:

Admiral Kichisaburo Nomura characterized the Allied Potsdam ultimatum to Japan as "the height of impertinence" in an interview broadcast Monday by the Japanese news agency. Nomura, who was the Nipponese ambassador to Washington before the war and was conducting "peace" talks with the American government at the time of the Pearl Harbor sneak attack, charged that the American Navy "had ambitiously dreamed of East Asiatic Hegemony from days in the past."

BERLIN:

The United States and Britain Monday gave the conquered Germans permission to free local trade unions and local political parties, but General Eisenhower warned the German people they would get full freedom only after they proved themselves willing to build democracy.

London:

Dr. Neils Bohr refugee Danish Scientist credited Monday by Secretary Stimson with assisting in the development of the Atomic Bomb escaped being apprehended by the Germans by fleeing Denmark in a fishing boat. Bohr arrived in Sweden about September 28, 1943 and immediately was surrounded by Swedish Police at the request of Danish Authorities to prevent his falling into the hands of German agents. He had halted his laboratory research on Atomic theories in 1940 as a protest against the German invasion. As the war took a turn for the worse against the Germans, the Nazis were anxious to force Bohr to work with them in the development of new explosives.

End of Press

Stenciled by Disbursing Office

August 8, 1945: Soviet Russia Declared war on Japan and invaded Machuris. President Harry S. Truman announced the secret of the atomic bomb would be shared only with Britain and Canada.

August 9: Another atom bomb is dropped on the Japanese city of Nagasaki.

August 14, 1945. Facing annihilation and possible global extinction, Emperor Hirohito announced defeat to his terrorized people, and Japan surrendered unconditionally.

Wilbur's letter of August 15, 1945, to his sister, carried little jubilance over the "victory". Mostly, it seemed, to merely convey a weary thankfulness that the holocaust had at last come to an end. The stamp of the Naval Censor was still upon the envelope:

W.A. Parker, EM 2/C
U.S.S. COLORADO, Box 11
c/o Fleet P.O.,S.F. Calif.
August 15, 1945

Dear Ruby,
 The mail has been rather slow lately but it came in again yesterday and I have your letter, which, together with the other good news, makes it a red letter day. It hardly seems possible that this old war can be over at last, does it?
 Expect there will be some big celebrations tonight. I don't suppose it will change things any here for a while, but at least it can't be long now.
 Most of us will be in for six months or so yet, I suppose. I have hopes I'll be out in 8 months at the most.
 That new road ought to be a good thing

for the folks, but I can't much blame them for
not wanting it through the front yard. Why
doesn't Dad try to get them to follow over the
hill up the creek where he started the road?
It seems it would be a better route anyhow. It
looks to me like a tough job just below the house
there.
 I'm so glad that Stanley is coming along so
well. Bet he has a time helping Grandpa as
soon as he gets to feeling well. It hardly
seems possible that he can be old enough to go
to school.
 I'm glad that Bill is getting somewhere with
the car. It might make a pretty good trade-in
car. If Bill wants to get a truck or pickup I
don't see why he doesn't trade it in instead of
the good car. Of course, he couldn't get nearly
as much for it but it would be nice to keep
your good car if you can. Please don't think
about paying me for it. I gave it to you, you
know, and will be only too glad if you can get
some good out of it. I imagine it is in pretty
poor shape and will cost you plenty to fix it up.
 Well, as usual, there doesn't seem like much
to write about. Everyone is counting up his
points, but no one seems to have enough to get
out. I expect they will lower the points in a
few months if everything goes right.
 Have you heard from Dorothy and Leslie? I
haven't for a long while. He shouldn't be
drafted now, and maybe they will be able to
really take a good vacation now.
 Nothing new has happened around the shop,
and I'm afraid I'm going to have to bring this
to a close. For now and Always, Yours, Wilbur

U.S.S. COLORADO

And now You've made HisTory!

Capt. W.S. Macaulay, U.S.Navy Commanding
Comdr. C.M. Hardison, U.S.Navy Executive Officer
Lt. Comdr. Jack O.Wheat, U.S.Navy Supply Officer
J.E. Wood, APC, U.S. Navy, Officer inCharge
       Commissary Section
  D.M. Patz, Chief Commissary Steward

Prior to receiving Wilbur's letter, Ruby Goodwin made an entry in her own journal:

"August 15, 1945 - With the dawn of this day it is certain that a cessation of open warfare between nations has come about. Japan has offered peace treaties, and says she will accept the terms of the Pottsdam Conference and, although the peace treaty is not yet signed, it was a jubilant day in the United States.

This, then, is the beginning of another peace ...how long will it last? Perhaps, at least long enough to let the present, war-suffering, men die and forget. Maybe the war mongers will wait for the next generation to grow up before starting another conflict. I wonder? Maybe Stanley will be old enough to be caught in the next great draft.

Why am I so depressed and pessimistic? Wilbur is *alive*! There is the bright anicipation of his homecoming; but I seem to dread seeing what the war may have done to him. I have the feeling it has killed something fine within him that can never be recovered.

It's close to a year now since he was home on furlough. I find myself wanting him home so much inspite of what the war may have done to him. I'm selfish, I just want him *Home!* And thank you, Lord, for his deliverance."

By Wilbur's next writing, censorship had been lifted. The envelope carried a big blue stamp upon it..."USS COLORADO in JAPAN"...for anyone who wished to read.

T.A. Parker EM 3
U.S.S. Colorado BB 55
c/o F.P.O. S.F. Calif.

air mail

USS COLORADO

IN JAPAN

Mrs. W.M. Goodwin
Fletcher Parks, Wyo.

Forwarded To Casper, Wyo.

W.A. Parker, EM 2/C
U.S.S. COLORADO, Box 11
c/o Fleet P.O., S.F. Calif.
Sept. 2, 1945

Dear Sister,
    I doubt there is much use in writing this if you are still at home as there isn't much to say other than what I wrote Mother; but then maybe you will be moved onto the new place by now.
    I haven't had much mail for some time but recieved Mother's and Ina's letters of the 17th yesterday. Mother said that Bill traded the Olds in on a Chevrolet. It was such a nice car it seems a shame, and I still think you should have traded the old Ford, but I guess Bill knows what he's doing. I've wondered how you made out with the papers on the old Ford as I haven't recieved anything to sign yet.
    Along the beach I can see many large buildings, and the numerous smoke stacks of Yokahama's factories. Also, I can make out the big cranes of the Navy Yard, but it's too hazy to see very clearly.
    The cooler climate is a pleasant relief after the hot sun of places further South. It has rained on us a good deal these last days, but we don't mind. It keeps us from sleeping top side, but the bunks in the compartment aren't too unbearably warm now.
    Work has slacked off a good deal with the end of the war. That's O.K. but with less work to do they are becoming much more strict with regulations. Well, I think it's mostly a bunch of bunk, but I should worry for I won't have to put up with it many more months now, or at least I hope not.
    It seems rather odd to be having a bright light top side in Tokyo. Boy! but we've been having picture shows - even in the rain!

Along the banks I can see many large buildings and the numerous smoke stacks of John Baur's factory. I make out the big Cranes Also I can make out the ship yard but it is too foggy to see very clearly. The cooler climate is a pleasant relief after the hot run of places further south. At Sea rained on us a good deal these last 2 days but not ver-

Beside what little work I do, I've been stringing shells and tinkering with knives and souvenirs. It hardly seems worth while to get ready to go up for another rate. I could hardly make it before I'll be back in civilian clothes again.

I've read a couple of good books on Alaska, and get more interested all the while.

I'm out of anything to say, and nearly out of paper, so will close.

With Love, Wilbur

As Ruby rejoiced over his letter, she turned the envelope over and wrote upon it:

As on the shore the bells do peal,
Speaks my heart, "No dream, but *real*."
The ship with steady prow
Brings him home, not *when?* but *NOW!*
The yesteryears with doubts and fears,
Are shed by these most happy tears!

World War II actually ended upon the date of this letter, September 2, 1945.

September 2, 1945, Japanese Foreign Minister Mamoru Shigemitsu and military leaders signed the surrender terms aboard the U.S.S. MISSOURI in Tokyo Bay.

With the peace treaty signed, and the war ended, censorship was lifted. Wilbur was anxious to get liberty so he could leave the U.S.S.COLORADO a while to go hunting souvenirs in Tokyo, Yakahama or Yohoshaka.

U.S.S. COLORADO
SURRENDER DINNER

Tomato Juice Cocktail

Salted Crackers

Stuffed Olives   Stuffed Celery   Sweet Pickles

Grilled Steak Colorado
Sunny Side Eggs
Roast Brown New Potatoes
Peas Parisene - Gravy

Cherry Pie
Strawberry Nut Sundae

Hot Rolls - Butter
Iced Fruit Juice

Cigars - Cigarettes

W. A. Parker, EM 2/C
U.S.S. COLORADO, Box 11
c/o Fleet P.O. - S.F. Calif.
Sept. 7, 1945

TOKYO BAY

My dear Sister,
Here we are still sitting in Tokyo Bay. It doesn't seem we are doing much good now, and the occupation appears to be nearly complete, so we have hopes of leaving soon.
They have quit censoring our mail now. I can hardly get back into the habit of licking my own stamps, and it just doesn't seem right to ramble on without watching what I say.
There isn't a great lot to say even at that, I fear. We were one of the first ships to come into the Bay, but it wasn't much like any of the other landings. Though, of course, we had to keep pretty much on the alert at first. There was never any occasion to fire. Things have pretty well slacked off now though, and last Wed. we had a big dinner to celebrate Japan's surrender. A little later than they celebrated in the States, I guess.
We had quite a few boys aboard that had been prisoners in Japan for a while. It was pretty interesting to talk to some of them. They didn't look too fat, but on the other hand, they didn't appear to be starved. I guess the Japs fed them about as good as they ate themselves so they could work them, but even that wasn't much. They have all left us now, and I think they caught plane rides back to the States.
For several days now they have been sending a small liberty party over to Yokohama and Yohesha-ka. We draw names from the hat to see who gets to go. I haven't been lucky so far. I would

sort of like to go and pick up some souvenirs, though, I guess they are pretty hard to get on account of the place being so burnt out. There are almost no stores open for business. Most of the fellows seem to find something, though I've a notion they just sort of walk off with them.

There hasn't been much going on around the shop. My circuit doesn't require much care now we quit firing the big guns; those things sure did shake up a lot of trouble. It's not much wonder though, and I think we have the record for the number of large shells fired as well as accuracy. We dropped over 60,000 tons of shells on Okinawa alone, which is a lot of shells in any man's way of thinking.

On Okinawa I had a chance when on liberty there, to see it close-range where some of our shells hit. A sixteen inch shell will dig a hole 12 or 15 feet deep.

Here about a week ago, I went to the dentist and got my teeth fixed. I had three more fillings put in. I sure hate that grinding and I'm glad it's over.

I haven't heard anything from Calif. for a long while, and sort of have a hunch Leslie and Dorothy are taking a trip home. I expect the factory work isn't so good now. By the time us fellows get out of the service I imagine it will be plenty hard to get a job, not only for us but for everyone. Well, I'll just hole up in a iceburg in Alaska...Ha!

Yes, Ina mentioned going to Alaska several times. I almost think she isn't kidding, but of course, she doesn't know what she is talking about.

Think I'm about run down and may just as well quit. Hope you are nicely settled and Stanley likes his school. Tell him, Uncle Wilbur says "Hello". Always Yours, Wilbur

WAR SUMMARY OF USS COLORADO

The following summary of the war activities of the U.S.S.COLORADO from the outbreak of war to the formal surrender of Japan in Tokyo Bay is being made available to all hands and information contained herein may be incorporated in personal correspondence, discussing in a general way the information incorporated herein, may be published in your hometown newspapers.

The U.S.S. COLORADO and her crew now are participating in the crowning event of almost four years of war in the Pacific---support of occupation operations of the Tokyo area of Japan. One of the battleships making up the Mightiest Array of Naval Power ever assembled, the COLORADO was among the first warships to steam into Sagami Bay within a few thousand yards of Japanese homeland beaches, and then through the narrow straits leading into Tokyo Bay itself to support amphibious and airborne landings in the Tokyo area.

To help reach this objective---the formal surrender of Japan and the occupation of the Japanese homeland---the COLORADO has taken part in 10 of the Pacific's most important invasion operations in the Island Hopping Strategy that led to the successful conclusion of the war. Here is the invasion route the COLORADO has helped establish:

1. NOVEMBER 20-29, 1943, Pre-invasion bombardment and occupation support of TARAWA in the GILBERT ISLANDS.

2. JANUARY 31 to FEBRUARY 6, 1944, Pre-invasion bombardment and occupation support of ROI and NAMUR, KWAJALEIN ATOLL, MARSHALL ISLANDS.

3. FEBRUARY 17-23, 1944, Preinvasion Bombardment and Occupation Support of ENIWETOK ATOLL in the MARSHALLS.

4. JUNE 14 to AUGUST 3, 1944, Pre-invasion Bombardment and Occupation Support of SAIPAN, GUAM and TINIAN in the MARIANAS.

5. NOVEMBER 19 to DECEMBER 3, 1944, Occupation support of LEYTE in the PHILIPPINES.

6. DECMBER 12 to DECEMBER 18, 1944, Pre-invasion Bombardment and Occupation Support of MINDORO ISLAND in the PHILLIPPINES.

7. JANUARY 2 to FEBRUARY 14, 1945, Pre-invasion Bombardment and Occupation Support of LUZON in the PHILIPPINES.

8. MARCH 21 to MAY 22, 1945, Pre-Invasion Bombardment and Occupation Support of OKINAWA in the RYUKYUS ISLANDS.

9. AUGUST 27, 1945 - Entered SAGAMI BAY, JAPANESE HOMELAND WATERS to Support Landing of Airborne Troops at ATSUGI AIRFIELD, 18 miles from TOKYO.

10. SEPTEMBER 1, 1945 - Entered TOKYO BAY to Support Occupation Operations in the TOKYO AREA.

During operations leading up to the surrender of Japan, the COLORADO's assigned task has been to support ground troops by bombardment of enemy positions, a contribution that has helped speed the invasion and occupation of strategic islands along the invasion route. Thousands of tons of explosive steel have been poured into menacing enemy installations, many of them well protected from field artillery by rugged terrain. The COLORADO has engaged in a comparatively new type of Naval Warfare, but one that has helped hasten the end of the PACIFIC WAR where amphibious operations were necessitated on a wide scale.

Target's of the COLORADO's heavy caliber guns have included gun emplacements, fortified caves, airfields, supply dumps, troop concentrations and other installations that had to be destroyed before the islands could be invaded and secured. Each of these invasions brought American forces closer to JAPAN, providing new bases for tightening and maintaining the complete undersea, surface and air blockade which cut off enemy forces; maintenance of the continuous supply line to the Fleet, ground troops and shore based air forces, and finally, the surrender of JAPAN, because submarine, surface ships and air attacks had destroyed its Navy and exposed the homeland to Naval blockade and its cities and Interior communications to destruction by bombardment.

Men serving on the COLORADO prior to PEARL HARBOR and have participated in all of the campaigns in which the ship has taken part are authorized to wear the following Campaign Medals; (1) American Defense Medal with one Star; (2) The American Area Campaign Medal; (3) The Asiatic-Pacific Area Campaign Medal with Six Stars, and (4) The PHILIPPINE Liberation Campaign Ribbon with One Star.

Men coming to the COLORADO since PEARL HARBOR are authorized to wear (1) The American Area Campaign Medal; (2) The Asiatic-Pacific Campaign

Medal with Stars in accordance with campaigns participated in on the basis of one Star for the GILBERTS, one for the MARSHALLS, one for the MARIANAS, two for the PHILIPPINES, and one for OKINAWA, and (3), The PHILLIPPINE Liberation Ribbon with one Star for those men who participated in the PHILIPPINES OPERATIONS.

Since the outbreak of the war, the U.S.S. COLORADO has steamed more than 150,000 miles in carrying out her orders and assignments. Early in 1942 she left the STATES and headed for the NEW HEBRIDES and FIJI ISLANDS to stand by with other units of the Fleet for any assignment that might be handed her in challenge of further Japanese moves in that direction. On this first wartime cruise the COLORADO and her crew were out more than 17 months, taking part in the invasion of TARAWA before returning to the STATES.

-:-   -:-   -:-

While Wilbur was sitting on the U.S.S. COLORADO in Tokyo Bay awaiting the time to be shipped stateside, Bill, Ruby, and Stanley left Granger, Wyoming to settle on a ranch near Cassa, Wyoming.

Each time Ruby recived one of her brother's letters she found herself in a state of anticipation. Maybe this one would say he was on his way home.

U.S.S. AMSTERDAM
Sunday, October 13, 1945

Dear Sister,
   Expect you think I'm never going to write. Well! at last I'm back with a line.
   I recieved your last letter and the papers to the car about a week ago in Pearl Harbor. Maybe I should have sent them right out but I thought it best to wait until I get to the States where I can get them signed by a Notary Public.
   I'm afraid I don't have any additional information on the car except perhaps this...a Ford doesn't have a Serial No. I'm not sure but what they stamped one on the frame...seems they did...on the driver's side, I believe...I think it is the same as the Engine No.
   Let's see! Guess I was in Tokyo Bay the last time I wrote. We pulled out soon after that, but I got one liberty in Tokyo before we left... stayed over all day and near ran my legs off! We rode miles and miles on the street cars, and never paid a cent. They sure did a good job of bombing over there. In fact, they didn't leave much at all. There are quite a few big department stores still standing, but none of them well-stocked. We nearly ran ourselves to death trying to find something to buy, and got very little then. After leaving Japan we stopped at Okinawa and picked up passengers. Thence we went to Pearl Harbor where I was transferred to this ship, the U.S.S. AMSTERDAM (a cruiser). I won't be on this for more than a few days yet (I hope), so don't send any mail here. In fact, don't send any at all as I have had my mail transferred to home.
   I should be getting out of this x x****------ place soon now, as I have the points, and am

almost back to the States. This ship goes to Portland, I think, and from there I'll be sent to Bremerton.

I'll try to write more often now, and keep you informed; let you know if to write or not, and *where*, when I find out more myself.

We'll soon be in port now. We are due in at 3, and it is about one now. Expect we could see land if it wasn't so foggy. Everyone aboard nearly is or has been sick on this trip. I was in sick bay for several days, and didn't eat a thing for 3 days. I feel O.K. now, but sure lost weight.

I had a couple of liberties while in Pearl Harbor, but didn't go in to Honolulu. Had some fun though, and got lots of good sunshine. It sure is nice there now.

Sure seems like it is getting cold here. Everyone is near to freezing. Will close for now. Love, Wilbur

<u>NEXT DAY</u>:
Well, we stopped in Astoria last night to let off the people that were sick, and early this morning we started on up the river to Portland. It sure is pretty, and we come quite near the banks in places. It doesn't seem the channel would be deep enough for a ship this size.

We're to reach Portland about one o'clock. I am supposed to leave the ship there about 2 o'clock, and take the train to Bremerton, but expect will be way behind time as usual.

That's about all for now. Better find the Post Office and get my things ready.
Yours, Wilbur

It kept Wilbur busy writing letters to keep his family informed of his next move. He'd better let his mother know, too, of his whereabouts.

U.S.S. AMSTERDAM
October 15, 1945

Dear Mother,
 Well, I'm back again. Didn't get around to writing you in Pearl H. but thought Doris' letter would do for you all.
 At last I'm back in the States. The old fir trees sure do look good.
 We stopped at Astoria last night to let off a bunch of patients that were in sick bay. Have been having quite an epidemic aboard, and about half the ones aboard were down at one time or another. I was sick for several days, and didn't eat a thing for three days. It sure took me down, but I feel O.K. again now.
 Early this morning we pulled out up the river for Portland. Are to arrive there about one o'clock. I'm to leave the ship and board the train for Bremerton about 2 o'clock but expect it will be closer to midnight. That's the way these things generally run.
 How are you fixed for money, Mother Dear? You had better hold tight because you may have recieved your last check from the Government. There can't be many more checks because I'll be getting out soon.
 I haven't heard from Leslie for months. Don't know what the heck's the matter with that guy. Dorothy must have layed down on him.
 Will write again and give you more dope when I know more myself. Love, Wilbur

Swan Island
Portland, Oregon
October 16, 1945

Dear Mother,

    We got off the ship soon after noon yesterday, and were put on a bus and brought out here, just a Navy camp a short way out of town.

    The barracks are good and so is the chow. Boy! what a sensation to sleep on that soft mattress with springs under it after sleeping on just a blanket on the cold steel deck!

    We were given liberty last evening after we got straightened around until eight this morning. I went down town and fooled around and didn't get in until after midnight.

    We are to muster at eight o'clock this evening with our baggage, so I guess we will be leaving for Bremerton.

    I took all my stuff but just my small suitcase and the stuff I may need, down to the Railway Express Office and shipped it to Wheatland this afternoon. I want you to have the mail man or someone drop around at the office there in Wheatland and pick it up. It weighs quite a bit...95#s is all in one sea bag, and the tags have Dad's name on them. I paid the charges, but you will have to pay the mail man, of course.

    I'm still feeling just a little low after that sick spell I had, but guess I'll come around all right. I can't seem to get my stomach straightened around to where I can eat right.

    Well, it's getting awfully close to time to muster, so guess I'd better see if I can get this mailed, which I probably can't at this time of day, and get my things together. Bye now...will be back again before too long with another line.
Love, Wilbur

Bremerton, Washington
October 18, 1945

Dear Sister,
 Just a line to say I'm getting along O.K. and should be out before long.
 Have been busy almost every moment of the time, and haven't got around to the papers for the car. In fact, I can't get off the station here in the day time, and nothing is open at night.
 After leaving the ship, we stayed over about 48 hrs. at Swan Island in Portland. Got liberty there but about all I got done was to take my sea bag down to the Railway Office and express it home. Sure was glad to get rid of it. It was such a nuisance. I nearly broke my back carrying it around. I'm still weak after that sick spell I had, but am feeling a little better each day.
 I guess the COLORADO hasn't pulled in yet. I don't see anything in the papers about it, and haven't seen or heard anything about it.
 When I first went to boot camp I thought these narrow two-decker bunks were pretty bad, but Boy! are they a luxury now after sleeping on the steel deck with just a blanket!
 Bye now...rained most of the time we were in Portland, but has been fairly nice here though it sure seems cold. That's All! As Ever, Wilbur

Mrs. A. M. Parker
Fletcher Park
Wyoming

W. A. Parker E M 2
Swan Island
Portland Oregon

of town.
The bunks are good and
so is the odors. Boy,
what a sensation to sleep
on that soft mattress
with springs under it
after sleeping on first
a blanket on the cold
steel deck.

As the U.S.S. COLORADO forged her way through her destined battles, Wilbur had used exertive forces of his own to steer his fatalistic course through the whole gamut of trials said to be every service man's lot.

On the long voyage home, he had a lot of time to meditate. Yes, he'd wallowed through all the prophesied Navy Steps, excepting the one of "the home going", and now he was into that.

He'd been:
1. reamed
2. needled
3. scalped
4. briefed
5. trapped
6. kamakazied
7. dear-johned
8. peace
9. stateside
10. the home going

He didn't know whether he was ending life or beginning it. At this moment all he was aware of was: He wasn't the same man he was at the beginning of his Naval training. He never would be that man again. His first problem may be in accepting himself as he now was. Also, another horrendous problem confronting him was to erase as best he could the faces of his dying comrades, the dead, stacked, men waiting to be buried at Pearl Harbor, and the watersoaked bodies of his dead sea buddies. He stood on the lifeless many a time while fixing the U.S.S. COLORADO's

ON THE U.S.S. COLORADO

"I'm not the same man I was...."

electrical circuits as schrapnel whined and splatted about him.

How long was the boom of the ship's heavy artillery to echo in his mind? How long would the war screams and fierce whine of an enemy suicide plane pierce his brain? He'd seen men turned into human torches by flame throwers. Nor did the blowing up of a colony of people take on any more meaning to the aggressor than dynamiting an ant hill in a garden patch.

Was it possible to put all this behind as if it never happened? Could he really build some kind of peace and life for himself? My, God, he was 31 years old! This meant, there was little youth left for him to build on. Yet, as he struggled through all his handicaps, he must never forget he was so much more fortunate than many of his crew who returned home minus arms or legs or both. Then there were the minds that trembled, limped, and failed after being a witness to the diabolic antics of human-kind during war.

"My, God," Wilbur reflected, "I've come through with *all* my parts. True, I've lost most of my hair due to tropical heat; but so far as I know I'm whole with only a schrapnel scar or two."

He could have claimed medals; but who wanted medals for the dastardly deeds he was forced to do?...medals for moments of bravery, when in order to save a comrade or his own life, he was forced into acts he wanted to erase forever from his mind!

Was it possible to emerge any way *but* mutilated from the insanity that is war? The worst wounds were those seared into the soul. Man's brutality to man would be scars carried to the grave. And he'd played his little part in making a torch of the human race, and its world a flaming pier.

Beneath the thundering guns of the U.S.S. COLO-RADO, he'd seen lush, tropical islands turned into charred clumps rearing from the sea.

How could one learn to think in an unthinking and unreasoning world? How could one establish morals where there were none? There were times when non-existence appeared the only sane and honorable state, and it carried much more appeal than a maimed body or mind. Was he like many others defaced and mangled inwardly? How could he come to know the truth about himself as he was today? Was it possible that his crumbling mental and moral state would become known to him by the reactions of his loved ones when he reached home?

How could he possibly deposit the horrible shreds of himself upon his parent's doorstep? Could his sister any better tolerate what he'd become? Why couldn't he go home to the mountains, unseen, unheard, unknown, while he struggled to see if any of these bloody strings could be brought and glued to any form of a whole?

At least, there was one thing he didn't have to worry about...the one of facing his girl in this ghastly shape. By the way of a Dear-John she'd let him know she was too young for him. He'd been afraid of this all along. He didn't blame her for her decision. This was just another aspect of War-Hell he had to face.

The letter was torn to shreds and cast somewhere in the Central Pacific, and like bits of all his war experiences it would remain afloat and suffering somewhere in his middle.

"One final question I should ask myself," he mused on, "When you come back from Hell, do you ever learn to laugh again?"

His Dad, Sam, once told him, "Son, when anyone loses all sense of humor he is lost."

Well, definitely, there was not a shred of humor left in him! Coming straight from Satan's howling inferno where he'd been slapped with blood, fire, and brimstone, the act of laughter would be a fiendish gesture.

Nevertheless, the memory of Amie McPherson and her laughing audience pushed into his groping mind. By, God, what he needed was a good, hog calling contest straight from Amie's ridiculous, though healing podium! Maybe Amie by the way of humor could get his mind and body back on a sane and even keel! However, even this therapeutic event was no longer available, for Amie had not lived to see the end of the war. She died back in September, 1944. Could it be she found it impossible to survive in a world so totally without humor?

Wilbur felt her absence as great a worldly loss as any man or woman killed in the war.

It was impossible to arrive at any conclusions. His mind wavered and staggered as did his body for like thousands of others on the homeward voyage he had come down with dysentery.

"I'm sick," he thought almost in as deep a despair as any he'd felt during the war. "All I know is I'm god-awful sick. All that matters is *I'M GOING HOME!*"

(the end)

U.S.S. COLORADO
The Service Record of

PARKER, Wilbur A.   EM2c
Name   Rate

shows that he is authorized to wear the following uniform decorations:

	BAR	STARS
American Defense	No	No
American Theater	Yes	No
Asiatic-Pacific	Yes	Six
European-African	No	No
Philippine Liberation	Yes	One

OTHER AWARDS

Good Conduct Ribbon - - - -
Participated Occupation of Japan;

Defacement of this card renders it void and the bearer liable to arrest and disciplinary action.

E. Ramsperger

E.J. RAMSPERGER, C.S.C., USN

EPILOGUE

From the time of his home-going, Wilbur never saw his ship the U.S.S. COLORADO again.

Although the last of the old battleships had been struck off the effective list in 1947, the TENNESEE, CALIFORNIA, COLORADO, MARYLAND and the WEST VIRGINIA had to be kept in reserve to placate Congress and public opinion. Despite their age they were put back on the effective list at the time of the Korean War to prove that the U.S. Navy was still up to strength, and there they remained until 1959 when permission to scrap them was finally give.

Not until 1961 did Wilbur come to know the fate of his ship the U.S.S. Colorado. The news came via of the Empire Magazine in the Denver Post:

"The USS COLORADO IS GONE. Once the most powerful battleship afloat, the 35,500-ton ship has been to sea for the last time. Recently she was cut into strips, blocks, sheets and tubes of steel at the Todd Shipyard, Seattle, Wash.

Commissioned in 1923, the COLORADO first saw battle action in November, 1943, against the Japanese stronghold of Tarawa. By the end of World War II her record included 10 campaigns. She was hit hard and often by the enemy and nearly 400 of her officers and men were killed or wounded.

But her fine record could not save the COLORADO.

Long before she fired her first shot in anger the era of the battle wagon was coming to a close. The end was foreseen in 1921 when Maj. Gen. Billy Mitchell proved aircraft could sink the big ships.

Following the war the COLORADO was deactivated and put into so-called "moth-ball fleet" at

Bremerton, Wash. Then in June, 1959, she was sold to a salvage company for scrap. In July of that year she made her last voyage...to the salvage dock.

As the scrapping crews stood by with torches ready the USS COLORADO was towed into Todd Shipyard to be whittled down to her very keel.--D.W.W."

Wilbur Parker left a special after-war, afterlife message to Ruby Goodwin among the many writings he willed her:

Dear Sister,

    Life's fragile light is gone
       I reach out to grasp this hand
Of yours, still trembling there,
       Holding you fast by the fireside...
Remember, Time past is not despair.

                      ----Wilbur Allen Parker

A BIT of AUTOBIOGRAPHY

I can relate my life, I'm sure, in three or four short paragraphs:

I was born in the mountainous North Laramie River Country, Albany County, State of Wyoming, U.S.A. My birthplace was my father's homestead cabin on the North Laramie River, Wyman, Wyoming, and I've lived in Wyoming all my life.

I've never liked biographies...mostly because I've never done anything to brag about.

How I'd love to boast about a glamorous, eventful, and fruitful life! However, to be truthful I'll have to confess it's been quite the opposite.

Prevarication inevitably catchs up with me, so here is a hilarious, *true* account of my life, which incidently has been a hand-to-mouth existence. In retrospect I've worked at so many occupations it's difficult to recall all of them...all very unimaginative and dull. Let's see *mmm m mn*...I've been a scrub woman, housewife, mother, hotel maid, waitress, store clerk... (I'm naming the most grueling jobs first). Slowly I evolved to a student, a teacher, school secretary, a bookkeeper, secretary to an accountant, and clerk to a judge.

I wouldn't need to cite all the foregoing. I do so because I think the lights and shadows of our experiences fall over our writing. Our way of existence may be the answer as to why we write as we do. Our writings are colored by what we are and where we've been. Our words reflect what we've done and our attitude towards what has happened to us.

Ruby Parker Goodwin
October 26, 1988